Microsoft

Microsoft PowerPoint 2016
Step by Step

Joan Lambert

PUBLISHED BY
Microsoft Press
A division of Microsoft Corporation
One Microsoft Way
Redmond, Washington 98052-6399

Library of Congress Control Number: 2015934869
ISBN: 978-0-7356-9779-9

Printed and bound in the United States of America.

First Printing

Microsoft Press books are available through booksellers and distributors worldwide. If you need support related to this book, email Microsoft Press Support at mspinput@microsoft.com. Please tell us what you think of this book at http://aka.ms/tellpress.

This book is provided "as-is" and expresses the author's views and opinions. The views, opinions, and information expressed in this book, including URL and other Internet website references, may change without notice.

Some examples depicted herein are provided for illustration only and are fictitious. No real association or connection is intended or should be inferred.

Acquisitions and Developmental Editor: Rosemary Caperton
Editorial Production: Online Training Solutions, Inc. (OTSI)
Technical Reviewers: Online Training Solutions, Inc. (OTSI)
Copyeditors: Jaime Odell, Kathy Krause, and Val Serdy (OTSI)
Indexers: Susie Carr and Angela Martin (OTSI)
Cover: Twist Creative • Seattle

Contents

Part 1: Get started with PowerPoint 2016

Give us feedback
Tell us what you think of this book and help Microsoft
improve our products for you. Thank you!
http://aka.ms/tellpress

Part 2: Insert and manage slide text

Part 3: Insert and manage visual elements

Part 4: Finalize presentations

Part 5: Use advanced PowerPoint functions

Give us feedback
Tell us what you think of this book and help Microsoft improve our products for you. Thank you!
http://aka.ms/tellpress

Introduction

Welcome! This *Step by Step* book has been designed so you can read it from the beginning to learn about Microsoft PowerPoint 2016 and then build your skills as you learn to perform increasingly specialized procedures. Or, if you prefer, you can jump in wherever you need ready guidance for performing tasks. The how-to steps are delivered crisply and concisely—just the facts. You'll also find informative, full-color graphics that support the instructional content.

Who this book is for

Microsoft PowerPoint 2016 Step by Step is designed for use as a learning and reference resource by home and business users of Microsoft Office programs who want to use PowerPoint to create and present slide presentations and printed materials. The content of the book is designed to be useful for people who have previously used earlier versions of PowerPoint and for people who are discovering PowerPoint for the first time.

The *Step by Step* approach

The book's coverage is divided into parts representing general PowerPoint skill sets. Each part is divided into chapters representing skill set areas, and each chapter is divided into topics that group related skills. Each topic includes expository information followed by generic procedures. At the end of the chapter, you'll find a series of practice tasks you can complete on your own by using the skills taught in the chapter. You can use the practice files that are available from this book's website to work through the practice tasks, or you can use your own files.

Download the practice files

Before you can complete the practice tasks in this book, you need to download the book's practice files to your computer from *http://aka.ms/powerpoint2016sbs /downloads*. Follow the instructions on the webpage.

 IMPORTANT PowerPoint 2016 is not available from the book's website. You should install that app before working through the procedures and practice tasks in this book.

You can open the files that are supplied for the practice tasks and save the finished versions of each file. If you later want to repeat practice tasks, you can download the original practice files again.

 SEE ALSO For information about opening and saving files, see "Open and navigate presentations" in Chapter 2, "Create and manage presentations."

The following table lists the practice files for this book.

Chapter	Folder	File
Part 1: Get started with PowerPoint 2016		
1: PowerPoint 2016 basics	Ch01	None
2: Create and manage presentations	Ch02	NavigateSlides.pptx
3: Create and manage slides	Ch03	AddRemoveSlides.pptx
		ApplyThemes.pptx
		ChangeBackgrounds.pptx
		CreateSections.pptx
		ImportOutline.docx
		RearrangeSlides.pptx
		ReuseSlides.pptx

Chapter	Folder	File
Part 2: Insert and manage slide text		
4: Enter and edit text on slides	Ch04	ApplyTextEffects.pptx
		CheckSpelling.pptx
		EditText.pptx
		EnterText.pptx
		FormatText.pptx
5: Present text in tables	Ch05	FormatTables.pptx
		InsertTables.pptx
		LinkTables.pptx
		ModifyTables.pptx
		NewEquipment.xlsx
Part 3: Insert and manage visual elements		
6: Insert and manage simple graphics	Ch06	Chickens.jpg
		DrawShapes.pptx
		EditPictures.pptx
		Fish.jpg
		Flamingos.jpg
		Flowers.jpg
		InsertPictures.pptx
		InsertScreens.pptx
		Penguins01.jpg, Penguins02.jpg
		Tiger01.jpg, Tiger02.jpg
		YellowBird.jpg

Chapter	Folder	File
Part 5: Use advanced PowerPoint functions		
11: Work in PowerPoint more efficiently	Ch11	None
12: Create custom presentation elements	Ch12	Background.jpg
		CreateThemes.pptx
		CustomizeMasters.pptx
		SaveTemplates.pptx
13: Save and share presentations	Ch13	AddComments.pptx
		RestrictAccess.pptx
		SaveSlides.pptx
		ShareSlides.pptx

Ebook edition

If you're reading the ebook edition of this book, you can do the following:

- Search the full text
- Print
- Copy and paste

You can purchase and download the ebook edition from the Microsoft Press Store at *http://aka.ms/powerpoint2016sbs/detail*.

Get support and give feedback

This topic provides information about getting help with this book and contacting us to provide feedback or report errors.

Errata and support

We've made every effort to ensure the accuracy of this book and its companion content. If you discover an error, please submit it to us at *http://aka.ms/powerpoint2016sbs/errata*.

If you need to contact the Microsoft Press Support team, please send an email message to *mspinput@microsoft.com*.

For help with Microsoft software and hardware, go to *http://support.microsoft.com*.

We want to hear from you

At Microsoft Press, your satisfaction is our top priority, and your feedback our most valuable asset. Please tell us what you think of this book at *http://aka.ms/tellpress*.

The survey is short, and we read every one of your comments and ideas. Thanks in advance for your input!

Stay in touch

Let's keep the conversation going! We're on Twitter at *http://twitter.com/MicrosoftPress*.

Part 1

Get started with PowerPoint 2016

PowerPoint 2016 basics

You can use PowerPoint 2016 to develop professional presentations for electronic delivery as on-screen slide shows, or for print delivery as slide decks with handouts and note pages. You can also use PowerPoint to quite easily lay out complex single-page presentations for production as flyers, posters, or postcards, or for delivery as electronic files, such as pictures.

PowerPoint presentations can be an effective way of providing information in small segments. Individual slides can include bullet points, pictures, charts, tables, and business diagrams. Professionally designed themes visually enhance your message and provide a professional, coordinated appearance.

The elements that control the appearance of PowerPoint and the way you interact with it while you create presentations are collectively referred to as the *user interface*. Some user interface elements, such as the color scheme, are cosmetic. Others, such as toolbars, menus, and buttons, are functional. The default PowerPoint configuration and functionality is based on the way that most people work with the app. You can modify cosmetic and functional user interface elements to suit your preferences and working style.

This chapter guides you through procedures related to starting PowerPoint, working in the PowerPoint user interface, and managing Office and app settings.

In this chapter

- Start PowerPoint
- Work in the PowerPoint user interface
- Manage Office and app settings

Practice files

No practice files are necessary to complete the practice tasks in this chapter.

Start PowerPoint

The way that you start PowerPoint 2016 is dependent on the operating system you're running on your computer. For example:

- In Windows 10, you can start PowerPoint from the Start menu, the All Apps menu, the Start screen, or the taskbar search box.

- In Windows 8, you can start PowerPoint from the Apps screen or Start screen search results.

- In Windows 7, you can start PowerPoint from the Start menu, All Programs menu, or Start menu search results.

You might also have a shortcut to PowerPoint on your desktop or on the Windows taskbar.

When you start PowerPoint without opening a specific presentation, the PowerPoint Start screen appears. The Start screen is a hybrid of the Open and New pages of the Backstage view. It displays links to recent files in the left pane, and new file templates in the right pane.

 TIP You can turn off the appearance of the Start screen if you want to go directly to a new, blank presentation. For information, see "Change default PowerPoint options" in Chapter 11, "Work in PowerPoint more efficiently."

To start PowerPoint by opening a presentation

1. Do either of the following:

   - In File Explorer, double-click the presentation.

      TIP File Explorer is the current version of the browsing utility that was formerly known as Windows Explorer. If you're working on a Windows 7 computer, use Windows Explorer whenever this book refers to File Explorer.

   - In Microsoft Outlook, double-click a presentation that is attached to an email message.

     TIP By default, PowerPoint opens presentations from online sources in protected mode.

To start PowerPoint on a Windows 10 computer

1. Click the **Start** button, and then click **All apps**.

2. In the app list, click any index letter to display the alphabet index, and then click **P** to scroll the app list to the apps starting with that letter.

3. Scroll the list if necessary, and then click **PowerPoint 2016** to start the app.

To start PowerPoint on a Windows 8 computer

1. From the **Start** screen, display the **Apps** screen.

2. Sort the **Apps** screen by name, and then click any index letter to display the alphabet index.

3. In the alphabet index, click **P** to scroll the app list to the apps starting with that letter. Then click **PowerPoint 2016** to start the app.

Work in the PowerPoint user interface

The PowerPoint user interface provides intuitive access to all the tools you need to develop a sophisticated presentation tailored to the needs of your audience. You can use PowerPoint 2016 to do the following (and much more):

- Create, import, format, and edit slide content, including text, pictures, tables, charts, shapes, symbols, equations, SmartArt business diagrams, audio recordings, and video recordings.

- Capture screenshots, screen recordings, and audio recordings.

- Organize and manage slides in sections.

- Animate slide content and the transitions between slides; managing the form, timing, and sound associated with animations.

- Document speaker notes for each slide.

- Control the layout of content by creating custom masters; precisely align slide elements by using gridlines and Smart Guides.

- Create, rehearse, present, and record custom slide shows.

- Save, export, and send presentations in a wide variety of formats.

- Create notes in a OneNote notebook that link to specific slide content.

When you're working with a presentation, it is displayed in an app window that contains all the tools you need to add and format content.

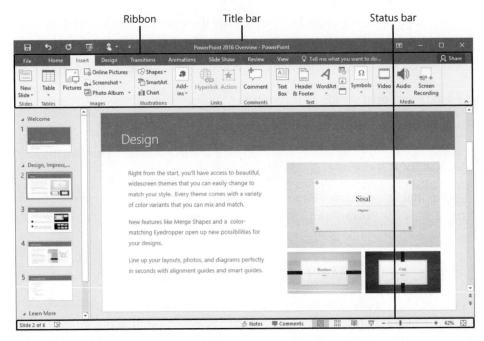

A presentation displayed in the app window

About Office

PowerPoint 2016 is part of the Microsoft Office 2016 suite of apps, which also includes Microsoft Access, Excel, Outlook, and Word. The apps in the Office suite are designed to work together to provide highly efficient methods of getting things done. You can install one or more Office apps on your computer. Some apps have multiple versions designed for different platforms. For example, you can install different versions of PowerPoint on a computer, a smartphone, an iPad, and an Android device; you can also work in a version of PowerPoint that is hosted entirely online. Although the core purpose of an app remains the same regardless of the platform on which it runs, the available functionality and the way you interact with the app might be different.

1

The app that is described and depicted in images throughout this book is a standard desktop installation of PowerPoint 2016 on a Windows 10 computer. It is available as part of the Office 2016 suite of apps, as a freestanding app, or as part of an Office 365 subscription.

Until recently, the standard way of acquiring Office software was to purchase a disc, packaged in a box, and install the software from the disc. In the recent past, the standard distribution model has changed to an online installation, often as part of an Office 365 subscription licensing package.

Office 365, which was originally available only to businesses, now has many subscription options designed for individual home and business users, students, households, small businesses, midsize businesses, enterprises, government agencies, academic institutions, and nonprofits; in other words, whatever your needs may be, there is an Office 365 subscription option that will be a close fit. Many of the Office 365 subscription options include licensing for the desktop Office apps and permit users to run Office on multiple devices, including Windows computers, Mac computers, Windows tablets, Android tablets, iPads, and smartphones.

If you have an Office 365 subscription and are working on a presentation that is stored on a Microsoft SharePoint site or in a Microsoft OneDrive folder, you'll also have access to PowerPoint Online. You can review and edit presentations in PowerPoint Online, which runs directly in your browser instead of on your computer. Office Online apps are installed in the online environment in which you're working and are not part of the desktop version that you install directly on your computer.

SEE ALSO For information about connecting to OneDrive and SharePoint sites, see "Manage Office and app settings" later in this chapter.

PowerPoint Online displays the contents of a presentation very much like the desktop app does, and offers a limited subset of the commands and content formatting options that are available in the full desktop app. If you're working with a presentation in PowerPoint Online and find that you need more functionality than is available, and you have the full version of PowerPoint installed on your computer, you can open the presentation in the full version.

Identify app window elements

The PowerPoint app window contains the elements described in this section. Commands for tasks you perform often are readily available, and even those you might use infrequently are easy to find.

Title bar

At the top of the app window, this bar displays the name of the active file, identifies the app, and provides tools for managing the app window, ribbon, and content.

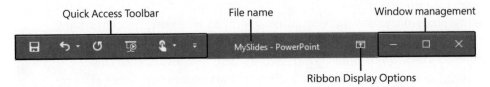

The title bar elements are always on the left end, in the center, and on the right end of the title bar

The Quick Access Toolbar at the left end of the title bar can be customized to include any commands that you want to have easily available. The default Quick Access Toolbar in the PowerPoint app window displays the Save, Undo, Redo/Repeat, and Start From Beginning buttons. On a touchscreen device, the default Quick Access Toolbar also includes the Touch/Mouse Mode button.

> **SEE ALSO** For information about Touch mode, see "Work with the ribbon and status bar" later in this topic.

You can change the location of the Quick Access Toolbar and customize it to include any command to which you want to have easy access.

> ✓ **TIP** You might find that you work more efficiently if you organize the commands you use frequently on the Quick Access Toolbar and then display it below the ribbon, directly above the workspace. For information, see "Customize the Quick Access Toolbar" in Chapter 11, "Work in PowerPoint more efficiently."

Four buttons at the right end of the title bar serve the same functions in all Office apps. You control the display of the ribbon by clicking commands on the Ribbon

Display Options menu, temporarily hide the app window by clicking the Minimize button, adjust the size of the window by clicking the Restore Down/Maximize button, and close the active presentation or exit the app by clicking the Close button.

> **SEE ALSO** For information about different methods of closing presentations and exiting PowerPoint, see "Save and close presentations" in Chapter 2, "Create and manage presentations."

Ribbon

The ribbon is located below the title bar. The commands you'll use when working with a presentation are gathered together in this central location for efficiency.

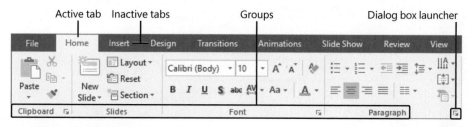

Your ribbon might display additional tabs

> **TIP** The available ribbon tabs and the appearance of the commands on the ribbon might differ from what is shown in this book, based on the apps that are installed on your computer, the PowerPoint settings and window size, and the screen settings. For more information, see the sidebar "Adapt procedure steps" later in this chapter.

Across the top of the ribbon is a set of tabs. Clicking a tab displays an associated set of commands arranged in groups.

Commands related to managing PowerPoint and presentations (rather than presentation content) are gathered together in the Backstage view, which you display by clicking the File tab located at the left end of the ribbon. Commands available in the Backstage view are organized on named pages, which you display by clicking the page tabs in the colored left pane. You redisplay the presentation and the ribbon by clicking the Back arrow located above the page tabs.

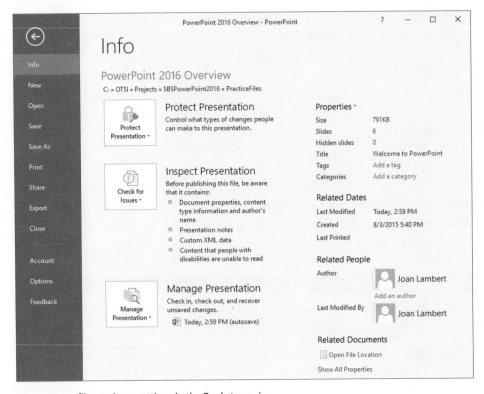

You manage files and app settings in the Backstage view

Commands related to working with presentation content are represented as buttons on the remaining tabs of the ribbon. The Home tab, which is active by default, contains the most frequently used commands.

When a graphic element such as a picture, table, or chart is selected on a slide, one or more *tool tabs* might appear at the right end of the ribbon to make commands related to that specific object easily accessible. Tool tabs are available only when the relevant object is selected.

> **TIP** Some older commands no longer appear as buttons on the ribbon but are still available in the app. You can make these commands available by adding them to the Quick Access Toolbar or the ribbon. For more information, see "Customize the Quick Access Toolbar" and "Customize the ribbon" in Chapter 11, "Work in PowerPoint more efficiently."

On each tab, buttons representing commands are organized into named groups. You can point to any button to display a ScreenTip that contains the command name, a description of its function, and its keyboard shortcut (if it has one).

ScreenTips can include the command name, keyboard shortcut, and description

> ✓ **TIP** You can control the display of ScreenTips and of feature descriptions in ScreenTips. For more information, see "Change default PowerPoint options" in Chapter 11, "Work in PowerPoint more efficiently."

Some buttons include an arrow, which might be integrated with or separate from the button. To determine whether a button and its arrow are integrated, point to the button to activate it. If both the button and its arrow are shaded, clicking the button displays options for refining the action of the button. If only the button or arrow is shaded when you point to it, clicking the button carries out its default action or applies the current default formatting. Clicking the arrow and then clicking an action carries out the action. Clicking the arrow and then clicking a formatting option applies the formatting and sets it as the default for the button.

Examples of buttons with separate and integrated arrows

When a formatting option has several choices available, they are often displayed in a gallery of images, called *thumbnails*, that provide a visual representation of each choice. When you point to a thumbnail in a gallery, the Live Preview feature shows you what the active content will look like if you click the thumbnail to apply the associated formatting. When a gallery contains more thumbnails than can be shown in the available ribbon space, you can display more content by clicking the scroll arrow or More button located on the right border of the gallery.

Related but less common commands are not represented as buttons in a group. Instead, they're available in a dialog box or pane, which you display by clicking the dialog box launcher located in the lower-right corner of the group.

 TIP To the right of the groups on the ribbon is the Collapse The Ribbon button, which is shaped like a chevron. For more information, see "Work with the ribbon and status bar," later in this topic.

Tell me what you want to do

Entering a term in the Tell Me What You Want To Do box located to the right of the ribbon tabs displays a list of related commands and links to additional resources online. Or you can press F1 to open the Help window for the current app.

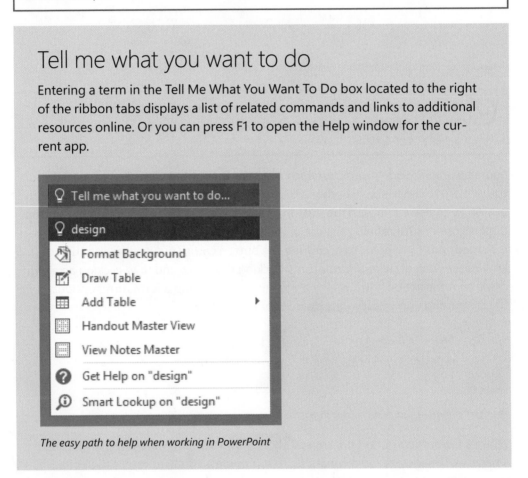

The easy path to help when working in PowerPoint

Status bar

Across the bottom of the app window, the status bar displays information about the current presentation and provides access to certain PowerPoint functions. You can

1

choose which statistics and tools appear on the status bar. Some items, such as Document Updates Available, appear on the status bar only when that condition is true.

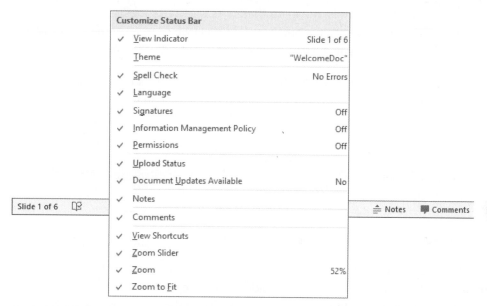

You can specify which items you want to display on the status bar

> 🔍 **SEE ALSO** For information about displaying updates when coauthoring a PowerPoint presentation, see "Coauthor presentations" in Chapter 13, "Save and share presentations."

The Notes and Comments buttons, View Shortcuts toolbar, Zoom Slider tool, and Zoom button are at the right end of the status bar. These tools provide you with convenient methods for changing the display of presentation content.

You can display and hide content, display different content views, and change the magnification from the status bar

> 🔍 **SEE ALSO** For information about changing the content view, see "Display different views of presentations" in Chapter 2, "Create and manage presentations." For information about entering notes, see "Add notes to slides" in Chapter 9, "Review presentations." For information about entering comments, see "Add and review comments" in Chapter 13, "Save and share presentations."

Work with the ribbon and status bar

The goal of the ribbon is to make working with presentation content as intuitive as possible. The ribbon is dynamic, meaning that as its width changes, its buttons adapt to the available space. As a result, a button might be large or small, it might or might not have a label, or it might even change to an entry in a list.

For example, when sufficient horizontal space is available, the buttons on the View tab of the PowerPoint app window are spread out, and you can review the commands available in each group.

At 1024 pixels wide, most button labels are visible

If you decrease the horizontal space available to the ribbon, small button labels disappear and entire groups of buttons might hide under one button that represents the entire group. Clicking the group button displays a list of the commands available in that group.

When insufficient horizontal space is available, labels disappear and groups collapse under buttons

When the ribbon becomes too narrow to display all the groups, a scroll arrow appears at its right end. Clicking the scroll arrow displays the hidden groups.

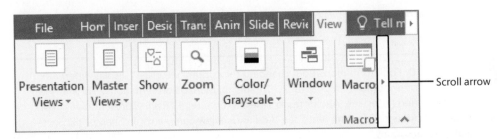

Scroll to display additional group buttons

The width of the ribbon depends on these three factors:

- **Window width** Maximizing the app window provides the most space for the ribbon.

- **Screen resolution** creen resolution is the size of your screen display expressed as pixels wide × pixels high. The greater the screen resolution, the greater the amount of information that will fit on one screen. Your screen resolution options are dependent on the display adapter installed in your computer, and on your monitor. Common screen resolutions range from 800 × 600 to 2560 × 1440 (and some are larger). The greater the number of pixels wide (the first number), the greater the number of buttons that can be shown on the ribbon.

- **The magnification of your screen display** If you change the screen magnification setting in Windows, text and user interface elements are larger and therefore more legible, but fewer elements fit on the screen.

You can hide the ribbon completely if you don't need access to any of its buttons, or hide it so that only its tabs are visible. (This is a good way to gain vertical space when working on a smaller screen.) Then you can temporarily redisplay the ribbon to click a button, or permanently redisplay it if you need to click several buttons.

If you're working on a touchscreen device, you can turn on Touch mode, which provides more space between buttons on the ribbon and status bar. (It doesn't affect the layout of dialog boxes or panes.) The extra space is intended to lessen the possibility of accidentally tapping the wrong button with your finger.

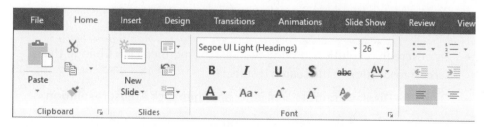

Touch mode has a greater amount of space on the ribbon and status bar

The same commands are available in Touch mode, but they're often hidden under group buttons.

 SEE ALSO For information about working with a modified ribbon, see the sidebar "Adapt procedure steps" later in this topic.

You can switch between Touch mode and Mouse mode (the standard desktop app user interface) from the Quick Access Toolbar. Switching any one of the primary Office apps (Access, Excel, Outlook, PowerPoint, and Word) to Touch mode turns it on in all of them.

To maximize the app window

1. Do any of the following:

    - Click the **Maximize** button.

    - Double-click the title bar.

    - Drag the borders of a non-maximized window.

    - Drag the window to the top of the screen. (When the pointer touches the top of the screen, the dragged window maximizes.)

To change the screen resolution

> ✅ **TIP** Methods of changing screen resolution vary by operating system, but you should be able to access the settings in Windows 10, Windows 8, and Windows 7 by using these methods.

1. Do any of the following:

    - Right-click the Windows 10 desktop, and then click **Display settings**. At the bottom of the **Display** pane of the **Settings** window, click the **Advanced display settings** link.

    - Right-click the Windows 8 or Windows 7 desktop, and then click **Screen resolution**.

    - Enter **screen resolution** in Windows Search, and then click **Change the screen resolution** in the search results.

    - Open the **Display** Control Panel item, and then click **Adjust resolution**.

2. Click or drag to select the screen resolution you want, and then click **Apply** or **OK**. Windows displays a preview of the selected screen resolution.

3. If you like the change, click **Keep changes** in the message box that appears. If you don't, the screen resolution reverts to the previous setting.

To completely hide the ribbon

1. Near the right end of the title bar, click the **Ribbon Display Options** button.

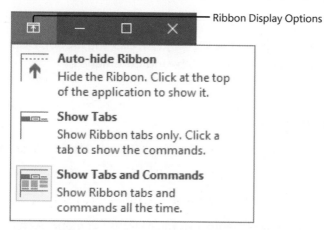

Ribbon Display Options

The Ribbon Display Options button is on the title bar so that it is available when the ribbon is hidden

2. On the **Ribbon Display Options** menu, click **Auto-hide Ribbon**.

 TIP To redisplay the ribbon, click the Ribbon Display Options button and then click Show Tabs or Show Tabs And Commands.

To display only the ribbon tabs

1. Do any of the following:

    *   Double-click any active tab name.

    *   Near the upper-right corner of the app window, click the **Ribbon Display Options** button, and then click **Show Tabs**.

    *   In the lower-right corner of the ribbon, click the **Collapse the Ribbon** button.

    *   Press **Ctrl+F1**.

To temporarily redisplay the ribbon

1. Click any tab name to display the tab until you click a command or click away from the ribbon.

To permanently redisplay the ribbon

1. Do any of the following:

    - Double-click any tab name.

    - Near the upper-right corner of the app window, click the **Ribbon Display Options** button, and then click **Show Tabs and Commands**.

    - Press **Ctrl+F1**.

To optimize the ribbon for touch interaction

1. On the Quick Access Toolbar, click or tap the **Touch/Mouse Mode** button, and then click **Touch**.

To specify the items that appear on the status bar

1. Right-click the status bar to display the Customize Status Bar menu. A check mark indicates each item that is currently enabled.

2. Click to enable or disable a status bar indicator or tool. The change is effected immediately. The menu remains open to permit multiple selections.

3. When you finish, click away from the menu to close it.

Adapt procedure steps

This book contains many images of user interface elements (such as the ribbons and the app windows) that you'll work with while performing tasks in PowerPoint on a Windows computer. Depending on your screen resolution or app window width, the PowerPoint ribbon on your screen might look different from that shown in this book. (If you turn on Touch mode, the ribbon displays significantly fewer commands than in Mouse mode.) As a result, procedural instructions that involve the ribbon might require a little adaptation.

Simple procedural instructions use this format:

1. On the **Insert** tab, in the **Illustrations** group, click the **Chart** button.

If the command is in a list, our instructions use this format:

1. On the **Transitions** tab, in the **Timing** group, click the **Sound** arrow and then, in the **Sound** list, click **Chime**.

If differences between your display settings and ours cause a button to appear differently on your screen than it does in this book, you can easily adapt the steps to locate the command. First click the specified tab, and then locate the specified group. If a group has been collapsed into a group list or under a group button, click the list or button to display the group's commands. If you can't immediately identify the button you want, point to likely candidates to display their names in ScreenTips.

Multistep procedural instructions use this format:

1. Display the presentation in Normal view.

2. Select the animated object or objects that you want to modify.

3. On the **Animations** tab, in the **Timing** group, click the **Start** arrow to display the list of start timing options.

4. In the **Start** list, click **After Previous**.

On subsequent instances of instructions that require you to follow the same process, the instructions might be simplified in this format because the working location has already been established:

1. In Normal view, select the animated objects that you want to modify.

2. On the **Animations** tab, in the **Start** list, click **After Previous**.

The instructions in this book assume that you're interacting with on-screen elements on your computer by clicking (with a mouse, touchpad, or other hardware device). If you're using a different method—for example, if your computer has a touchscreen interface and you're tapping the screen (with your finger or a stylus)—substitute the applicable tapping action when you interact with a user interface element.

Instructions in this book refer to user interface elements that you click or tap on the screen as *buttons*, and to physical buttons that you press on a keyboard as *keys*, to conform to the standard terminology used in documentation for these products.

When the instructions tell you to enter information, you can do so by typing on a connected external keyboard, tapping an on-screen keyboard, or even speaking aloud, depending on your computer setup and your personal preferences.

Manage Office and app settings

You access app settings from the Backstage view; specifically, from the Account page and the PowerPoint Options dialog box.

The Account page of the Backstage view in PowerPoint displays information about your installation of PowerPoint (and other apps in the Office suite) and the resources you connect to. This information includes:

- Your Microsoft account and links to manage it.
- The current app window background and theme.
- Storage locations and services (such as Facebook and LinkedIn) that you've connected Office to.
- Your subscription information and links to manage the subscription, if you have Office through an Office 365 subscription.
- The app version number and update options.

Account information in PowerPoint

1

Microsoft account options

If you use Office 365, Skype, OneDrive, Xbox Live, Outlook.com, or a Windows Phone, you already have a Microsoft account. (Microsoft account credentials are also used by many non-Microsoft products and websites.) If you don't already have a Microsoft account, you can register any existing account as a Microsoft account, sign up for a free Outlook.com or Hotmail.com account and register that as a Microsoft account, or create an alias for an Outlook.com account and register the alias.

TIP Many apps and websites authenticate transactions by using Microsoft account credentials. For that reason, it's a good idea to register a personal account that you control, rather than a business account that your employer controls, as your Microsoft account. That way, you won't risk losing access if you leave the company.

Two ways you can personalize the appearance of your PowerPoint app window are by choosing an Office background and an Office theme. (These are specific to Office and aren't in any way associated with the Windows theme or desktop background.) The background is a subtle design that appears in the title bar of the app window. There are 14 backgrounds to choose from, or you can choose to not have a background.

Backgrounds depict a variety of subjects

At the time of this writing, there are three Office themes:

- **Colorful** Displays the title bar and ribbon tabs in the color specific to the app, and the ribbon commands, status bar, and Backstage view in light gray

- **Dark Gray** Displays the title bar and ribbon tabs in dark gray, and the ribbon commands, status bar, and Backstage view in light gray

- **White** Displays the title bar, ribbon tabs, and ribbon commands in white, and the status bar in the app-specific color

There are rumors that another theme will be released in the near future, but it hasn't yet made an appearance.

 TIP The images in this book depict the No Background option to avoid interfering with the display of any user interface elements, and the Colorful theme.

From the Connected Services area of the page, you can connect Office to Facebook, Flickr, and YouTube accounts to access pictures and videos; to SharePoint sites and OneDrive storage locations; and to LinkedIn and Twitter accounts to share presentations. You must already have an account with one of these services to connect Office to it.

Until you connect to storage locations, they aren't available to you from within PowerPoint. For example, when inserting a picture onto a slide, you will have the option to insert a locally stored picture or to search online for a picture. After you connect to your Facebook, SharePoint, and OneDrive accounts, you can also insert pictures stored in those locations.

The changes that you make on the Account page apply to all the Office apps installed on all the computers associated with your account. For example, changing the Office background in PowerPoint on one computer also changes it in Outlook on any other computer on which you've associated Office with the same account.

Some of the settings on the Account page are also available in the PowerPoint Options dialog box, which you open from the Backstage view. This dialog box also contains hundreds of options for controlling the way PowerPoint works. Chapter 11, "Work in PowerPoint more efficiently," provides in-depth coverage of these options. It's a good idea to familiarize yourself with the dialog box content so you know what you can modify.

1

To display your Office account settings

1. With PowerPoint running, click the **File** tab to display the Backstage view.

2. In the left pane of the Backstage view, click **Account**.

To manage your Microsoft account settings

1. Display the **Account** page of the Backstage view.

2. In the **User Information** area, click any of the links to begin the selected process.

To change the app window background for all Office apps

1. Display the **Account** page of the Backstage view.

2. In the **Office Background** list, point to any background to display a live preview in the app window, and then click the background you want.

To change the app window color scheme for all Office apps

1. Display the **Account** page of the Backstage view.

2. In the **Office Theme** list, click **Colorful**, **Dark Gray**, or **White**.

To connect to a cloud storage location or social media service

1. Display the **Account** page of the Backstage view.

2. At the bottom of the **Connected Services** area, click **Add a service**, click the type of service you want to add, and then click the specific service.

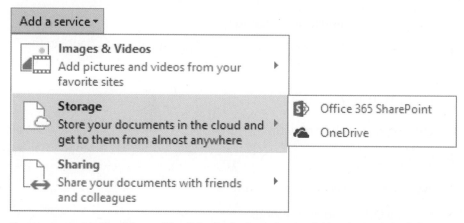

You can connect to OneDrive and OneDrive for Business sites by clicking the OneDrive link

To manage your Office 365 subscription

1. Display the **Account** page of the Backstage view.

2. In the **Product Information** area, click the **Manage Account** button to display the sign-in page for your Office 365 management interface.

3. Provide your account credentials and sign in to access your options.

To manage Office updates

1. Display the **Account** page of the Backstage view.

2. Click the **Update Options** button, and then click the action you want to take.

You can install available updates from the Backstage view before the automatic installation occurs

To open the PowerPoint Options dialog box

1. In the left pane of the Backstage view, click **Options**.

Skills review

In this chapter, you learned how to:

- Start PowerPoint

- Work in the PowerPoint user interface

- Manage Office and app settings

Practice tasks

No practice files are necessary to complete the practice tasks in this chapter.

Start PowerPoint

Perform the following tasks:

1. Using the technique that is appropriate for your operating system, start PowerPoint.

2. When the **Start** screen appears, press the **Esc** key to create a new blank presentation.

Work in the PowerPoint user interface

Start PowerPoint, create a new blank presentation, maximize the app window, and then perform the following tasks:

1. On each tab of the ribbon, do the following:

   - Review the available groups and commands.

   - Display the ScreenTip of any command you're not familiar with. Notice the different levels of detail in the ScreenTips.

   - If a group has a dialog box launcher in its lower-right corner, click the dialog box launcher to display the associated dialog box or pane.

2. Change the width of the app window and notice the effect it has on the ribbon. When the window is narrow, locate a group button and click it to display the commands.

3. Maximize the app window. Hide the ribbon entirely, and notice the change in the app window. Redisplay the ribbon tabs (but not the commands). Temporarily display the ribbon commands, and then click away from the ribbon to close it.

4. Use any of the procedures described in this chapter to permanently redisplay the ribbon tabs and commands.

5. Display the status bar shortcut menu, and identify the tools and statistics that are currently displayed on the status bar. Add any indicators to the status bar that will be useful to you.

6. Keep the presentation open in PowerPoint for use in the next set of practice tasks.

Manage Office and app settings

With a new blank presentation open in PowerPoint, perform the following tasks:

1. Display the **Account** page of the Backstage view and review the information that is available there.

2. Expand the **Office Background** list. Point to each background to display a live preview of it. Then click the background you want to apply.

3. Apply each of the Office themes, and consider its merits. Then apply the theme you like best.

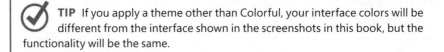 **TIP** If you apply a theme other than Colorful, your interface colors will be different from the interface shown in the screenshots in this book, but the functionality will be the same.

4. Review the services that Office is currently connected to. Expand the **Add a service** menu and point to each of the menu items to display the available services. Connect to any of these that you want to use.

5. Click the **Update Options** button and note whether updates are currently available to install.

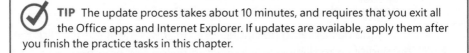 **TIP** The update process takes about 10 minutes, and requires that you exit all the Office apps and Internet Explorer. If updates are available, apply them after you finish the practice tasks in this chapter.

6. On the **Update Options** menu, click **View Updates** to display the *What's New and Improved in Office 2016* webpage in your default browser. Review the information on this page to learn about any new features that interest you.

7. Return to PowerPoint and open the **PowerPoint Options** dialog box.

8. Explore each page of the dialog box. Notice the sections and the settings in each section. Note the settings that apply only to the current file.

9. Review the settings on the **General** page, and modify them as necessary to fit the way you work. Then close the dialog box.

10. Close the presentation without saving changes.

Create and manage presentations

2

PowerPoint makes it easy to efficiently create effective presentations for a wide variety of audiences. PowerPoint presentations are no longer used solely by business executives to present information at board meetings. They're commonly used in business and educational settings to share information, not only in group presentations, but also in electronic communications and online settings. Even primary school students are assigned PowerPoint presentations as homework projects. Whether you need to give a report about a research study, present a budget to a board of directors, or convince management to invest in a new piece of equipment, PowerPoint helps you get the job done in a professional, visually appealing way.

The sophisticated presentation features of PowerPoint are easy to find and use, so even novice users can work productively with PowerPoint after only a brief introduction. Many of the processes you perform with slide content are similar to processes you use in Microsoft Word documents and Microsoft Excel workbooks, so if you already use another Microsoft Office app, you might be familiar with them. Processes that are specific to the creation and management of slides are unique to PowerPoint.

This chapter guides you through procedures related to creating presentations, opening and navigating presentations, displaying different views of presentations, displaying and editing presentation properties, and saving and closing presentations.

In this chapter

- Create presentations
- Open and navigate presentations
- Display different views of presentations
- Display and edit presentation properties
- Save and close presentations

Practice files

For this chapter, use the practice files from the PowerPoint2016SBS\Ch02 folder. For practice file download instructions, see the introduction.

Create presentations

When creating a new presentation, you can start by using a blank presentation or by using a presentation that is based on a template. Unlike the templates provided for Word and Excel, most PowerPoint templates are design templates that control thematic elements (colors, fonts, and graphic effects) and slide layouts rather than content templates that provide purpose-specific placeholder content. Each template has a corresponding theme, so you can create a presentation based on one template but then entirely change its appearance by applying a different theme.

When you start PowerPoint, the app displays a Start screen that gives you options for opening an existing presentation or creating a new one.

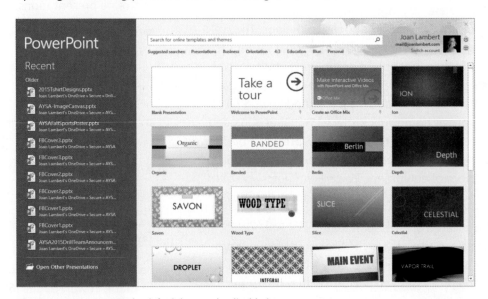

The Start screen appears by default but can be disabled

> ⚠ **IMPORTANT** The templates that appear by default in your installation of PowerPoint might be different from those shown in images in this book. The templates can change depending on your use of PowerPoint and the installation of program updates.

There are a few different ways to start a new presentation. If you press the Esc key when this screen appears, PowerPoint starts a blank presentation for you. You can also select from among the presentation thumbnails and links to create presentations based on the following sources:

■ **Blank presentation** If you want to build and format a presentation from scratch, you can start with a presentation based on the Blank Presentation template. A new, blank presentation contains only a blank title page; it's up to you to add slides and slide content, apply a theme, and make any necessary custom configuration changes. Creating attractive, functional presentations from scratch can be time-consuming and requires quite a bit of knowledge about PowerPoint. You'll learn the skills you need while you work through this book.

> **SEE ALSO** For information about themes, see "Apply themes" in Chapter 3, "Create and manage slides."

■ **Design template** You can save time by basing your presentation on one of the many design templates that come with PowerPoint. A design template is a blank presentation with a theme already applied to it. Sometimes it includes background graphic elements and specialized slide layouts. Some templates supply only a title slide and leave it to you to add the other slides you need; other templates supply an example of each of the available slide layouts.

■ **Content template** You can preview and download many prepopulated presentation templates from the Office website. These templates provide not only the design elements but also suggestions for content that is appropriate for different types of presentations, such as reports or product launches. After you download a template, you simply customize the content provided in the template to meet your needs.

An important thing to be aware of when you create a presentation in PowerPoint is that you have the choice of two slide aspect ratios, which are referred to (slightly inaccurately) as slide sizes. The default slide size is Widescreen (16:9), which is optimized for displays such as those found on many laptop screens and desktop monitors these days.

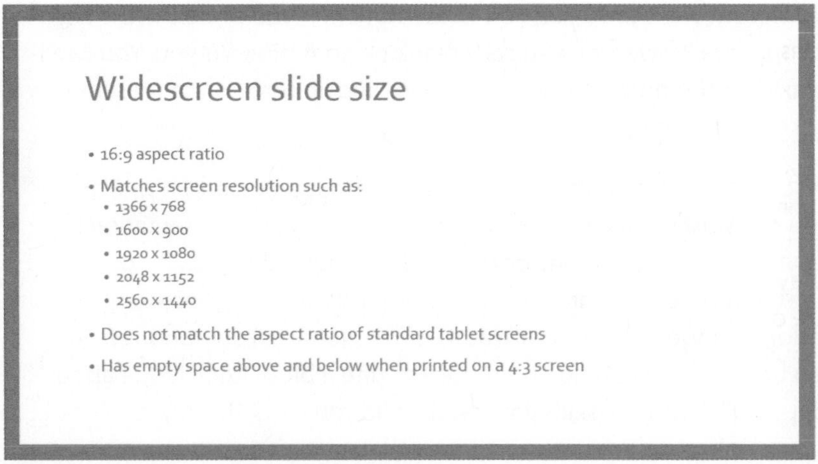

Widescreen slide size

- 16:9 aspect ratio
- Matches screen resolution such as:
  - 1366 x 768
  - 1600 x 900
  - 1920 x 1080
  - 2048 x 1152
  - 2560 x 1440
- Does not match the aspect ratio of standard tablet screens
- Has empty space above and below when printed on a 4:3 screen

Widescreen slides are shorter than Standard slides

The alternative slide size is Standard (4:3), which is optimized for wide rectangular screens such as that of the iPad.

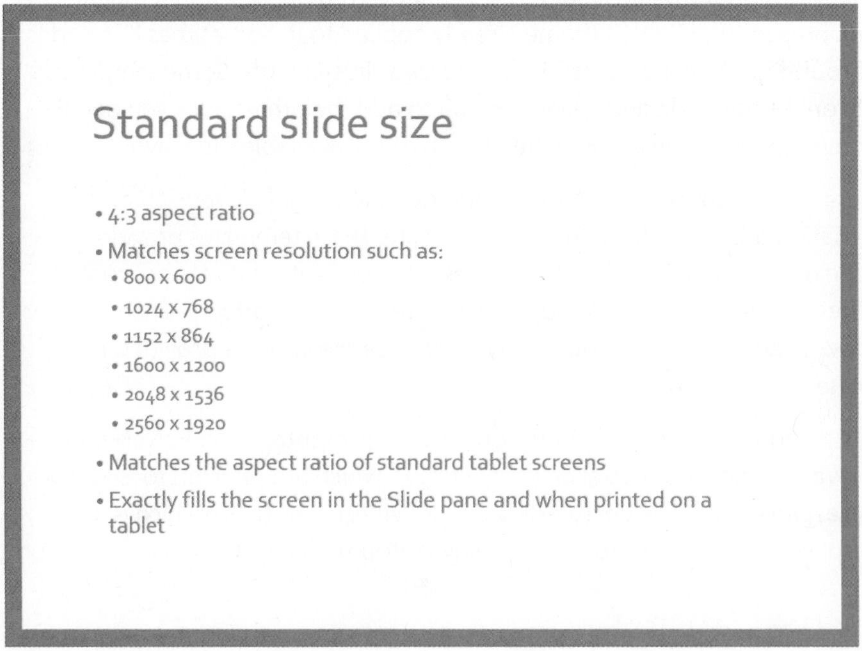

Standard slide size

- 4:3 aspect ratio
- Matches screen resolution such as:
  - 800 x 600
  - 1024 x 768
  - 1152 x 864
  - 1600 x 1200
  - 2048 x 1536
  - 2560 x 1920
- Matches the aspect ratio of standard tablet screens
- Exactly fills the screen in the Slide pane and when printed on a tablet

Standard slides fit tablet screens

2

The actual size (dimensions) of the slide aren't as important as its aspect ratio. By default, the slides in presentations you create based on the Blank Presentation template are set to Widescreen size.

 SEE ALSO For more information about slide sizes, see "Configure slides for presentation or printing" in Chapter 9, "Review presentations."

When you display the built-in templates on the New page of the Backstage view, the default slide size of each template is apparent from its thumbnail. Most of the templates are 16:9, but you can easily filter the templates to display only those that are formatted specifically for 4:3 slides.

Before you begin adding content to a new presentation, you should consider how the presentation will be viewed and choose the most appropriate slide size. It's advisable to select the slide size before you select the presentation template. You can change the slide size after you create the slide deck, but doing so might cause graphic elements (especially those on master slides) to look different, and text and other slide elements to not fit on slides as intended.

Whether you create a blank presentation or a presentation that is based on a design template, the presentation exists only in your computer's memory until you save it.

 SEE ALSO For information about saving presentations, see "Save and close presentations" later in this chapter.

To create a new blank presentation

1. Start PowerPoint.

2. When the Start screen appears, press the **Esc** key.

Or

1. If PowerPoint is already running, click the **File** tab to display the Backstage view.

2. In the left pane of the Backstage view, click **New** to display the New page.

3. On the **New** page of the Backstage view, click the **Blank Presentation** thumbnail.

To preview presentation design templates

1. Display the Backstage view, and then, in the left pane, click **New**.

2. On the **New** page, scroll the pane to view the presentation design templates that were installed with PowerPoint.

3. Click any thumbnail to open a preview window that displays the title slide of the selected design with alternative color schemes and graphic backgrounds.

Each design template has multiple color variants and slide layouts

4. Do any of the following:

   - Click the **More Images** arrows to display other slide layouts for the template.

   - Click any of the thumbnails in the right half of the preview window to apply that color scheme to the slide layouts of the selected template.

   - Click the arrows to the left and right of the preview window to preview other design templates.

   - Click the **Create** button to create a presentation based on the template that is active in the preview window.

   - In the upper-right corner of the preview window, click the **Close** button to close the preview window without creating a presentation.

To display only presentation templates that are optimized at the 4:3 slide size

1. On the **New** page of the Backstage view, below the **Search** box, click **4:3**.

Common filters are available below the Search box

To create a presentation based on a default design template

1. Display the **New** page of the Backstage view.

2. Scroll the pane to locate the design you want to use.

3. Do either of the following:

   • Double-click the thumbnail to create the presentation.

   • Click the thumbnail to preview the design template, and then click the **Create** button in the preview window to create the presentation.

   PowerPoint displays the new presentation in Normal view. The title slide is visible in the Thumbnails pane and in the Slide pane.

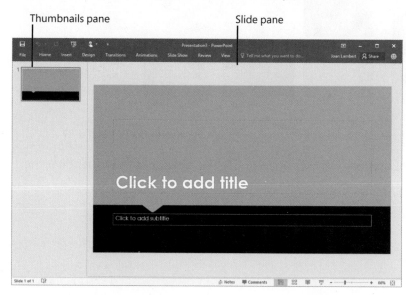

The title slide of a new presentation

> **TIP** The Notes pane is below the Slide pane but is collapsed by default. For information about working in the Notes pane, see "Add notes to slides" in Chapter 9, "Review presentations."

To create a presentation based on an online template

1. Display the **New** page of the Backstage view.

2. In the search box at the top of the page, enter a term related to the template content or design you're looking for, and then click the **Search** button.

   Or

   Below the search box, click one of the suggested searches.

You can enter a color as a search term to display templates that feature that color

3. In the **Category** list, click any category or categories to further filter the templates.

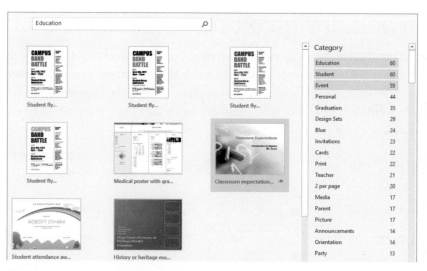

Clicking multiple categories applies multiple filters

> **TIP** PowerPoint displays applied category filters in colored bars at the top of the Category list. To remove a filter, point to it and then click the X that appears to the right of the category name, or double-click the category name.

4. Scroll the pane to locate a design that fit your needs.

5. Click any thumbnail to preview the design template, and click the **More Images** arrows to see the content defined as part of the template. Then click the **Create** button in the preview window to create the presentation.

   Or

   Double-click any thumbnail to create a presentation based on the template.

To disable the display of the Start screen

1. In the Backstage view, click **Options** to open the **PowerPoint Options** dialog box.

2. On the **General** page of the dialog box, clear the **Show the Start screen when this application starts** check box.

3. Close the **PowerPoint Options** dialog box.

Open and navigate presentations

The Start screen that appears by default when you start PowerPoint displays a list of presentations you worked on recently, and a link to open other existing presentations. If the presentation you want to open appears on the Start screen, you can open it directly from there. Otherwise, you open presentations from the Open page of the Backstage view.

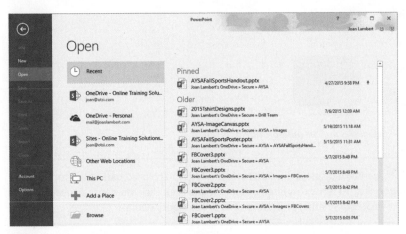

The Open page includes all the locations you've linked to from an Office program

When a presentation is open, you can move among slides by clicking or tapping elements in several areas of the app window, including the Thumbnails pane in Normal view and the Slide pane in Normal view or Slide Sorter view. You can also move among slides by rotating the wheel button on a mouse.

The scroll bar indicates the position of the current slide in the presentation

To open a recent presentation

1. Start PowerPoint.

2. On the Start screen, in the **Recent** list, click the file name of the presentation you want to open.

Or

1. With PowerPoint running, click the **File** tab to display the Backstage view.

2. In the left pane of the Backstage view, click **Open** to display the **Open** page.

3. In the right pane of the **Open** page, scroll the presentation list if necessary to locate the presentation you want to open, and then click the presentation file name to open it.

To open any existing presentation

1. Start PowerPoint.

2. On the Start screen, at the bottom of the left pane, click **Open Other Presentations** to display the **Open** page of the Backstage view.

   Or

With PowerPoint running, display the Backstage view, and then click **Open** to display the **Open** page.

The Places list includes all the locations you've linked to from an Office program

3. In the **Places** list, click the local or network storage location where the presentation is stored.

4. Navigate to the presentation storage folder by using one of the following methods:

   - In the right pane, click a recent folder. Then click any subfolders until you reach the folder you want.

   - In the left pane, click **Browse** to open the **Open** dialog box. Then click folders in the Navigation pane, double-click folders in the file pane, or enter the folder location in the Address bar.

5. Double-click the presentation you want to open.

2

 TIP In the Open dialog box, clicking a file name and then clicking the Open arrow displays a list of alternative ways to open the selected file. To look through a presentation without making any inadvertent changes, you can open the file as read-only, open an independent copy of the file, or open it in Protected view. You can also open the file in a web browser. In the event of a computer crash or other similar incident, you can tell PowerPoint to open the file and try to repair any damage.

To move back or forward one slide while working in a presentation

1. Use any of the following techniques

   - In the **Slide** pane, on the scroll bar, click above or below the scroll box.

   - Below the **Slide** pane scroll bar, click the **Previous Slide** or **Next Slide** button.

Previous Slide and Next Slide buttons

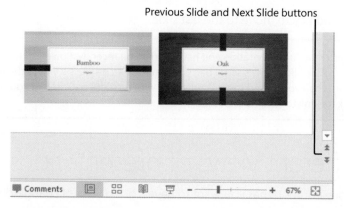

Use the Previous Slide and Next Slide buttons or the thumbnails to move more quickly among slides

   - Press the **Page Up** or **Page Down** key.

 SEE ALSO For information about moving among slides in Reading view, see "Display different views of presentations" later in this chapter.

To move among slides while working in a presentation

1. Use any of the following techniques:

   - In the **Thumbnails** pane, click the slide you want to display.

   - In the **Slide** pane, drag the scroll bar up or down.

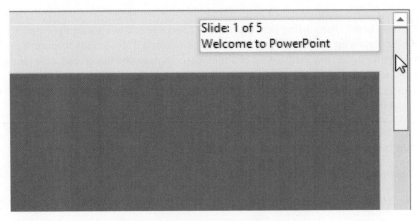

A tooltip displays the slide that will be shown if you stop dragging

- Press the **Home** key to move to the first slide.
- Press the **End** key to move to the last slide.

> **✓ TIP** When you open a presentation you have worked on recently, PowerPoint displays a flag adjacent to the Slide pane's scroll bar. Clicking the flag displays a link to the slide you were working on when you closed the presentation, with the date and time of your last change. Simply click the link to jump to that slide.

Display different views of presentations

The elements of a presentation that you want to have a good view of change depending on what you're currently doing with the presentation. You can switch among standard presentation views, adjust the elements shown in each view, and change the magnification of the content in the app window.

Display standard views

PowerPoint has six views in which you can create, organize, and preview presentations. The views are:

- **Normal view** This view includes the Thumbnails pane on the left side of the app window, the Slide pane on the right side of the window, and an optional Notes pane at the bottom of the window. You insert, cut, copy, paste, duplicate, and delete slides in the Thumbnails pane, create slide content in the Slide pane, and record slide notes in the Notes pane.

2

SEE ALSO For information about working with notes, see "Add notes to slides" in Chapter 9, "Review presentations."

- **Notes Page view** This is the only view in which you can create speaker notes that contain elements other than text. Although you can add speaker notes in the Notes pane in Normal view, you must be in Notes Page view to add graphics, tables, diagrams, or charts to your notes.

- **Outline view** This view displays a text outline of the presentation in the Outline pane and the active slide in the Slide pane. You can enter text either directly on the slide or in the outline.

SEE ALSO For information about working with outlines, see "Enter text on slides" in Chapter 4, "Enter and edit text on slides."

- **Reading view** In this view, which is ideal for previewing the presentation, each slide fills the screen. You can click buttons on the navigation bar to move through or jump to specific slides.

In Reading view, the navigation bar and View Shortcuts toolbar are at the right end of the status bar

- **Slide Show view** This view displays the presentation as a full-screen slide show, beginning with the current slide. It displays only the slides and not the presenter tools.

- **Slide Sorter view** This view displays thumbnails of all the slides in the presentation. In this view, you manage the slides, rather than the slide content. You can easily reorganize the slides, group them into sections, and apply transitions to one or multiple slides. You can also apply transitions from one slide to another, and specify how long each slide should remain on the screen.

SEE ALSO For information about changing the order of slides, see "Rearrange slides and sections" in Chapter 3, "Create and manage slides." For information about applying transitions, see "Add and manage slide transitions" in Chapter 8, "Add sound and movement to slides."

The views you'll use most frequently when developing presentations are Normal view and Slide Sorter view.

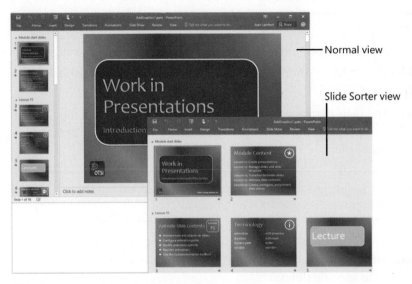

The primary presentation development views

 SEE ALSO For information about creating more elaborate notes, see "Add notes to slides" in Chapter 9, "Review presentations."

View options are available from the View Shortcuts toolbar near the right end of the status bar and from the View tab of the ribbon.

View Shortcuts toolbar

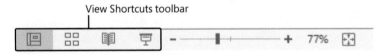

The active view is shaded

To review a presentation (or deliver it to an audience), you display it in Slide Show view. In this view, each slide fills the screen, and PowerPoint implements transitions, animations, and media effects the way you have specified. You can start the slide show from the first slide or from the currently active slide.

TIP You can control the default look of a presentation by working with the masters displayed in Slide Master view, Handout Master view, or Notes Master view. For information about masters, see "Customize slide masters and layouts" in Chapter 12, "Create custom presentation elements."

2

To switch among development views of a presentation

1. Do either of the following:

   - On the **View Shortcuts** toolbar, click the **Normal** or **Slide Sorter** button.

      TIP Clicking the Normal button while it is active switches between Normal and Outline views.

   - On the **View** tab, in the **Presentation Views** group, click the **Normal** or **Slide Sorter** button.

To display a presentation in Slide Show view from the first slide

1. Do either of the following:

   - On the **Slide Show** tab, in the **Start Slide Show** group, click the **From Beginning** button. (When you point to this button, the ScreenTip that appears says *Start From Beginning*.)

   - Press **F5**.

To display a presentation in Slide Show view from the current slide

1. Do any of the following:

   - On the **View Shortcuts** toolbar, click the **Slide Show** button.

   - On the **Slide Show** tab, in the **Start Slide Show** group, click the **From Current Slide** button. (When you point to this button, the ScreenTip that appears says *Start from This Slide*.)

   - Press **Shift+F5**.

SEE ALSO For information about delivering a presentation to an audience, see "Present slide shows" in Chapter 10, "Prepare and deliver presentations."

To navigate a presentation in Slide Show view

1. Do any of the following:

    *   Move the mouse to display the **Slide Show** toolbar. Then click the **Previous** or **Next** button on the toolbar.

Previous and Next buttons

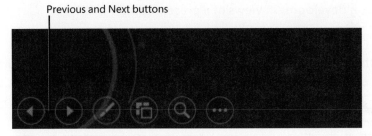

The Slide Show toolbar hides itself until you activate it

    *   Press the **N** (for *next*), **Enter**, **Right Arrow**, **Down Arrow**, or **Page Down** key to move forward one slide.

    *   Press the **P** (for *previous*), **Backspace**, **Left Arrow**, **Up Arrow**, or **Page Up** key to move back one slide.

    *   Press the **Home** key to display the first slide.

    *   Press the **End** key to display the last slide.

    *   Press the **Esc** key to return to Normal or Slide Sorter view.

 SEE ALSO For more information about the Slide Show tools, see "Present slide shows" in Chapter 10, "Prepare and deliver presentations."

To display a presentation in Reading view

1. Do either of the following:

    *   On the **View Shortcuts** toolbar, click the **Reading View** button.

    *   On the **View** tab, in the **Presentation Views** group, click the **Reading View** button.

To navigate a presentation in Reading view

1. Do any of the following:

    -   Press the **N** (for *next*), **Enter**, **Right Arrow**, **Down Arrow**, or **Page Down** key to move forward one slide.

    -   Press the **P** (for *previous*), **Backspace**, **Left Arrow**, **Up Arrow**, or **Page Up** key to move back one slide.

    -   Press the **Home** key to display the first slide.

    -   Press the **End** key to display the last slide.

    -   Press the **Esc** key or click the **Normal** or **Slide Sorter** button on the **View Shortcuts** toolbar to return to Normal or Slide Sorter view.

Display program elements

You can change the space available for the app window elements by adjusting the relative sizes of the panes or collapsing the ribbon.

 TIP Any changes you make to a view, such as adjusting the sizes of panes, are saved with the presentation that is open at the time and do not affect other presentations.

To adjust the size of the Thumbnails pane in Normal view

1. Do either of the following:

    -   Point to the right border of the **Thumbnails** pane, and drag right or left to resize or hide the **Thumbnails** pane.

    -   When the **Thumbnails** pane is hidden, click the **Thumbnails** button at the top of the bar to redisplay it.

 TIP When you adjust the width of the Thumbnails pane, the size of the slide thumbnails is adjusted accordingly—that is, there are more small thumbnails in a narrow pane and fewer large thumbnails in a wide pane.

To show or hide the Notes pane in Normal view

1. On the status bar, click the **Notes** button.

To adjust the size of the Notes pane in Normal view

1. Point to the border between the **Slide** pane and the **Notes** pane, and when the pointer changes to a bar with opposing arrows, drag up or down to resize or hide the **Notes** pane.

To hide the ribbon in Normal, Outline, or Slide Sorter views

1. Do any of the following:

   - At the right end of the ribbon, click the **Collapse the Ribbon** button, which resembles an upward-pointing arrow.

   - Press **Ctrl+F1**.

   Collapsing the ribbon hides the groups and buttons but leaves the tab names visible.

To temporarily redisplay the ribbon

1. Click any tab name.

   The ribbon remains visible until you click a button on it or click away from it.

To permanently redisplay the ribbon

1. Do any of the following:

   - Double-click any tab name.

   - Click any tab name and then click the **Pin the ribbon** button, which resembles a pushpin.

   - Press **Ctrl+F1**.

Change the display of content

You can easily switch among multiple open presentations. If you want to compare or work with the content of multiple presentations, you can simplify the process by displaying the presentations next to each other.

2

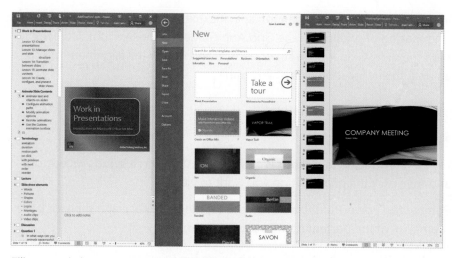

Tiling app windows simplifies the process of comparing, copying, or moving content

To help you to more precisely position and align slide elements, you can display rulers, gridlines, and guides in the Slide pane, and change the magnification of the current slide.

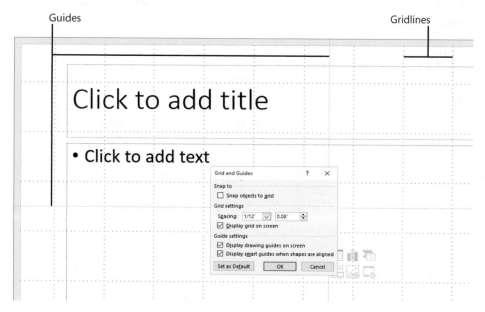

Use gridlines and guides to more precisely position objects

Gridlines are faint dotted lines that mark off specific units of measure on a slide. You can adjust the spacing of gridlines in the Grid And Guides dialog box, but you can't move them on the slide. Guides are a set of vertical and horizontal alignment tools that you can drag to any location in the Slide pane.

To display a different open presentation

1. Do either of the following:

   - On the **View** tab, in the **Window** group, click the **Switch Windows** button, and then click the presentation you want to view.

   - Point to the **PowerPoint** button on the Windows taskbar, and then click the thumbnail of the presentation you want to display.

To display multiple open presentations at the same time

1. On the **View** tab, in the **Window** group, click the **Arrange All** button.

To display or hide the ruler, gridlines, and guides

1. On the **View** tab, in the **Show** group, select or clear the **Ruler**, **Gridlines**, or **Guides** check boxes.

To modify the spacing of gridlines

1. On the **View** tab, click the **Show** dialog box launcher to open the **Grid and Guides** dialog box.

2. In the **Grid settings** area, change either the fractional or unit measurement of the **Spacing** setting. Then click **OK**.

To change the magnification of content in the app window

1. On the **View** tab, in the **Zoom** group, click the **Zoom** button to open the **Zoom** dialog box.

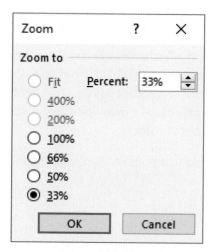

You can select a magnification or enter a specific percentage

2. In the **Zoom** dialog box, select a **Zoom to** option or enter a specific percentage in the **Percent** box, and then click **OK**.

Or

1. In the zoom controls at the right end of the status bar, do any of the following:

    *   At the left end of the slider, click the **Zoom Out** button to decrease the zoom percentage.

    *   At the right end of the slider, click the **Zoom In** button to increase the zoom percentage.

    *   At the right end of the status bar, click the **Fit slide to current window** button.

Clicking the Fit Slide To Current Window button is a quick way to view the entire slide at the largest size that fits in the Slide pane

Display and edit presentation properties

Properties are file attributes or settings, such as the file name, size, creation, date, author, and read-only status. Some properties exist to provide information to computer operating systems and apps. You can display properties within a presentation (for example, you can display the slide number on a slide). PowerPoint automatically tracks some of the properties for you, and you can set others.

You can examine the properties that are attached to a presentation from the Info page of the Backstage view.

Properties ▾	
Size	764KB
Slides	11
Hidden slides	2
Words	164
Notes	1
Title	Company Meeting
Tags	Add a tag
Comments	Add comments
Multimedia clips	0
Presentation format	Widescreen
Template	Vapor Trail
Status	Add text
Categories	Add a category
Subject	Specify the subject
Hyperlink Base	Add text
Company	Online Training Solutio...

Related Dates

Last Modified	Today, 10:37 PM
Created	Today, 10:35 PM
Last Printed	Today, 10:37 PM

Related People

Manager	Specify the manager
Author	Joan Lambert

Some of the properties stored with a typical presentation

You can change or remove basic properties in the default Properties pane or expand the Properties pane to make more available, or display the Properties dialog box to access even more properties.

To display presentation properties

1. Display the **Info** page of the Backstage view. The standard properties associated with a presentation are displayed in the **Properties** area of the right pane.

2. At the bottom of the **Properties** pane, click **Show All Properties** to expand the pane.

3. At the top of the **Properties** pane, click **Properties** and then click **Advanced Properties** to display the **Properties** dialog box.

To edit presentation properties

1. In the **Properties** pane, click the value for the property you want to edit to activate the content box. (Note that not all properties are available to edit. Those that can be edited will display an edit box when you point to them. Nothing happens if you click one that can't be edited.)

2. Enter or replace the property value, and then press **Enter**.

Or

1. In the **Properties** dialog box, do either of the following:

    *   On the **Summary** page, click the box to the right of the property you want to modify, and then enter or replace the property value.

    *   On the **Custom** page, select the property you want to modify in the **Name** list, and then enter or replace the property value in the **Value** box.

Save and close presentations

You save a presentation the first time by clicking the Save button on the Quick Access Toolbar or by displaying the Backstage view and then clicking Save As. Both actions open the Save As page, where you can select a storage location.

Save your presentation in an online location to access it from anywhere

> **TIP** Many countries have laws that require that certain types of digital content be accessible to people with various disabilities. If your presentation must be compatible with assistive technologies, you need to know the final file format(s) of your presentation before you create it and start adding content. Some types of content are visible in a PowerPoint file in Normal view but not in other accessible file formats such as tagged PDFs. Before basing a presentation on a template you have not used before, test it for accessibility.

You can save the presentation in a folder on your computer or, if you have an Internet connection, in a folder on your Microsoft OneDrive. If your company is running Microsoft SharePoint, you can add your SharePoint OneDrive or a different SharePoint location so that it is available from the Places pane of the Save As page, just like any other folder.

> **SEE ALSO** For information about OneDrive, see the sidebar "Save files to OneDrive" later in this chapter.

Clicking Browse at the bottom of the left pane displays the Save As dialog box, in which you assign a name to the file.

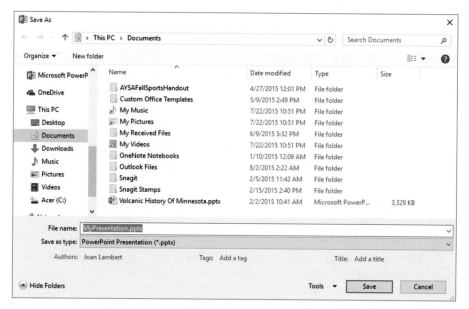

2

Use standard Windows techniques in either the Address bar or the Navigation pane to navigate to the folder you want

 TIP If you want to create a new folder in which to store the file, click the New Folder button on the dialog box's toolbar.

After you save a presentation for the first time, you can save changes simply by clicking the Save button on the Quick Access Toolbar. The new version of the presentation then overwrites the previous version.

If you want to keep both the new version and the previous version, display the Save As page, and then save a new version with a different name in the same location or with the same name in a different location. (You cannot have two files with the same name in the same folder.)

TIP By default, PowerPoint periodically saves the presentation you are working on. To adjust the time interval between saves, display the Backstage view, and click Options. In the left pane of the PowerPoint Options dialog box, click Save, and then specify the period of time in the Save AutoRecover Information Every box.

Every time you open a presentation, a new instance of PowerPoint starts. If you have more than one presentation open, clicking the Close button at the right end of a presentation's title bar closes that presentation and exits that instance of PowerPoint. If you have only one presentation open and you want to close the presentation but leave PowerPoint running, display the Backstage view and then click Close.

To save a presentation

1. On the Quick Access Toolbar, click the **Save** button to display the **Save As** page of the Backstage view.

2. Select a storage location, and then in the right pane, click **Browse** to open the **Save As** dialog box.

    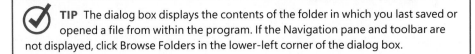 **TIP** The dialog box displays the contents of the folder in which you last saved or opened a file from within the program. If the Navigation pane and toolbar are not displayed, click Browse Folders in the lower-left corner of the dialog box.

3. Use standard Windows techniques to navigate to your file folder.

4. In the **File name** box, enter a name for your presentation, and then click **Save** to store the file in your file folder.

Or

1. Press **Ctrl+S** to save an existing presentation without changing the file name or location.

    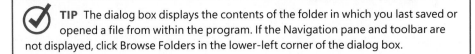 **TIP** Programs that run on Windows use file name extensions to identify different types of files. For example, the extension .pptx identifies PowerPoint 2016, 2013, 2010, and 2007 presentations. Windows programs do not display these extensions by default, and you shouldn't enter them in the File Name box. When you save a file, PowerPoint automatically adds whatever extension is associated with the type of file selected in the Save As Type box.

To close a presentation

1. Do any of the following:

   - At the right end of the title bar, click the **Close** button to close the presentation and the app window.

   - Display the Backstage view, and then click **Close** to close the presentation without exiting the app.

   - On the **Windows Taskbar**, point to the **PowerPoint** button to display thumbnails of all open presentations, point to the thumbnail of the presentation you want to close, and then click the **Close** button that appears in its upper-right corner.

Compatibility with earlier versions

The Microsoft Office 2016 programs use file formats based on XML. By default, PowerPoint 2016 files are saved in the .pptx format.

You can open a .ppt file created with an earlier version of PowerPoint in PowerPoint 2016, but the newer features of PowerPoint are not available. The presentation name appears in the title bar with [Compatibility Mode] to its right. You can work in this mode, or you can convert the presentation to the current format by clicking the Convert button on the Info page of the Backstage view, or by saving the presentation as a different file in the PowerPoint Presentation format.

If you work with people who are using a version of PowerPoint earlier than 2007, you can save your presentations in a format that they will be able to use by changing the Save As Type setting in the Save As dialog box to PowerPoint 97-2003 Presentation.

Save files to OneDrive

Whether you're working in a corporate environment or at home, you have the option of saving files to OneDrive. The OneDrive location you save to might be part of your company's SharePoint environment, or it might be a cloud-based storage location that is associated with your Microsoft account. Saving a file in either type of OneDrive location provides the option of sharing the file with other people.

To save a presentation to OneDrive, display the Save As page of the Backstage view, click your OneDrive, and then specify the OneDrive folder in which you want to save the file. If your OneDrive doesn't already appear in the list of locations, click Add A Place, click OneDrive, and then enter the credentials associated with the OneDrive you want to access.

When you save a PowerPoint presentation to OneDrive, you and other people with whom you share the presentation can work on it by using a local installation of PowerPoint or by using PowerPoint Online, which is available in the OneDrive environment.

SEE ALSO For information about PowerPoint Web App, see Chapter 1, "PowerPoint 2016 basics."

Microsoft provides free OneDrive storage to Microsoft account holders. If you already have a Microsoft account, you can access your OneDrive directly from any Office program, or from *onedrive.live.com*. If you don't yet have a Microsoft account, you can configure any existing email account as a Microsoft account at *signup.live.com*. (If you don't yet have an email account that you want to configure for this purpose, you can get a new account there, too.)

OneDrive for Business is available as part of a SharePoint 2016 environment, and your storage there will be managed by your company or SharePoint provider.

Skills review

In this chapter, you learned how to:

- Create presentations
- Open and navigate presentations
- Display different views of presentations
- Display and edit presentation properties
- Save and close presentations

Practice tasks

The practice file for these tasks is located in the PowerPoint2016SBS\Ch02 folder. You can save the results of the tasks in the same folder.

Create presentations

Do not start PowerPoint before beginning this task.

1. Start PowerPoint and create a new, blank presentation.

2. Display the available presentation design templates.

3. Preview a template that you like.

4. Without closing the preview window, preview the next or previous template.

5. From the preview window, create a presentation based on the currently displayed template. Notice that the unsaved blank presentation closes.

6. Leave the presentation open and continue to the next task.

Open and navigate presentations

Complete the following tasks:

1. From the Backstage view, open the **NavigateSlides** presentation.

2. Navigate among the slides by using the **Thumbnails** pane, and then by using the **Previous Slide** and **Next Slide** buttons.

3. Use a keyboard method to move to the last slide of the presentation.

4. Leave the presentations open and continue to the next task.

Display different views of presentations

Complete the following tasks:

1. Display the **NavigateSlides** presentation in Slide Sorter view and select Slide **2**.

2. Display the presentation in Slide Show view, beginning with Slide 2.

3. Move forward through the presentation to its end. Then return to Slide Sorter view.

4. Display the presentation in Reading view. Use any method to navigate to the fourth slide, and then use the most efficient method to return to the first slide.

5. Display the presentation in Normal view. Hide the **Thumbnails** pane and display the **Notes** pane.

6. Redisplay the **Thumbnails** pane and hide the ribbon.

7. Arrange the two presentations side by side on the screen.

8. In the **NavigateSlides** presentation, display the gridlines. Notice that they appear in both open presentations.

9. In the **NavigateSlides** presentation, change the spacing of the gridlines to **1"**. Notice that this modification affects only the active presentation.

10. Switch to the presentation you created in the first practice task. Display the guides, and then move them so they align with the upper-left corner of the slide content area. Notice the effect of these actions in the other open presentation.

11. Set the magnification of the active presentation to **60%** and notice the effect of this action in the other open presentation.

12. Leave the presentations open and continue to the next task.

Display and edit presentation properties

Maximize the NavigateSlides window, and then complete the following tasks:

1. Display all the presentation properties.

2. Edit the **Subject** property, entering **Colors** as the subject of the presentation.

3. Leave the presentations open and continue to the next task.

Save and close presentations

Complete the following tasks:

1. Save the **NavigateSlides** presentation as **MyPresentation**, and then close it.

2. Close the presentation you created in the first task without saving it.

Create and manage slides

When you create a presentation from a design template, the only slide that is immediately available is the title slide. It's up to you to add more slides for the content that you want the presentation to include. You can create slides based on slide templates that are designed to hold specific types of content, or you can copy existing slides from other presentations.

When the presentation you're developing has multiple slides, you can organize them into sections. Sections are not visible to the audience, but they make it easier to work with slide content in logical segments. A logical presentation and an overall consistent look, punctuated by variations that add weight exactly where it is needed, can enhance the likelihood that your intended audience will receive the message you want to convey.

This chapter guides you through procedures related to adding and removing slides, dividing presentations into sections, rearranging slides and sections, applying themes, and changing slide backgrounds.

> ✓ **TIP** The content in this chapter is about slides in general, rather than the content of the slides. Chapters 4 through 8 of this book are about working with the various types of slide content.

In this chapter

- Add and remove slides
- Divide presentations into sections
- Rearrange slides and sections
- Apply themes
- Change slide backgrounds

Practice files

For this chapter, use the practice files from the PowerPoint2016SBS\Ch03 folder. For practice file download instructions, see the introduction.

Add and remove slides

The appearance and structure of slides is defined by the slide layouts associated with the slide master that is part of the design template. Slide layouts define the elements on specific types of slides, such as:

- Slide backgrounds and incorporated graphics.

- Text box locations, sizes, and formats.

- Default paragraph and character formats for each text box location.

- Standard headers or footers.

> **TIP** Text boxes can contain static content that can't be changed by the presentation author (for example, a company logo), or they can serve as placeholders that define the default formatting of content entered within the text box.

A slide master could have only one slide layout, but most have unique slide layouts for slides that display the presentation title, section titles, and various combinations of slide titles and content, and a blank slide with only the background. Each slide layout is named; the name suggests the primary application of the slide layout, but you aren't limited to that suggestion; you can enter any type of content in any slide layout and modify the layout of any slide. The slide layouts that are available in a presentation are displayed on the New Slide menu.

> **SEE ALSO** For information about working with slide masters and slide layouts, see "Customize slide masters and layouts" in Chapter 12, "Create custom presentation elements."

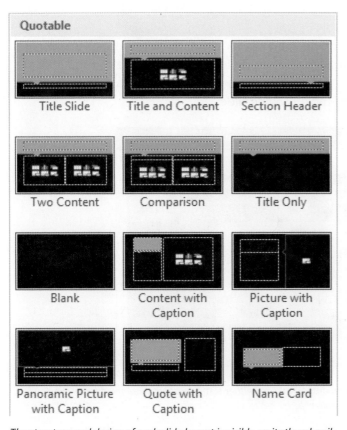

The structure and design of each slide layout is visible on its thumbnail

You can modify the built-in slide layouts, create your own slide layouts, or create entirely new sets of slide layouts called slide masters, and you can reset slides to match their slide layouts, or apply different slide layouts to existing slides.

3

Insert new slides

When you create a new slide, PowerPoint inserts it after the currently active slide. In a new presentation based on a standard PowerPoint template, a slide you add after the title slide has the Title And Content layout, and a slide added after a slide other than the title slide has the layout of the preceding slide.

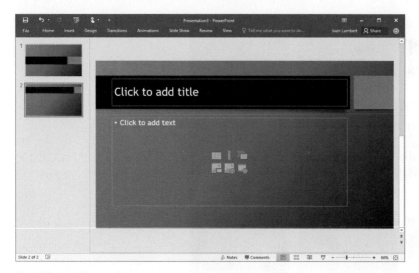

The Title And Content layout accommodates a title and either text or graphic content—a table, chart, diagram, picture, clip art image, or media clip

If you want to add a slide that has a different layout, you can select the layout when you insert the slide or you can change the slide layout after you create the slide.

To add a slide based on the default slide layout

1. Select the slide after which you want to add the new slide.

2. Do either of the following:

   - On the **Home** tab, in the **Slides** group, click the **New Slide** button (not its arrow).

   - Press **Ctrl+M**.

> **TIP** You can reset slide content to the slide layout defaults by clicking the Reset button in the Slides group on the Home tab. If you add content to a slide and then realize that the content would work better with a different layout, you can change the slide layout by clicking the Layout arrow in the Slides group, and then clicking the slide layout you want to apply.

To add a slide based on any slide layout

1. Select the slide after which you want to add the new slide.

2. On the **Home** tab, in the **Slides** group, click the **New Slide** arrow to display the **New Slide** gallery and menu.

3. In the gallery, click a slide layout thumbnail to add a slide based on that slide layout.

3

Copy and import slides and content

You can reuse slides from one presentation in another, in one of two ways: you can copy the slides from the original presentation to the new presentation, or you can use the Reuse Slides tool, which displays the content of an original presentation and allows you to choose the slides you want to insert in the new presentation.

Within a presentation, you can duplicate an existing slide to reuse it as the basis for a new slide. You can then customize the duplicated slide instead of having to create it from scratch.

If you frequently include a certain type of slide in your presentations, such as a slide that introduces you to the audience, you don't have to re-create the slide for each presentation. You can easily reuse a slide from one presentation in a different presentation. (You can use the same techniques to reuse a slide from someone else's presentation to standardize the appearance or structure of slide content with other members of your organization.) The slide takes on the formatting of its new presentation unless you specify otherwise.

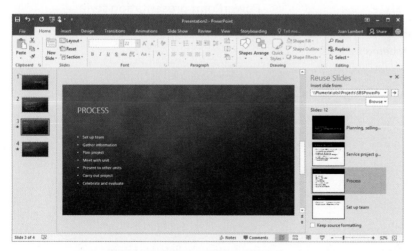

PowerPoint automatically applies the new theme to reused slides

If the content of your presentation exists in a document, you can configure that content in outline format and then import the outline into PowerPoint. For the import process to work smoothly, format the document content that you want to port into the presentation as headings. PowerPoint converts some styles into slide headings, converts some styles into bullet points, and ignores other styles.

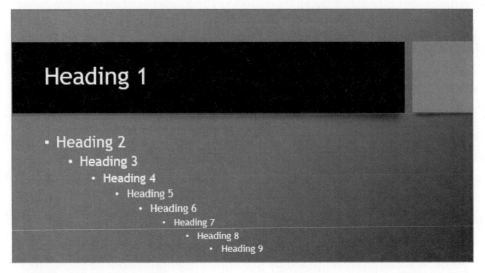

A slide created from an imported outline

The following table illustrates how PowerPoint converts Word document styles to PowerPoint slide elements.

Word document style	PowerPoint presentation style
Title, Subtitle, Heading 1, any bulleted list level, or any numbered list level	Slide title
Heading 2	First-level bulleted list item
Heading 3	Second-level bulleted list item
Heading 4	Third-level bulleted list item
Heading 5	Fourth-level bulleted list item
Heading 6	Fifth-level bulleted list item
Heading 7	Sixth-level bulleted list item
Heading 8	Seventh-level bulleted list item
Heading 9	Eighth-level bulleted list item

To select a single slide

1. Do any of the following:

    - In Normal view, click the slide in the **Thumbnails** pane.

    - In Outline view, click the slide header in the **Outline** pane.

    - In Slide Sorter view, click the slide in the **Slide** pane.

3

To select multiple slides

1. In Normal view, Outline view, or Slide Sorter view, click the first slide you want to select.

2. Do either of the following:

    - To select a contiguous series of slides, press and hold the **Shift** key, and then click the last slide you want to select.

    - To select noncontiguous slides, press and hold the **Ctrl** key, and then click each additional slide you want to select.

To insert a copy of a slide immediately following the original slide

1. Display the presentation in Normal view.

2. In the **Thumbnails** pane, right-click the slide that you want to copy, and then click **Duplicate Slide**.

To insert a copy of one or more slides anywhere in a presentation

1. Display the presentation in Normal view or Slide Sorter view.

2. Do either of the following to copy a slide or slides:

    - Select the slide thumbnail or thumbnails, and then press **Ctrl+C** or, on the **Home** tab, in the **Clipboard** group, click the **Copy** button.

    - Right-click a slide thumbnail, and then click **Copy**.

3. Do either of the following to insert the slide copy or copies:

    - Click the thumbnail that you want to insert the slide copy or copies after, or click the empty space after the thumbnail. Then press **Ctrl+V** or, on the **Home** tab, in the **Clipboard** group, click the **Paste** button.

- Right-click where you want to insert the slide copy or copies, and then, in the **Paste Options** section of the shortcut menu, click the **Use Destination Theme** button or the **Keep Source Formatting** button.

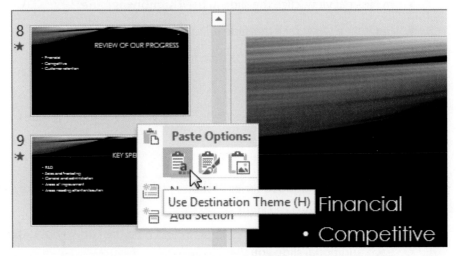

You can match the destination theme, retain the source theme, or paste as a picture

 TIP When PowerPoint displays the paste options, press H to use the destination style or K to use the source style.

4. Repeat step 3 to paste additional copies of the slide or slides into the presentation.

To insert a slide from another presentation

1. Open the source and destination presentations in PowerPoint. Display each presentation in Normal view or Slide Sorter view.

2. Display the two PowerPoint windows side by side.

3. In the source presentation, select the slide or slides you want to copy.

4. Drag the selection to the destination presentation. A horizontal line between slide thumbnails in Normal view or a vertical line between thumbnails in Slide Sorter view indicates the location at which PowerPoint will insert the slides.

   PowerPoint creates copies of the slides and applies the destination theme to the copies.

Or

1. Display the destination presentation in Normal view.

2. On the **Home** tab or **Insert** tab, in the **Slides** group, click the **New Slide** arrow.

3. On the **New Slide** menu, below the gallery, click **Reuse Slides** to open the **Reuse Slides** pane on the right side of the screen.

4. Click the **Browse** button, and then click **Browse File**. In the **Browse** dialog box, browse to the folder that contains the presentation you want to use slides from, and then double-click the presentation.

> **TIP** If you've previously connected to the presentation you want to import slides from, you can click the down arrow in the Insert Slide From box to expand the list, and then click the presentation in the list, or click the presentation file name in the Open section of the Reuse Slide pane.

Or

Click the **Browse** button, and then click **Browse Slide** Library. In the **Select a Slide Library** window, browse to the slide library that contains the slide or slides you want to insert.

> **SEE ALSO** For information about slide libraries, see the sidebar "SharePoint slide libraries" in this topic.

The Reuse Slides pane displays thumbnails of the available slides.

5. In the **Reuse Slides** pane, click the thumbnail of each slide you want to use to insert that slide into your presentation.

> **TIP** The reused slide takes on the design of the presentation in which it is inserted. If you want the slide to retain the formatting from the source presentation instead, select the Keep Source Formatting check box at the bottom of the Reuse Slides pane.

6. Close the **Reuse Slides** pane.

To prepare a source document to import as a presentation

1. Enter the content that you want to appear on the slides (and any other content) in a document.

2. Review the styles applied to the content you want to include in the presentation.

    -   Title, Subtitle, Heading 1, and any list items will convert to slide titles.

    -   Heading 2 through Heading 8 will convert to bulleted list items.

3. Save and close the document.

To create a presentation by importing a Word document

1. On the **Open** page of the Backstage view, click **Browse**.

2. In the file type list, click **All Files (*.*)**.

3. Browse to the folder that contains the Word document that contains the slide title and bullet point information.

4. Double-click the document to create a new presentation.

5. Select all the slides in the new presentation, and then on the **Home** tab, in the **Slides** group, click the **Reset** button.

6. Apply the design template you want.

 SEE ALSO For information about applying design templates to presentations, see "Create presentations" in Chapter 2, "Create and manage presentations."

To create slides in an existing presentation by importing a Word document

1. Select the slide after which you want to insert the new slides.

2. On the **Home** tab or **Insert** tab, in the **Slides** group, click the **New Slide** arrow.

3. On the **New Slide** menu, below the gallery, click **Slides from Outline** to open the **Insert Outline** dialog box, which resembles the **Open** dialog box.

4. Use standard Windows techniques to browse to the folder that contains the Word document you want to use for the slide titles and content.

5. Double-click the document to insert slides based on its content.

3

SharePoint slide libraries

If your organization uses a version of Microsoft SharePoint that supports slide libraries, you and your colleagues can store individual slides or entire presentations in a slide library so they are available for use by anyone who has access to the library. At the time of this writing, the current versions of SharePoint (SharePoint Server 2013 and SharePoint Online 2013) don't support the creation of new slide libraries but you can publish slides to and insert slides from legacy libraries.)

To store slides in a slide library, follow these steps:

1. On the **Share** page of the Backstage view, click **Publish Slides**, and then click the **Publish Slides** button.

2. In the **Publish Slides** dialog box, select the check box of each slide you want to publish. (Click the **Select All** button to select the entire presentation.)

3. In the **Publish To** box, enter or paste the URL of the slide library (or click the **Browse** button and browse to the slide library).

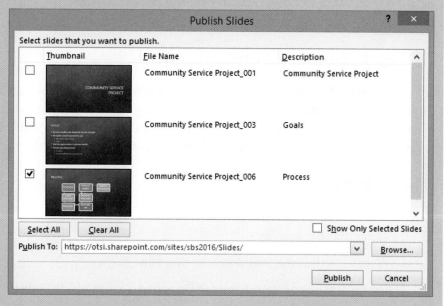

Each slide is published individually

4. Click **Publish**.

Hide and delete slides

If you create a slide and then later realize that you don't need it, you can delete it. If you don't need the slide for a presentation to a specific audience but might need it later, you can hide the slide instead. Hidden slides aren't presented in slide shows. They remain available from the Thumbnails pane, but their thumbnails are dimmed and slide numbers crossed through with a backslash.

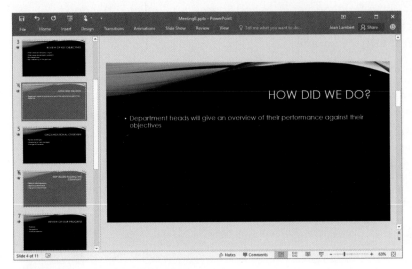

You can edit the content of hidden slides

When you select a hidden slide, the Hide Slide button on the Slide Show tab is shaded to indicate that the command is in effect. You can edit a hidden slide in the Slide pane just as you can any other, so you might use this feature to keep a slide that you're still working on hidden until it's final. You can unhide a slide to include it in the slide show.

To hide or unhide slides

1. Select the slide or slides you want to hide or unhide.

2. Do either of the following:

    - Right-click the selection, and then click **Hide Slide**.

    - On the **Slide Show** tab, in the **Set Up** group, click the **Hide Slide** button.

 TIP The name of the Hide Slide command and button doesn't change; when a hidden slide is active, the command and button are shaded.

To delete slides

1. Right-click a single slide, and then click **Delete Slide**.

Or

1. Select the slide or slides you want to delete.
2. Do any of the following:
   - Right-click the selection, and then click **Delete Slide**.
   - On the **Home** tab, in the **Clipboard** group, click **Cut**.
   - Press the **Delete** key.

 TIP When you add or delete slides in a presentation, PowerPoint renumbers all the subsequent slides.

Divide presentations into sections

To make it easier to organize and format a longer presentation, you can divide it into sections. In both Normal view and Slide Sorter view, sections are designated by titles above their slides. They do not appear in other views, and they do not create slides or otherwise interrupt the flow of the presentation.

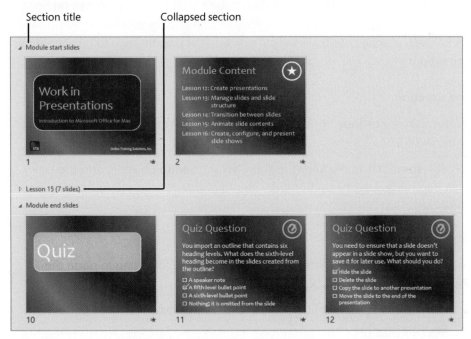

You can rename, remove, move, collapse, and expand sections

Because you can collapse entire sections to leave only the section titles visible, the sections make it easier to focus on one part of a presentation at a time.

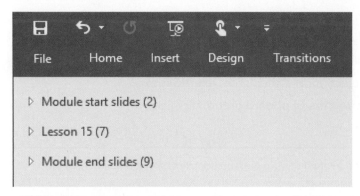

You can collapse sections to provide an "outline" of long presentations, with the number of slides in each section displayed in parentheses

 TIP If you're collaborating with other people on the development of a presentation, sections are a convenient way of assigning slides to different people.

Some templates include a slide layout, similar to the title slide layout, that is specifically designed for section divider slides. If you divide a long presentation into sections based on topic, you might want to transfer your section titles to these slides to provide guidance to the audience or to mark logical points in the presentation to take breaks or answer questions.

To create a section

1. In Normal view or Slide Sorter view, select the slide that you want to be first in the new section.

2. On the **Home** tab, in the **Slides** group, click the **Section** button, and then click **Add Section** to insert a section title named *Untitled Section* before the selected slide.

To rename a section

1. In Normal view or Slide Sorter view, do either of the following to open the **Rename Section** dialog box:

   • Right-click the section title you want to change, and then click **Rename Section**.

- On the **Home** tab, in the **Slides** group, click the **Section** button, and then click **Rename Section**.

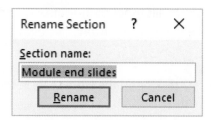

The current section name is selected so that you can easily replace it

2. In the **Section name** box, replace or edit the existing section name, and then click the **Rename** button.

To collapse or expand one slide section

1. In Normal view or Slide Sorter view, click the arrow that precedes the section title.

 TIP A right-pointing arrow indicates a collapsed section, an arrow that points to the lower-right corner indicates an expanded section.

To collapse or expand all slide sections

1. Do either of the following:

- On the **Home** tab, in the **Slides** group, click the **Section** button, and then click **Collapse All** or **Expand All**.

- Right-click any section name, and then click **Expand All** or **Collapse All**.

Rearrange slides and sections

After you have added several slides to a presentation, you might want to rearrange their order so that they more effectively communicate your message.

You can rearrange a presentation by moving individual slides or entire sections of slides.

To move a slide within a presentation

1. In Normal view or Slide Sorter view, drag the slide thumbnail to its new posi-
    tion. Notice as you drag that the other thumbnails move to indicate where the
    selected slide will appear when you release the mouse button.

Or

1. Select the slide thumbnail, and then press **Ctrl+X** or on the **Home** tab, in the
    Clipboard group, click **Cut**.

2. Do either of the following:

    *   Click the slide thumbnail that you want to insert the cut slide after, and then
        press **Ctrl+V** or, in the **Clipboard** group, click **Paste**.

    *   Click between the other slide thumbnails to insert a thin red marker (hori-
        zontal in Normal view or vertical in Slide Sorter view) where you want to
        move the slide. Then press **Ctrl+V** or, in the **Clipboard** group, click **Paste**.

Or

1. Right-click the slide thumbnail, and then click **Cut**.

2. Right-click between the other slide thumbnails where you want to move the
    slide.

> **TIP** The thin red destination marker appears only when you click between
> thumbnails, not when you right-click between thumbnails.

3. In the **Paste Options** section of the shortcut menu, click the **Use Destination
    Theme** button or the **Keep Source Formatting** button.

> **TIP** When PowerPoint displays the paste options, press H to use the destination
> style or K to use the source style.

To move a section within a presentation

1. Click the title of the section of slides you want to move, to select all the slides in
    the section.

2. Drag the section to its new location.

Or

1. Right-click the section title, and then click **Move Section Up** or **Move Section Down** to move the section and all its slides before the preceding section or after the following section.

 TIP The Move Section commands aren't available on the Section menu; they are available only on the shortcut menu that appears when you right-click a section title.

3

To merge a section into the preceding section by removing the section divider

1. Click the title of the section of slides you want to ungroup.

2. On the **Home** tab, in the **Slides** group, click the **Section** button, and then click **Remove Section**.

Or

1. Right-click the section title, and then click **Remove Section**.

To merge all sections by removing all section dividers

1. On the **Home** tab, in the **Slides** group, click the **Section** button, and then click **Remove All Sections**.

To delete a section of slides

1. Click the title of the section of slides you want to delete, to select all the slides in the section.

2. Press the **Delete** key.

Or

1. Right-click the section title, and then click **Remove Section & Slides**.

If the selected section is collapsed, PowerPoint prompts you to confirm the deletion

2. If PowerPoint prompts you to confirm the deletion, click **Yes** to delete the section title and all the slides in the section.

 TIP The Remove Section & Slides command isn't available on the Section menu; it is available only on the shortcut menu that appears when you right-click a section title.

Apply themes

The appearance of every presentation that you create is governed by a theme—a combination of colors, fonts, effect styles, and background graphics or formatting that coordinates the appearance of all the presentation elements. Even a blank presentation has a theme: the Office theme, which has a white slide background, a standard set of text and accent colors, and the Office font set, which uses Calibri Light for headings and Calibri for body text.

PowerPoint and the other Office 2016 apps share a common set of themes and theme elements. This enables you to easily produce coordinated print and presentation materials. Approximately 30 of these themes are available to you from the PowerPoint Themes gallery. Many of the themes come with predefined variants, which have a different color scheme or background graphic.

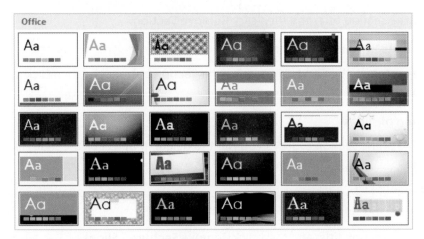

The built-in Office themes for PowerPoint

Each thumbnail in the PowerPoint Themes gallery displays a sample of the font set in the form of an uppercase and lowercase letter A (*Aa*) and the color scheme in the form of colored blocks over the default title slide. Title slides frequently have background graphics that set the tone for the presentation. The standard slides associated with the theme will often have a more-subtle background graphic that coordinates with the title slide background. You can choose to hide the background graphic and use only a colored background if you want to.

You can change the theme that is applied to an entire presentation or to only one section of the presentation. If you like the colors of one theme, the fonts of another, and the effects of another, you can mix and match theme elements. You can also create your own themes.

SEE ALSO For information about creating themes and custom theme elements, see "Create custom themes" in Chapter 12, "Create custom presentation elements."

When you're working in Normal view you can use the Live Preview feature to see how your presentation would look with a different theme applied. Simply point to any theme and pause. PowerPoint temporarily applies the selected formatting to the slide in the Slide pane. This makes it easy to try different themes and theme elements until you find the ones you want.

To apply a standard theme to a presentation

1. Display the presentation in Normal view.

2. On the **Design** tab, in the **Themes** group, click the **More** button (below the scroll arrows) to display the menu that includes the **Office** theme gallery and any custom templates on your computer.

3. Point to thumbnails in the gallery to display the theme names in tooltips and preview the effect of applying the themes to your presentation.

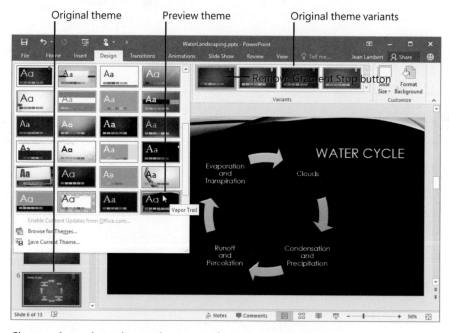

Choose a theme that enhances the content of your presentation

4. Click a **theme** thumbnail to apply that theme to the entire presentation.

To change the color scheme of the presentation

1. On the **Design** tab, in the **Variants** group, click a variant thumbnail.

Or

1. On the **Design** tab, in the **Variants** group, click the **More** button (below the scroll arrows) to expand the **Variants** menu.

2. On the **Variants** menu, click **Colors**, and then click the color set you want to apply.

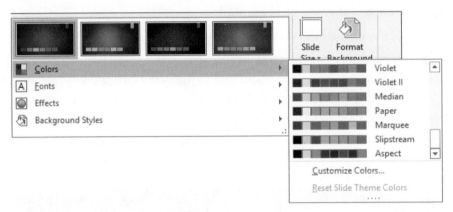

Choose from the dozens of standard color schemes

> **TIP** Changing the color scheme, font set, or effect style of a presentation doesn't change the theme that is applied to the presentation.

To change the font set of the presentation

1. On the **Design** tab, in the **Variants** group, click the **More** button (below the scroll arrows) to expand the **Variants** menu.

2. On the **Variants** menu, click **Fonts**, and then click the font set you want to apply.

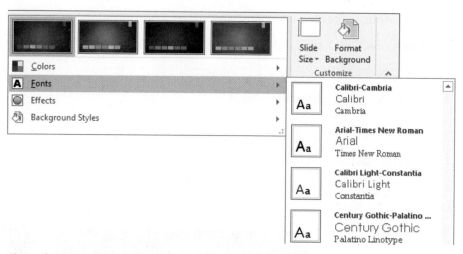

Choose from same-font or complementary-font heading/body font combinations

To change the effect style of the presentation

1. On the **Design** tab, in the **Variants** group, click the **More** button (below the scroll arrows) to expand the **Variants** menu.

2. On the **Variants** menu, click **Effects**, and then click the effect style you want to apply.

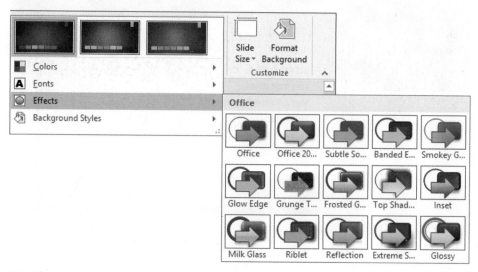

The effect style preview color coordinates with the current color scheme

To apply a theme or theme variant to only part of a presentation

1. Create a section that contains the slides you want to have a different theme.

2. Click the section header to select the section.

3. Apply the theme or theme element.

Change slide backgrounds

The presentation theme includes a standard background. The background might be a color or it might include a background graphic.

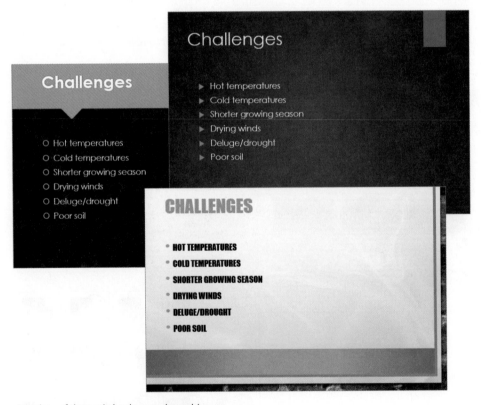

A variety of thematic background graphics

You can customize slide backgrounds by removing the background graphic and fill-ing the slide background with a solid color, a color gradient, a texture, a pattern, or a picture of your choice. You make these changes in the Format Background pane.

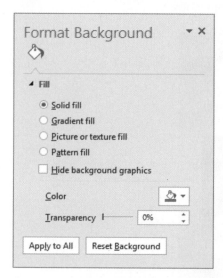

You can control the color, texture, pattern, or picture in the background of one or all slides

Each of the options in the Format Background pane has specific settings that appear when you select the option.

A solid color background is a good choice for readability, but if you want to add some interest without a lot of distraction, you can use a color gradient in which a solid color gradually changes to another. PowerPoint offers several light-to-dark and dark-to-light gradient patterns based on the color scheme.

You can also create custom gradients of two, three, or more colors. Each change in color within a gradient is controlled by a gradient stop. For each gradient stop, you can specify the location and specific color (including the transparency and brightness of the color). A color gradient can have from 2 to 10 gradient stops.

A gradient can include up to 10 color changes

If you want something fancier than a solid color or a color gradient, you can give the slide background a texture or pattern. PowerPoint comes with several built-in textures that you can easily apply to the background of slides.

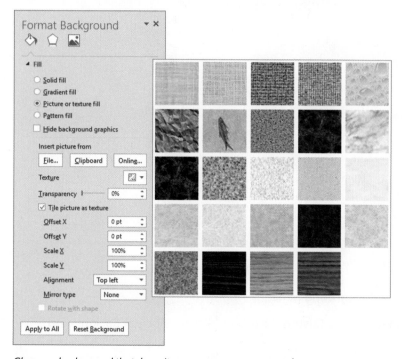

Choose a background that doesn't overpower your presentation

If none of these meets your needs, you might want to use a picture of a textured surface. For a dramatic effect, you can even incorporate a picture of your own, although these are best reserved for small areas of the slide rather than the entire background.

If you prefer to use a simple pattern rather than a texture, you can choose from 48 patterns and set the background and foreground color to your liking.

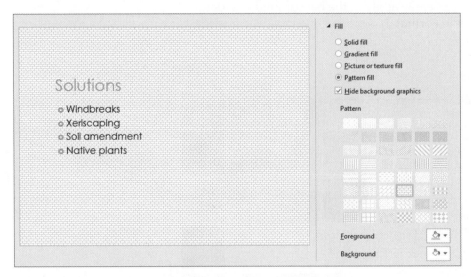

Click any pattern to preview it on the slide

To display the Format Background pane

1. On the **Design** tab, in the **Customize** group, click the **Format Background** button.

To close the Format Background pane

1. Do either of the following:

    • In the upper-right corner of the pane, click the **Close** button (the X).

    • To the right of the pane name, click the down arrow, and then click **Close**.

To apply a background change to all slides

1. In the **Format Background** pane, configure the slide background formatting you want.

2. At the bottom of the pane, click the **Apply to All** button.

To remove the slide background graphic applied by a theme

1. Display the **Format Background** pane.

2. In the **Format Background** pane, select the **Hide background graphics** check box.

To apply a solid background color to one or more slides

1. In the **Format Background** pane, click **Solid fill**.

2. Click the **Color** button to display the color palette.

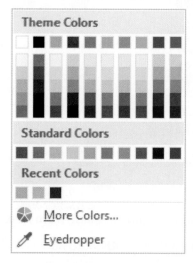

The color palette displays theme colors, standard colors, and recently used colors

> **SEE ALSO** For information about the colors you can use, see the sidebar "Non-theme colors" later in this topic.

3. Click a theme color variant, a solid color, or a recent color, or click **More Colors** and select a custom color.

4. Move the **Transparency** slider to adjust the background color transparency, or set a specific transparency percentage.

> **SEE ALSO** For information about printing slides without background colors and images, see "Print presentations and handouts" in Chapter 9, "Review presentations."

To apply a gradient background color to one or more slides

1. In the **Format Background** pane, click **Gradient fill**.

2. Click the **Preset gradients** button, and then click a gradient option based on the current color palette.

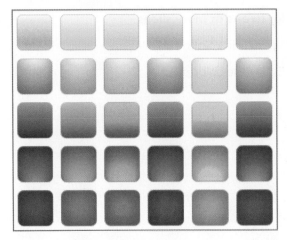

Preset color gradients offer linear and radial variants of the theme accent color

Or

1. In the **Type** list, click **Linear**, **Radial**, **Rectangular**, **Path**, or **Shade from title**.

2. In the **Direction** list, click the direction you want the gradient to flow.

3. If you chose the **Linear** type, you can specify the angle you want the gradient to move along. Enter the angle in the **Angle** box.

4. If you want to add gradient stops, do either of the following in the **Gradient Stops** area:

   • Click the **Add gradient stop** button, and then reposition the marker that appears on the slider.

   • Click the slider in the approximate location where you want to insert the gradient stop.

Add Gradient Stop button

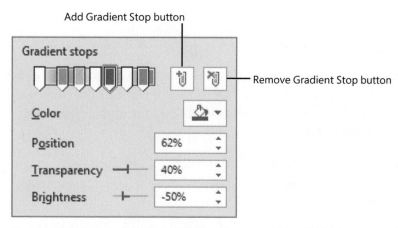

Remove Gradient Stop button

3

You can precisely control a color by adjusting the transparency and brightness

5. If you want to remove gradient stops, do either of the following in the **Gradient Stops** area:

   • On the slider, click the marker for the gradient stop you want to remove. Then click the **Remove gradient stop** button.

   • Drag the gradient stop marker off of the slider.

6. In the **Gradient stops** area, set the color, position, transparency, and brightness for each color in the gradient. Note the following:

   • You can select a color swatch or match an existing color by using the eye-dropper tool to select a color.

   • You can change the transparency and brightness by moving the markers on the sliders, by entering specific percentages, or by scrolling the dials.

To apply a textured background to one or more slides

1. In the **Format Background** pane, click **Picture or texture fill**.

2. Click the **Texture** button to display the texture gallery. You can select from a variety of textures, including fabric, marble, granite, wood grain, and Formica-like textures in various colors.

3. In the texture gallery, click the texture you want to apply.

4. Move the **Transparency** slider to adjust the background color transparency, or set a specific transparency percentage.

Non-theme colors

Although using themes enables you to create presentations with a color-coordinated design, you can also use colors that aren't part of the theme. Whenever you apply a color to any presentation element, you can choose from among these options:

- Six shades of each of the 10 theme colors
- Ten standard colors that are available in all Office documents, regardless of the theme
- Non-standard colors that you've used recently
- The Standard color palette that offers permutations of primary, secondary, and tertiary colors in a hexagonal color wheel

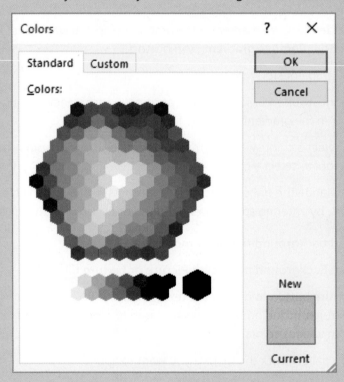

Colors from the Standard color wheel remain the same in any Office document regardless of the color scheme

- A custom color model on which you can select from permutations of primary and secondary colors or specify colors by RGB (Red, Green, and Blue) or HSL (Hue, Saturation, and Luminescence) values

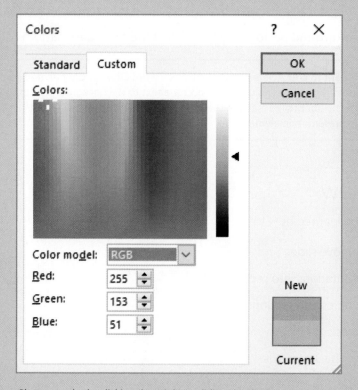

Choose a color by clicking the rainbow, sliding the shade scale, or entering an RGB or HSL value

If you want to make a selected element the same color as one that is used elsewhere on the same slide, display the color menu, click Eyedropper, and then click the color you want.

To apply a patterned background to one or more slides

1. In the **Format Background** pane, click **Pattern fill**.

2. In the **Pattern** palette, click one of the 48 pattern swatches.

3. Click the **Foreground** button, and then select the primary pattern color.

4. Click the **Background** button, and then select the secondary pattern color.

> ✓ **TIP** If you want to add a watermark, such as the word *Draft* or *Confidential*, to the background of your slides, you need to add the text to the background of the slide master. For information about slide masters, see "Customize slide masters and layouts" in Chapter 12, "Create custom presentation elements."

Skills review

In this chapter, you learned how to:

- Add and remove slides

- Divide presentations into sections

- Rearrange slides and sections

- Apply themes

- Change slide backgrounds

Practice tasks

The practice files for these tasks are located in the PowerPoint2016SBS\
Ch03 folder. You can save the results of the tasks in the same folder.

Add and remove slides

Open the AddRemoveSlides presentation in PowerPoint, and then perform the
following tasks:

1. Add two slides after the title slide. First, add a slide that has the default **Title and Content** layout. Then add a slide that has the **Two Content** layout.

2. Add 7 more slides, so you have a total of 10 slides. Use each slide layout at least once.

3. In Normal view, delete slide **3**.

4. Switch to Slide Sorter view, and then delete slides **5** through **8**. The presentation now contains five slides.

5. Add seven slides to the end of the presentation by inserting the content of the **ImportOutline** document.

6. Use the **Reuse Slides** feature to insert the first slide from the **ReuseSlides** presentation as slide **2** in the **AddRemoveSlides** presentation. Then close the **Reuse Slides** pane.

7. Insert a duplicate copy of slide **2** as slide **3**.

8. Hide slide **2**, and then delete slide **8**.

9. Save and close the presentation.

Divide presentations into sections

Open the CreateSections presentation in Normal view, and then perform the following tasks:

1. Divide the presentation into two sections:

    - A section that contains slides **1** through **3**

    - A section that contains slides **4** through **12**

2. Change the name of the first section to **Introduction**.

3. Switch to Slide Sorter view, and then change the name of the second section to **Process**.

4. Collapse both sections, and then expand only the **Process** section.

5. Save and close the presentation.

Rearrange slides and sections

Open the RearrangeSlides presentation in Normal view, and then perform the following tasks:

1. Move the first slide in the **Step 1** section so that it is the third slide in the Introduction section. Then delete the last slide in the Introduction section.

2. Switch to **Slide Sorter** view and scroll through the presentation, noticing the sections.

3. Collapse the sections, and then rearrange them so that the sections for steps 1 through 7 are in order and the End section is at the end of the presentation.

4. Merge the **End** section into the **Step 7** section.

5. Save and close the presentation.

Apply themes

Open the ApplyThemes presentation in Normal view, and then perform the following tasks:

1. On slide **1**, click the slide title. On the **Home** tab, in the **Font** group, notice that the title font is blue-gray, 44-point, Times New Roman.

2. Apply the **Ion** theme to the presentation. On the **Home** tab, in the **Font** group, notice that the title font is now white, 72-point, Century Gothic.

3. Switch to **Slide Sorter** view, and adjust the magnification to display all the slides.

4. Apply the **Circuit** theme to the presentation. Notice that the slide background is blue.

5. Apply the **gray** variant of the Circuit theme to the **Past** section of the presentation.

6. Apply the **red** variant of the Circuit theme to the **Present** section of the presentation.

7. Apply the **green** variant of the Circuit theme to the **Future** section of the presentation.

8. Save and close the presentation.

Change slide backgrounds

Open the ChangeBackgrounds presentation, and then perform the following tasks:

1. Apply a gradient fill background to slide **1**.

2. Change the gradient type to **Rectangular** and set the direction to **From Top Left Corner**.

3. Configure the gradient to have the following four gradient stops:

Stop	Color	Position	Transparency	Brightness
1	Light Green	5%	0%	-10%
2	White	45%	0%	90%
3	Light Blue	75%	0%	0%
4	Purple	100%	20%	0%

4. Apply the custom gradient fill to all slides in the presentation.

5. Change the background of only slide **1** to the **Water droplets** texture, and set the **Transparency** of the texture to **25%**.

6. Save and close the presentation.

Part 2

Insert and manage slide text

Enter and edit text on slides

Later chapters of this book describe ways to add fancy effects to electronic presentations so that you can really grab the attention of your audience. However, no amount of animation, jazzy colors, and supporting pictures convey your message if the words on the slides are inadequate to the task.

Because of the way elements on a PowerPoint slide float independently, PowerPoint presentations offer simpler options for creatively presenting information than Microsoft Word documents and have become an alternative delivery format for reports.

For most of your presentations, text is the foundation on which you will build everything else. Even if you follow the current trend of building presentations that consist primarily of pictures, you still need to make sure that titles and any other words on your slides do their job, and do it well.

This chapter guides you through procedures related to entering text on slides; moving, copying, and deleting text; formatting characters and paragraphs; applying WordArt text effects; and checking spelling and choosing the best wording.

In this chapter

- Enter text on slides
- Move, copy, and delete text
- Format characters and paragraphs
- Apply WordArt text effects
- Check spelling and choose the best wording

Practice files

For this chapter, use the practice files from the PowerPoint2016SBS\Ch04 folder. For practice file download instructions, see the introduction.

Enter text on slides

On each slide in a presentation, PowerPoint indicates with placeholders the type and position of the objects on the slide. For example, a slide might have placeholders for a title and for a bulleted list with bullet points and one or more levels of secondary subpoints. You can enter text into the existing placeholders and place additional text onto slides.

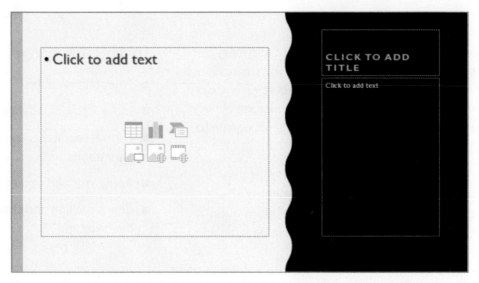

PowerPoint uses placeholders to indicate where the text you enter will appear on the slide

Enter text in placeholders

You can enter text directly into a placeholder on a slide in the Slide pane in Normal view; or you can switch to Outline view, where the entire presentation is displayed in outline form, and then enter text in the Outline pane.

When you point to a text placeholder or to an outline, the pointer changes to an I-beam. When you click, a blinking cursor appears, indicating where characters will appear when you enter them. As you enter text, it appears both on the slide and on the slide thumbnail (Normal view) or in the outline (Outline view).

PowerPoint provides an AutoFit feature to size text to fit its placeholder. By default, if you enter more text than will fit in a placeholder, PowerPoint reduces the size of the text so that it fits the placeholder. When PowerPoint reduces text to fit a placeholder, the AutoFit Options button appears to the left of the placeholder. You can control the AutoFit feature for each individual placeholder, or you can configure it for all place-holders from the AutoFormat As You Type page of the AutoCorrect dialog box.

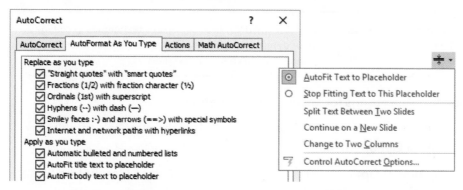

Manage the way that extra text fits into a placeholder

> **TIP** The AutoFit Options menu for a bulleted list placeholder includes additional options that allow you to split the list between two slides or change it to a two-column list, which is ideal for a long list of short entries.

To enter text in a placeholder

1. Do either of the following:

   - Display the slide in Normal view. Click the placeholder, and then enter the text.

   - Display the slide in Outline view, and enter text directly in the **Outline** pane.

To demote the current text by one level

1. Do either of the following:

   - With the cursor at the beginning of the paragraph, press **Tab**.

   - On the **Home** tab, in the **Paragraph** group, click the **Increase List Level** button.

To promote the current text by one level

1. Do either of the following:

   - With the cursor at the beginning of the paragraph, press **Shift+Tab**.

   - On the **Home** tab, in the **Paragraph** group, click the **Decrease List Level** button.

> ✓ **TIP** In the Outline pane, you can use the demote and promote techniques to change a slide title to a bulleted list item or demote a numbered list item to a lower level. Pressing Enter next to a first-level entry in the Outline pane creates a new slide.

To change AutoFit settings for an individual placeholder

1. Click the **AutoFit** button that appears to the left of the placeholder to display the AutoFit Options menu.

2. On the **AutoFit Options** menu, click either **AutoFit Text to Placeholder** or **Stop Fitting Text to This Placeholder**.

Or

1. In the **Format Shape** pane, click **Text Options**.

2. Display the **Text Box** page of settings.

3. Click **Do not Autofit**, **Shrink text on overflow**, or **Resize shape to fit text**.

To change the default AutoFit settings for all placeholders

1. Click the **AutoFit** button to display the AutoFit Options menu, and then click **Control AutoCorrect Options** to display the AutoFormat As You Type tab of the AutoCorrect dialog box.

2. On the **AutoFormat As You Type** tab, select or clear the options to automatically fit title text and body text to placeholders. Then click **OK**.

> 🔍 **SEE ALSO** For information about modifying the AutoCorrect options, see the "Manage proofing options" section of "Change default PowerPoint options" in Chapter 11, "Work in PowerPoint more efficiently."

Insert nonstandard characters

The text that you want to present on a slide might include characters that aren't available on a standard keyboard, such as copyright or trademark symbols, currency symbols, Greek letters, or letters with accent marks. Or you might want to add arrows or graphic icons to convey meaning. You can insert a variety of nonstandard characters, including mathematical operators.

PowerPoint gives you easy access to a huge array of symbols that you can easily insert into any slide. Like graphics, symbols can add visual information or eye-appeal to a slide. However, they are different from graphics in that they are actually characters of a specific font alphabet—usually one of the Wingdings family of fonts.

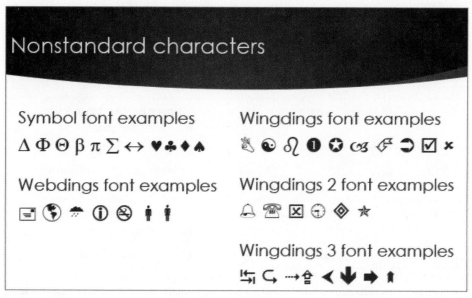

A sampling of the hundreds of available symbols

You can insert some common symbols by entering specific key combinations such as those shown in the following table. The AutoCorrect and AutoFormat functions replace the key combinations with the symbols.

Symbol	Description	Key combination
©	Copyright	(c)
®	Registered trademark	(r)
™	Trademark	(tm)
€	Euro	(e)
…	Ellipsis	… (three periods)
—	Em dash	-- (two hyphens followed by a word and space) Or Ctrl+Alt+Minus Sign on numeric keypad
–	En dash	- (space hyphen space followed by a word and space) Or Ctrl+Minus Sign on numeric keypad
1st, 2nd, 3rd, 4th, and so on	Ordinal numbers	1st, 2nd, 3rd, 4th, and so on followed by a space
¼, ½, ¾, and so on	Fractional numbers	1/4, 1/2, 3/4, and so on

> **TIP** You can review and control the AutoCorrect options from the Proofing page of the PowerPoint Options dialog box. For more information, see the "Manage proofing options" section of "Change default PowerPoint options" in Chapter 11, "Work in PowerPoint more efficiently."

You can insert several hundred other symbols from the Symbol dialog box by first selecting a font that includes symbols, and then selecting and inserting the symbol you want. You can insert accented characters from the Symbol dialog box by selecting them from the characters available for the font you're working in. Fonts might include Latin, Greek, Coptic, Cyrillic, and many other extended character sets.

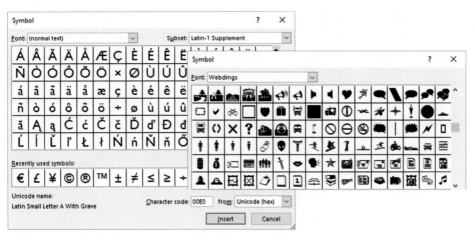

Many special characters and symbols are available

To insert a symbol

1. Position the cursor where you want to insert the symbol.

2. On the **Insert** tab, in the **Symbols** group, click the **Symbol** button to open the Symbol dialog box.

3. In the dialog box, click the **Font** list, and then click a symbol font such as **Symbol**, **Webdings**, or **Wingdings** to display the characters of that font. Scroll the character pane up and down to display additional characters.

> **TIP** The Recently Used Symbols area of the Symbol dialog box is dynamic. If the symbol you want to insert is among those in this area, you can insert it from there.

4. Do either of the following to insert a symbol at the cursor:

    -   Click the symbol you want to insert, and then click **Insert**.

    -   Double-click the symbol.

To insert a special character

1. Position the cursor where you want to insert the special character.

2. On the **Insert** tab, in the **Symbols** group, click the **Symbol** button.

3. In the **Symbol** dialog box, click the **Font** list, and then click the font you're working in.

4. In the **Subset** list, click the subset of characters you want to display.

> ✓ **TIP** Subsets include groups such as Latin Extended, Greek Extended, General Punctuation, Superscripts and Subscripts, Currency Symbols, Combining Diacritical Marks, Geometric Shapes, and many others.

5. Do either of the following to insert a character at the cursor:

- Click the character you want to insert, and then click **Insert**.
- Double-click the character.

Add supplementary text to slides

The size and position of the placeholders on a slide, and the formatting of the content within the placeholders, are dictated by the slide layout. You can modify slide content, and you can reset modified content that is within the placeholders to the defaults by reapplying the slide layout.

If you want to add text outside of a placeholder, you can create an independent text box and enter the text there. You can move, size, and format text boxes by using the same techniques that you do with shapes.

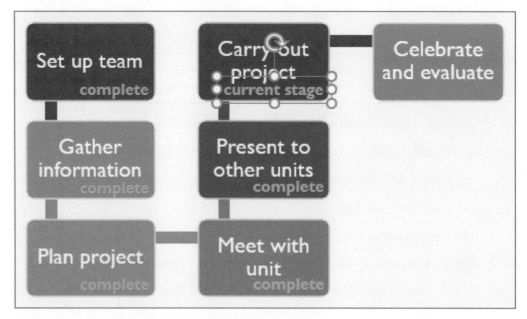

You can add supplementary text by inserting a text box

The text that you enter into a text box takes on the default formatting associated with text boxes. You can format the text by using all the usual text-formatting methods. If you want to change the default text box formatting for the presentation that you're working in, you can do so.

> ✅ **TIP** The information in text boxes cannot be accessed by some assistive technology devices that make presentations accessible to people with disabilities. If your presentation must be compatible with these devices, avoid putting important information in text boxes.

4

To insert a text box

1. On the **Insert** tab, in the **Text** group, click the **Text Box** button.

2. Do either of the following:

   - Click the slide where you want the text box to appear, and then enter the text. The width of the text box expands to fit what you enter on one line.

   - On the slide, drag a box where you want the text box to appear, and then enter the text. The box adjusts to the height of one line, but maintains the width you specified. When the text reaches the right boundary of the box, the height of the box expands by one line so that the text can wrap. As you continue entering text, the width of the box stays the same, but the height grows as necessary to accommodate all the text.

To set the default formatting for text boxes

1. Apply the formatting that you want to set as the default.

2. Select the text box.

3. Right-click the border of the selected text box, and then click **Set As Default Text Box**.

Insert equations

You can insert mathematical symbols, such as those for pi or sigma, the same way you would insert any other symbol. But you can also create entire mathematical equations on a slide.

You can insert some predefined equations by selecting them from a menu. The available predefined equations include Area of Circle, Binomial Theorem, Expansion of a Sum, Fourier Series, Pythagorean Theorem, Quadratic Formula, Taylor Expansion, Trig Identity 1, and Trig Identity 2.

Each equation has Professional and Linear forms. The Professional form displays the equation on multiple line levels, whereas the Linear form displays it on only one line. PowerPoint uses the Linear form when you insert the equation in a bulleted list item, and otherwise uses the Professional form.

Examples of standard equations

- ▶ **Binomial theorem (Linear form)**
  - ▶ $(x + a)^n = \sum_{k=0}^{n} \binom{n}{k} x^k a^{n-k}$
- ▶ **Expansion of a sum (Linear form)**
  - ▶ $(1 + x)^n = 1 + \frac{nx}{1!} + \frac{n(n-1)x^2}{2!} + \cdots$
- ▶ **Fourier series (Professional form)**
  - $f(x) = a_0 + \sum_{n=1}^{\infty} \left(a_n \cos\frac{n\pi x}{L} + b_n \sin\frac{n\pi x}{L} \right)$

The Professional and Linear form options are available by name in other Office apps

If you need something other than these standard equations, you can build your own equations by using a library of mathematical symbols. You build the equation by using the commands on the Design tool tab in the Equation Tools tab group.

Add a slide footer

If you want the same identifying information to appear at the bottom of every slide, you can insert it in a footer.

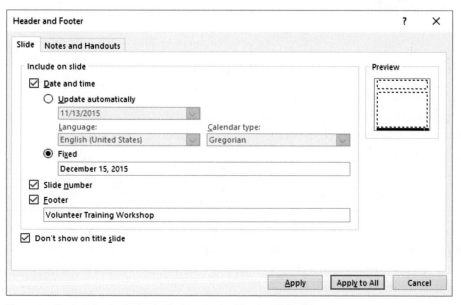

- **Provide appropriate skills development**
- **Meet genuine needs**

December 15, 2015   **Volunteer Training Workshop**   2

A slide footer provides fixed information on every slide

From the Header And Footer dialog box, you can configure the footer to display simple information such as the date and time, the slide number, and custom text.

You enter the text for the footer in the Header And Footer dialog box

4

To add standard footer information to every slide in a presentation

1. On the **Insert** tab, in the **Text** group, click the **Header & Footer** button to display the Slide tab of the Header And Footer dialog box.

2. Do any of the following:

   - In the **Include on slide** area, select the **Date and time** check box. Then click **Update automatically**, and click the format you want to display the date and time in, or click **Fixed**, and then enter the date and time as you want to display them.

   - Select the **Slide number** check box.

   - Select the **Footer** check box, and then in the text box, enter the text you want to display at the bottom of the page.

   - Select the **Don't show on title slide** check box.

3. Click **Apply to All**.

Move, copy, and delete text

After you enter text, you can use standard techniques to change it at any time. It's easy to modify a few characters, but if you want to edit more than that efficiently, you need to know how to select text. Selected text appears highlighted on the screen.

> **TIP** Many instructional materials incorrectly refer to selecting text as *highlighting text*, which is misleading. To highlight text is to apply the Highlight character format.

You can select content by using the mouse, using the keyboard, tapping, or combining multiple tools. When you select content, PowerPoint displays the Mini Toolbar, from which you can quickly format the selection or perform other actions, depending on the type of content you select.

> **SEE ALSO** For information about turning off the display of the Mini Toolbar, see the "Manage general Office and PowerPoint options" section of "Change default PowerPoint options" in Chapter 11, "Work in PowerPoint more efficiently."

You can move or copy selected text on a slide, within a presentation, or between presentations by using these methods:

- You can drag a selection from one location to another. This method is easiest to use when you can display the original location and destination on the screen at the same time.

- You can cut or copy the text from the original location to the Clipboard and then paste it from the Clipboard into the new location. There are multiple methods for cutting, copying, and pasting text. No matter which method you use, when you cut text, PowerPoint removes it from its original location. When you copy text, PowerPoint leaves the original text intact.

> **TIP** Clicking the Paste arrow on the Home tab displays the Paste menu of options for controlling the way PowerPoint inserts content that you paste onto a slide. The available options vary depending on the type of content that you have cut or copied to the Clipboard. For example, when you are pasting text, the Paste menu includes buttons for adopting the destination theme, keeping source formatting, pasting unformatted text, or pasting the content as a picture. Pointing to a button displays the paste option name in a ScreenTip, and a preview of how the source content will look if you use that option to paste it at the current location.

The Clipboard is a temporary storage area that is shared by the Office apps. You can display items that have been cut or copied to the Clipboard in the Clipboard pane.

The Clipboard stores items that have been cut or copied from any Office app

You can cut and copy content to the Clipboard and paste the most recent item from the Clipboard without displaying the Clipboard pane. If you want to work with items other than the most recent, you can display the Clipboard pane and then do so.

If you make a change and then realize that you made a mistake, you can easily reverse, or undo, one or more recent changes. You can redo changes that you've undone, or repeat your most recent action elsewhere in the presentation.

> ✓ **TIP** When moving and copying text in the Outline pane, you can hide bullet points under slide titles so that you can display more of the presentation at one time. Double-click the icon of the slide whose bullet points you want to hide. Double-click again to redisplay the bullet points. To expand or collapse the entire outline at once, right-click the title of a slide, point to Expand or Collapse, and then click Expand All or Collapse All.

In addition to moving and copying text, you can also simply delete it. The easiest way to do this is by using the Delete key or the Backspace key. However, when you delete text by using one of these keys, the text is not saved to the Clipboard and you can't paste it elsewhere.

Format text placeholders

The text placeholders on slide layouts provide a consistent appearance and location of slide content. Usually, you won't want to change the formatting of a presentation's text placeholders. However, if you want to draw attention to a slide or one of its elements, you can do so effectively by making specific placeholders stand out.

When a placeholder is selected, the Format tool tab appears on the ribbon, because placeholders are actually text-box shapes that can be manipulated like any other shape. You can outline or fill the placeholder, or add a visual effect to it, by using the commands in the Shape Styles group. Your changes affect only the selected placeholder, not corresponding placeholders on other slides.

TIP If you want to make changes to the same placeholder on every slide, make the adjustments on the presentation's master slide. For more information about working with master slides, see "Customize slide masters and layouts" in Chapter 12, "Create custom presentation elements."

To select text

1. Do any of the following:

   - To select adjacent words, lines, or paragraphs, drag through the text.

   - Position the cursor at the beginning of the text you want to select, and then do any of the following:

     - To select one character at a time, hold down the **Shift** key and then press the **Left Arrow** or **Right Arrow** key.

     - To select one word at a time, hold down the **Shift** and **Ctrl** keys and then press the **Left Arrow** or **Right Arrow** key.

     - To select one line at a time, hold down the **Shift** key and then press the **Up Arrow** or **Down Arrow** key.

     - To select any amount of adjacent content, hold down the **Shift** key and then click at the end of the content that you want to select.

   - To select a word, double-click anywhere in the word. PowerPoint selects the word and the space immediately after the word, but not any punctuation after the word.

   - To select a bulleted list item, click the bullet either on the slide or in the **Outline** pane.

   - To select all the text on a slide, click its slide icon in the **Outline** pane.

   - To select all the objects on a slide, click in any placeholder, and then click its border, which becomes solid instead of dashed. Click the **Select** button, and then click **Select All**.

   - To select a paragraph, triple-click anywhere in the paragraph.

   - To select non-adjacent words, lines, or paragraphs, select the first text segment and then hold down the **Ctrl** key while selecting the next text segment.

   - To select all the content in the current placeholder, do either of the following:

     - On the **Home** tab, in the **Editing** group, click the **Select** button, and then click **Select All**.

     - Press **Ctrl+A**.

4

To release a selection

1. Click anywhere in the window other than the selection area.

To cut text to the Clipboard

1. Select the text, and then do any of the following:

    -   On the **Home** tab, in the **Clipboard** group, click the **Cut** button.
    -   Right-click the selection, and then click **Cut**.
    -   Press **Ctrl+X**.

To copy text to the Clipboard

1. Select the text, and then do any of the following:

    -   On the **Home** tab, in the **Clipboard** group, click the **Copy** button.
    -   Right-click the selection, and then click **Copy**.
    -   Press **Ctrl+C**.

To paste the most recent item from the Clipboard

1. Position the cursor where you want to insert the text, and then do either of the following:

    -   On the **Home** tab, in the **Clipboard** group, click the **Paste** button.
    -   Press **Ctrl+V**.

Or

1. Right-click where you want to insert the text, and then in the **Paste Options** section of the menu, click a paste option.

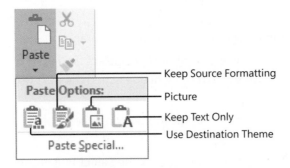

You can control the format of content as you paste it

To move text

1. Do either of the following:

    - Cut the text from the original location, and then paste it into the new location.

    - Drag the text from the original location to the new location.

To copy text from one location to another

1. Do either of the following:

    - Copy the text from the original location, and then paste it into the new location.

    - Hold down the **Ctrl** key and drag the text from the original location to the new location.

> **TIP** To drag selected text, point to it, hold down the mouse button and move the pointer to the insertion location (indicated by a thick vertical line), and then release the mouse button.

To display the Clipboard pane

1. On the **Home** tab, click the **Clipboard** dialog box launcher.

To manage cut and copied items in the Clipboard pane

1. Do any of the following:

    - To paste an individual item at the cursor, click the item, or point to the item, click the arrow that appears, and then click **Paste**.

    - To paste all the items stored on the Clipboard at the same location, click the **Paste All** button at the top of the **Clipboard** pane.

    - To remove an item from the Clipboard, point to the item in the **Clipboard** pane, click the arrow that appears, and then click **Delete**.

    - To remove all items from the Clipboard, click the **Clear All** button at the top of the **Clipboard** pane.

To control the behavior of the Clipboard pane

1. At the bottom of the pane, click **Options**, and then click the display option you want.

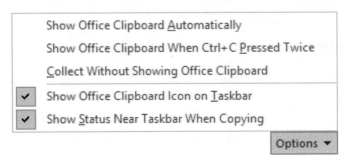

Clipboard pane display options

To undo your last editing action

1. Do either of the following:

   • On the Quick Access Toolbar, click the **Undo** button.

   • Press **Ctrl+Z**.

To undo two or more actions

1. On the Quick Access Toolbar, in the **Undo** list, click the first action you want to undo. Word reverts that action and all those that follow.

> ✓ **TIP** By default, you can undo up to 20 actions at a time from the Undo list. You can change that number from the Advanced page of the PowerPoint Options dialog box. For information, see the "Manage advanced options" section of "Change default PowerPoint options" in Chapter 11, "Work in PowerPoint more efficiently."

To restore your last editing action

1. Do either of the following:

   • On the Quick Access Toolbar, click the **Redo** button.

   • Press **Ctrl+Y**.

> **TIP** The Redo button appears on the Quick Access Toolbar, to the right of Undo. When you point to the Undo or Redo button, the name in the ScreenTip reflects your last editing action—for example, Redo Drag And Drop.

To delete only one or a few characters

1. Position the cursor immediately to the left of the text you want to delete.
2. Press the **Delete** key once for each character you want to delete.

Or

1. Position the cursor immediately to the right of the text you want to delete.
2. Press the **Backspace** key once for each character you want to delete.

To delete any amount of text

1. Select the text you want to delete.
2. Press the **Delete** key or the **Backspace** key.

Format characters and paragraphs

The alignment and spacing of paragraphs in a presentation's text placeholders are controlled by the template on which the presentation is based. For an individual paragraph, you can change these and other settings, which are collectively called *paragraph formatting*. After clicking anywhere in the paragraph to select it, you can make changes by using the commands in the Paragraph group on the Home tab.

> **TIP** If you want to make multiple changes to a paragraph's formatting, open the Paragraph dialog box so that you can make all the changes in one place. In this dialog box, you can also indent individual bullet points without changing them to subpoints.

In addition to changing the look of paragraphs, you can manipulate the look of individual words by manually applying settings that are collectively called *character formatting*. After selecting the characters you want to format, you make changes by using the commands in the Font group on the Home tab.

To make it quick and easy to apply the most common paragraph and character formatting, PowerPoint displays the Mini Toolbar when you select text. This toolbar contains buttons from the Font and Paragraph groups on the Home tab, but they're all in one place adjacent to the selection. If you don't want to apply any of the Mini Toolbar formats, simply ignore it and use the ribbon to make the changes you want.

You can quickly apply formatting by clicking buttons on the Mini Toolbar

After you format the text on a slide, you might find that you want to adjust the way lines break to achieve a more balanced look. This is often the case with slide titles, but bullet points and regular text can sometimes benefit from a few manually inserted line breaks.

> ⚠️ **IMPORTANT** This fine-tuning should wait until you have taken care of all other formatting of the slide element because changing the font, size, and other attributes of text can affect how it breaks.

To apply character attributes to text

1. Select the text you want to style, and then do any of the following:

   - On the **Home** tab, in the **Font** group, click the **Bold**, **Italic**, **Underline**, **Text Shadow**, or **Strikethrough** button.

   - On the **Mini Toolbar**, click any of the equivalent formatting buttons.

   - Use any of the following keyboard shortcuts:

     - To style selected text as bold, press **Ctrl+B**.

     - To style selected text as italic, press **Ctrl+I**.

     - To style selected text as underline, press **Ctrl+U**.

To change text casing

1. On the **Home** tab, in the **Font** group, click the **Change Case** button, and then click the case you want.

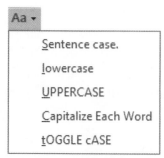

You can choose from several case options

To increase or decrease the space between characters

1. In the **Font** group, click the **Character Spacing** button, and then do either of the following:

   - Click the spacing option you want.

   - Click **More Spacing** to display the Character Spacing page of the Font dialog box, and then specify the space you want between characters.

To change the font color of existing text

1. Select the text you want to format.

2. On the **Home** tab, in the **Font** group, click the **Font Color** arrow.

3. In the **Standard Colors** palette, click any color swatch.

> **TIP** The colors available in the Theme Colors palette are determined by the theme that is part of the presentation's design. For information about using colors that are not available in the Theme Colors or Standard Colors palette, see the sidebar "Non-theme colors" in Chapter 3, "Create and manage slides."

To increase the font size of existing text

1. Select the text you want to format.

2. Do either of the following:

   - In the **Font** group, click the **Increase Font Size** button.

   - Press **Ctrl+Shift+>**.

> **TIP** If you turn off AutoFit so that you can manually size text, you can drag the handles around a selected placeholder to adjust its size to fit its text.

To clear formatting from text

1. Select the text you want to format.

2. Do either of the following:

   - In the **Font** group, click the **Clear All Formatting** button.

   - Press **Ctrl+Spacebar**.

To convert bulleted list items to regular text paragraphs

1. Select the bulleted list items that you want to convert.

2. Do either of the following:

   - On the **Home** tab, in the **Paragraph** group, click the active **Bullets** button.

   - Click the **Bullets** arrow, and then click **None** in the gallery.

To convert a bulleted list to a numbered list or a numbered list to a bulleted list

1. Select the bulleted or numbered list items, and then click the **Bullets** or **Numbering** button, respectively.

To change the style of bullets or numbering

1. Click the **Bullets** or **Numbering** arrow, and then click the style you want in the gallery.

To change the alignment of text

1. On the **Home** tab, in the **Paragraph** group, click any of the following alignment buttons:

   - To align text along the placeholder's left edge, click the **Align Left** button.

   - To align text in the middle of the placeholder, click the **Center** button.

   - To align text against the placeholder's right edge, click the **Align Right** button.

   - To align text against both the left and right edges, adding space between words to fill the line, click the **Justify** button. (This option works only if the paragraph contains more than one line.)

   - To align text vertically at the top, in the middle, or at the bottom of the placeholder, click the **Align Text** button.

   Or

1. Use any of the following keyboard shortcuts:

   - To left-align text, press **Ctrl+L**.

   - To center text, press **Ctrl+E**.

   - To right-align text, press **Ctrl+R**.

To change line spacing

1. On the **Home** tab, in the **Paragraph** group, click the **Line Spacing** button, and then click the spacing you want.

To format a paragraph by using settings in the Paragraph dialog box

2. On the **Home** tab, click the **Paragraph** dialog box launcher to open the Paragraph dialog box.

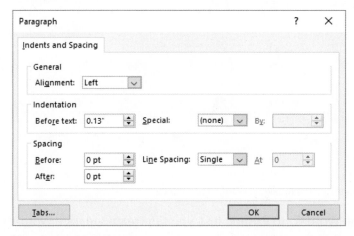

In the Paragraph dialog box, you can set alignment, indentation, line spacing, and paragraph spacing all in one place

3. Do any of the following:

   - In the **General** area, change the **Alignment** setting to **Left**, **Centered** or **Right**.

   - In the **Spacing** area, enter a number in the **Before** or **After** box.

   - In the **Spacing** area, change the **Line Spacing** setting.

To insert a line break in a paragraph

1. Press **Shift+Enter**.

Apply WordArt text effects

PowerPoint includes 20 artistic text effects that are referred to as *WordArt*. Unlike the somewhat clumsy WordArt of the past that inserted independent objects with rather garish designs, WordArt now consists of predefined artistic text effects that you can apply to any text (or insert independently). Applying a WordArt text effect retains the original font and font size but adds various font color, gradient, outline, dimensional, and reflection elements.

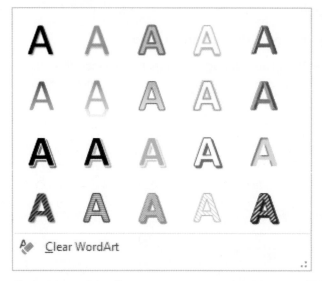

The WordArt gallery offers easy access to several WordArt text effects

In addition to applying WordArt to existing text, you can create separate WordArt text objects. These are simply text boxes that contain only the WordArt-formatted text. You can modify and format them just as you do any other text boxes.

 SEE ALSO For information about working with text boxes, see "Add supplementary text to slides" earlier in this chapter.

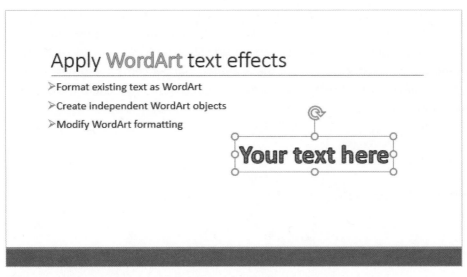

WordArt text effects can help to add visual interest to your presentation

You can leave the WordArt effects as-is or customize any of them by modifying the settings in the WordArt Styles group on the Format tool tab. As with other color effects, WordArt fill, outline, and glow colors are based on the presentation color scheme. If you change the theme or color scheme, these will automatically update to match other color scheme–controlled elements.

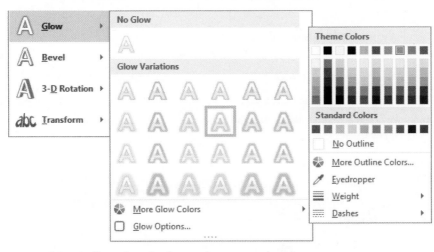

Outline, fill, and effect colors all reference the current color scheme

The most interesting feature of WordArt formatting is the text effects that you can apply. (You can actually apply these text effects to any text, not only to text that has a WordArt format applied.) The text effects include Shadow, Reflection, Glow, Bevel, 3-D Rotation, and Transform. Some of these are familiar concepts and others are unique to WordArt—in particular, transformation, which is reminiscent of the original WordArt options.

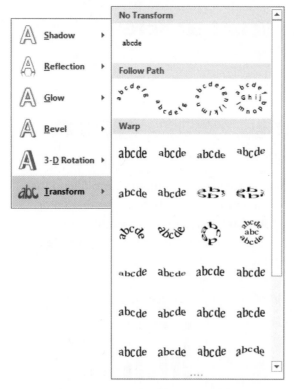

You can choose from several text effects, including Transform text effects, which result in a warping of the text

In each of the text effect categories, you can choose a preformatted option or create a unique combination. If you're working with an independent WordArt object, you can modify the object size, shape, and sometimes structure by moving the size handles on the object frame.

**Long ago
and far away
WordArt was born**

You can change the appearance of WordArt by applying text effects

To apply a WordArt effect to existing text

1. Select the text that you want to format.

2. On the **Format** tool tab, in the **WordArt Styles** group, click the **More** button to display the WordArt Styles gallery.

3. In the gallery, click the WordArt effect that you want to apply.

To insert a WordArt text object

1. On the **Insert** tab, in the **Text** group, click the **WordArt** button.

2. In the **WordArt** gallery, click the WordArt style that you want, to insert a text box that contains placeholder text in the middle of the slide.

3. Replace the placeholder text with your own text.

To modify WordArt formatting

1. Select the WordArt object or formatted text.

2. On the **Format** tool tab, in the **WordArt Styles** group, do any of the following:

   - In the **WordArt Styles** gallery, click a different WordArt style.

   - On the **Text Fill** menu, select a different color or a picture, gradient, or texture fill for the lettering.

   - On the **Text Outline** menu, select a different color, weight, or pattern for the letter outlines.

   - On the **Text Effects** menu, modify the shadow, reflection, glow, bevel, rotation, or transformation of the text.

To change the size and angles of a WordArt object

1. Click the WordArt object to activate its handles.

2. Do any of the following:

   - Drag the side or corner handles (hollow circles) to change the size or aspect ratio of the object.

   - Drag the angle handles (yellow circles) to change the angles or curves of the text within the object.

   - Drag the rotate handle (circling arrow) to rotate the object on the slide.

3. Click away from the object to display the effect of your changes.

Configure AutoCorrect options

PowerPoint uses the AutoCorrect feature to identify and automatically correct many common capitalization and spelling errors. For example, if you enter *teh* instead of *the* or *WHen* instead of *When*, or don't capitalize the first word of a paragraph, AutoCorrect immediately corrects the entry.

You can customize AutoCorrect to recognize misspellings you routinely enter or to ignore text you do not want AutoCorrect to change. You can also create your own AutoCorrect substitutions to automate the entry of frequently used text. For example, you might want AutoCorrect to substitute your organization's name when you enter only an abbreviation.

To reverse an AutoCorrect change, do either of the following:

- Immediately after AutoCorrect makes the change, click the **Undo** button on the Quick Access Toolbar or press **Ctrl+Z**.

- Point to the AutoCorrect change, point to the bar that appears below it, and then click the arrow to display the AutoCorrect Options menu. On the menu, click the appropriate correction option.

SEE ALSO For information about adding words to the AutoCorrect list, see "Change default PowerPoint options" in Chapter 11, "Work in PowerPoint more efficiently."

Check spelling and choose the best wording

The AutoCorrect feature is useful if you frequently enter the same misspelling. However, most misspellings are the result of erratic finger-positioning errors or memory lapses. You can use one of the following two methods to ensure that the words in your presentations are spelled correctly in spite of these random occurrences.

By default, the PowerPoint spelling checker checks the spelling of the entire presentation—all slides, outlines, notes pages, and handout pages—against its built-in dictionary. To draw attention to words that are not in its dictionary and that might be misspelled, PowerPoint underlines them with a red wavy underline. You can right-click a word with a red wavy underline to display a menu with a list of possible spellings and actions. You can choose the correct spelling from the menu, tell PowerPoint to ignore the word, or add the word to a supplementary dictionary (explained later in this topic).

4

- Set up team
- Gather infermation
  - information
  - Ignore All
  - Add to Dictionary
- Plan project

PowerPoint flags any misspelled or unknown words

TIP To turn off this behind-the-scenes spell-checking, open the PowerPoint Options dialog box, click Proofing, and clear the Check Spelling As You Type check box.

Instead of dealing with potential misspellings while you're creating a presentation, you can check the entire presentation in one session by clicking the Spelling button in the Proofing group on the Review tab. PowerPoint then works its way through the presentation. If it encounters a word that is not in its dictionary, it displays the word in the Spelling pane. After you indicate how PowerPoint should deal with the word—by ignoring it, ignoring all instances of it, adding it to the supplementary dictionary, changing it to the suggested spelling, or changing all instances of it to the suggested spelling—it moves on and displays the next word that is not in its dictionary, and so on.

The Spelling pane offers suggestions to correct the flagged word

> **TIP** PowerPoint alerts you to the fact that there are spelling errors in a presentation by placing an X over the spelling indicator at the left end of the status bar.

If PowerPoint flags a word or phrase that is written in another language, you can mark it as such. Then, PowerPoint will cease to flag that word or phrase as a misspelling.

You can mark a flagged word or phrase as a foreign word

You cannot make changes to the main dictionary in PowerPoint, but you can add correctly spelled words that are flagged as misspellings to the PowerPoint supplementary dictionary (called *CUSTOM.DIC*). You can also create and use custom dictionaries and use dictionaries from other Microsoft apps.

PowerPoint can check your spelling, but it can't alert you if you're not using the best wording. Language is often contextual. The language you use in a presentation to members of a club is different from the language you use in a business presentation. To make sure you're using words that best convey your meaning in any given context, you can use the Thesaurus feature to look up alternative words, called *synonyms*, for a selected word.

The Thesaurus pane suggests several synonyms for the selected word

> **TIP** For many words, the quickest way to find a suitable synonym is to right-click the word and point to Synonyms. You can then either click one of the suggested words or click Thesaurus to open the Thesaurus pane.

Find and replace text and fonts

If you suspect that you might have used an incorrect word or phrase through-out a presentation—for example, if you have repeatedly used an inaccurate company name—you can click the buttons in the Editing group on the Home tab to do the following:

- To locate each occurrence of a word, part of a word, or a phrase, click the **Find** button to open the Find dialog box. Enter the text, and then click **Find Next**. You can specify whether PowerPoint should locate only matches with the exact capitalization, or *case*—in other words, if you specify *person*, you don't want PowerPoint to locate *Person*. You can also tell PowerPoint whether it should locate only matches for the entire text—in other words, if you specify *person*, you don't want PowerPoint to locate *personal*.

- To locate each occurrence of a word, part of a word, or a phrase and replace it with something else, click the **Replace** button to open the Replace dialog box. Enter the text you want to find and what you want to replace it with, click **Find Next**, and then click **Replace** to replace the found occurrence or **Replace All** to replace all occurrences. Again, you can specify whether to match capitalization and whole words.

TIP If you are working in the Find dialog box and you want to replace instead of find, click Replace at the bottom of the dialog box to open the Replace dialog box with any settings you have already made intact.

You can also click the Replace arrow, and in the Replace list, click Replace Fonts to open the Replace Font dialog box. Here, you can specify the font you want to change and the font you want PowerPoint to replace it with.

To correct spelling errors on a slide

1. Right-click any word that has a wavy red underline. PowerPoint displays suggested spelling corrections at the top of the shortcut menu.

2. Click any of the suggested corrections to replace the word.

To use the Thesaurus to find a synonym

1. Select or click in a word.

2. Do either of the following to open the Thesaurus pane and display synonyms for the selected word:

   - On the **Review** tab, in the **Proofing** group, click the **Thesaurus** button.

   - Press **Shift+F7**.

> **TIP** If the pane doesn't show an obvious substitute for the selected word, click a possible replacement word in the Thesaurus list to display synonyms for that word.

3. Point to the word you want to use, click the arrow that appears, and then click **Insert**.

To mark a word as written in a specific language

1. Select a word that has a wavy red underline.

2. On the **Review** tab, in the **Language** group, click the **Language** button, and then click **Set Proofing Language**.

3. In the **Language** dialog box, click the language. Then click **OK**.

To check the spelling of an entire presentation

1. If you want to begin checking from the beginning of the presentation, press **Ctrl+Home** to move there.

2. To begin the review, do either of the following:

   - On the **Review** tab, in the **Proofing** group, click the **Spelling & Grammar** button.

   - Press **F7**.

   The Spelling pane opens and displays the first possible error. The corresponding text on the slide is highlighted.

3. In the **Spelling** pane, review the explanation and the suggested responses, and then do any of the following:

    - If the selection is identified as a possible spelling error, do any of the following:

        - Click **Ignore** to continue the review without changing the highlighted word or **Ignore All** to continue and to ignore other instances of the word in the current presentation.

        - Click **Add** to add the word to the custom dictionary on your computer.

        - Select the correct spelling of the word in the suggestions list, and then click **Change** to change only this instance of the word or **Change All** to change all instances of this word in the document.

    - If the selection is identified as a duplicated word, do either of the following:

        - Click **Ignore** to continue the review without making a change.

        - Click **Delete** to delete the highlighted instance of the duplicated word.

    - If the selection is identified as a possible grammatical or formatting error, do either of the following:

        - Click **Ignore** to continue the review without making a change.

        - Select the correct usage in the suggestions list, and click **Change** to change the selection to the new usage.

    When you click a button to fix or ignore the issue, the spelling and grammar checker moves to the next word that Word does not recognize.

4. After the last selection has been addressed, Word displays a message indicating that it has finished checking the spelling and grammar of the document. Click **OK** to close the message box.

To manage the custom dictionary

1. From the Backstage view, open the **PowerPoint Options** dialog box.

2. Display the **Proofing** page. In the **When correcting spelling in Microsoft Office programs** section of the Proofing page, click the **Custom Dictionaries** button.

3. The **Custom Dictionaries** dialog box displays the dictionaries that Office apps consult. Select the dictionary that has *(default)* after the name. Then click the **Edit Word List** button.

4. In the dialog box for the selected dictionary, do any of the following:

   - To review the content of the dictionary, scroll the **Dictionary** pane.

   - To remove a word from the dictionary, click it in the **Dictionary** pane, and then click **Delete**.

   - To clear the entire dictionary, click **Delete All**.

   - To add a word to the dictionary, enter it in the **Word(s)** box and then click **OK**.

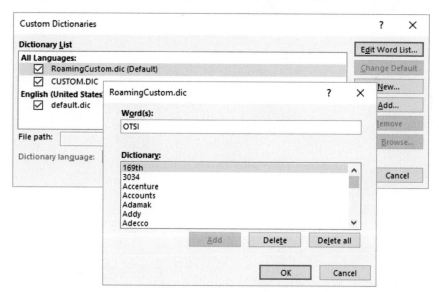

The dictionary includes words that you've added from the Spelling pane or entered manually

Skills review

In this chapter, you learned how to:

- Enter text on slides
- Move, copy, and delete text
- Format characters and paragraphs
- Apply WordArt text effects
- Check spelling and choose the best wording

Practice tasks

The practice files for these tasks are located in the PowerPoint2016SBS
\Ch04 folder. You can save the results of the tasks in the same folder.

Enter text on slides

Open the EnterText presentation and perform the following tasks:

1. Display slide **1** in Normal view, and then in the placeholder, enter **Wide World Importers** as the presentation title.

2. Insert a registered trademark (®) symbol after *Wide World Importers*.

3. In the subtitle placeholder, enter **Where we are, where we are going, how we are going to get there...and how long it is going to take.**

4. If it's not already configured to do so, change the AutoFit settings so text does not automatically fit in the placeholder.

5. Display slide **2** in Outline view.

6. In the **Outline** pane, next to the slide 2 location, enter **Expanding to the UK.**

7. After *UK*, enter **(£)*** (pound symbol surrounded by parentheses followed by an asterisk).

8. Press **Enter**, and then press **Tab** to create a first-level bullet.

9. Enter **Preparing for a buying trip**, and then press **Enter**.

10. Enter the following three bullet points, pressing **Enter** after each:

    -   **Traveling internationally**
    -   **Meeting the client**
    -   **Know your needs**

11. Demote the *Know your needs* bullet to a second-level bullet point.

12. Insert a text box in the lower-right corner of the slide, and then enter ***Short-term strategy.**

13. Reduce the size of the text in the text box to **12** point and set that size as the default for all text boxes.

14. Add a slide footer that includes the text **Wide World Importers** and set it so that it does not appear on the title slide.

15. Close the presentation.

Move, copy, and delete text

Open the EditText presentation, and then perform the following tasks:

1. Display slide **2** in Normal view and, in the first bullet, delete the word *buying*.

2. Switch to Outline view.

3. In the **Outline** pane, in the second bullet point on slide **6**, replace the word *good* with the word **lasting**. Notice that the text is replaced in both the Outline pane and the Slide pane.

4. On slide **5**, move the entire *Know the culture* bullet point by cutting it from its current location and pasting it to the left of *Know your customers* on slide **3**.

5. Switch to Normal view, and then on slide **3**, in the **Slide** pane, move the *Know your needs* bullet point and its subpoints as a unit by dragging it to the left of *Read the Buyer Manuals*.

6. Undo the action in step 5.

7. Restore that editing action.

8. Close the presentation.

Format characters and paragraphs

Open the FormatText presentation, and then perform the following tasks:

1. On slide **1**, select *Flowers in nature and arrangements*, and use the **Mini Toolbar** to make the words italic.

2. Display slide **2**, select the entire bulleted list and then increase the font size until the setting in the **Font Size** box is **32**.

3. Clear the formatting to return the font size to **24** (the original size).

4. Change the font color to yellow.

5. Convert the bullet points to regular text paragraphs.

6. Select all the paragraphs, and then open the **Paragraph** dialog box.

7. Change the **Alignment** setting to **Centered**.

8. In the **Spacing** area, enter **0** in the **Before** box, and then increase the **After** setting to **24 pt**.

9. Change the **Line Spacing** setting to **Exactly**, change the **At** setting to **30 pt**, and then click **OK**.

10. On slide **7**, insert a line break to the left of the word *of*.

11. Close the presentation.

Apply WordArt text effects

Open the ApplyTextEffects presentation, and then perform the following tasks:

1. On slide **1**, select the *Litware, Inc.* text.

2. Display the **WordArt Styles** gallery, and then click **Fill – White, Background 2, Inner Shadow**.

3. Display slide **5** and insert a WordArt text object with **Gradient Fill – Gray** style.

4. Replace the placeholder text with **Objective: Author Satisfaction**.

5. Select the WordArt object and on the **Text Fill** menu, click the **Purple Accent 1** swatch.

6. On the **Text Outline** menu, click the **Black, Text 1** swatch.

7. On the **Text Effects** menu, on the **Shadow** submenu, click **Perspective Diagonal Upper Right**.

8. Resize the WordArt object to make it smaller.

9. Rotate the WordArt object so that it runs diagonally across the slide, from the upper-left to the lower-right.

10. Close the presentation.

Check spelling and choose the best wording

Open the CheckSpelling presentation, and then perform the following tasks:

1. On slide **3**, replace *infermation*, which PowerPoint has flagged as a possible error with a red wavy underline, with **information**.

2. On slide **6**, identify the phrase *Médecins Sans Frontières* as a French (France) phrase.

3. Display slide **1**.

4. Check the spelling of the entire presentation, and then do the following:

   a. Change the word *Persue* to **Pursue**

      The spelling checker then stops on the word *CSCom*, suggesting *Como* as the correct spelling. For purposes of this task, assume that this is a common abbreviation for *Community Service Committee*.

   b. Add the term *CSCom* to the CUSTOM.DIC dictionary.

   c. Delete the duplicated word *to*.

   d. Change the word *employes* to **employees**.

   e. Change the word *succeful* to **successful**.

5. This presentation still has spelling problems—words that are spelled correctly but that aren't correct in context. Proof the slides and correct these errors manually.

6. Remove CSCom from the supplementary dictionary.

7. On slide **1**, replace the word *executing* with the word **completing** by using the **Thesaurus** pane.

8. Close the presentation.

Present text in tables

5

When you want to present a lot of data on a PowerPoint slide in an organized and easy-to-read format, a table is often your best choice. Tables provide a tidy structure for the presentation of text and numeric information in rows and columns, so that identifying categories or individual items and making comparisons is easier.

You can insert a table on any PowerPoint slide, regardless of whether it includes a content placeholder. If the information you want to present is already in a tabular format—for example, in a Microsoft Word document or a Microsoft Excel workbook—you can copy the existing table to your slide and then modify it as necessary to fit your presentation. If you want to preserve the formulas in an Excel table, it's best to embed the worksheet as an object on the PowerPoint slide.

After you insert a table, whether blank or from another source, you can modify its structure and formatting.

This chapter guides you through procedures related to inserting tables, formatting tables, modifying table structure, and embedding and linking to Excel content.

In this chapter

- Insert tables
- Format tables
- Modify table structure
- Embed and link to Excel content

Practice files

For this chapter, use the practice files from the PowerPoint2016SBS\Ch05 folder. For practice file download instructions, see the introduction.

Insert tables

You can insert a blank table from a content placeholder or from the Insert tab of the ribbon. You can specify the number of rows and columns you want to start with, and then modify the table as necessary to fit its content.

 TIP As an alternative to inserting a table, you can "draw" a table by using a pencil tool. This is a more difficult method and doesn't seem to offer any efficiencies.

After you specify the number of columns and rows you want in the blank table, PowerPoint creates the table structure. By default, the table matches the color scheme of the presentation theme. The first row is formatted as a header row, and the subsequent rows are banded. You can then add data, add or remove rows and columns, change the table elements that are emphasized, and change the table formatting.

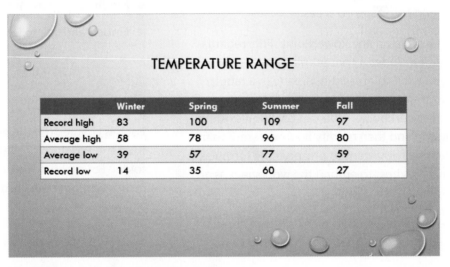

TEMPERATURE RANGE

	Winter	Spring	Summer	Fall
Record high	83	100	109	97
Average high	58	78	96	80
Average low	39	57	77	59
Record low	14	35	60	27

The default header and banded row formatting

 TIP The box at the intersection of each row and column is called a *cell*. Often the first row of a table is used for column headings, and the leftmost column is used for row headings.

If the table you want to use already exists in a Word document, or in an Excel workbook, you can copy the original table and paste it onto the slide, rather than re-creating the table. When you paste a table from another source onto a slide, a Paste Options button appears. Clicking the button displays a menu of options for pasting the table.

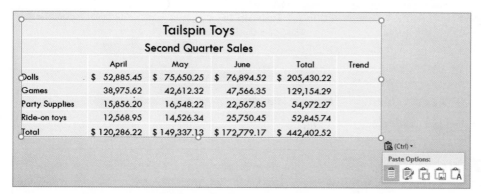

Applying the destination styles to the pasted table

On the Paste Options menu for a table, you can choose from these options:

- **Use Destination Styles** This is the default option. It applies the fonts, colors, and effects of the slide theme to the table. The table can be modified.

- **Keep Source Formatting** This option retains the original formatting of the table. The table can be modified.

- **Embed** This option inserts an image of the table that is linked to the original source document or workbook. Double-clicking the image opens the source file (if it's available) in which you can make changes to the table content.

> **SEE ALSO** For information about embedding linked tables on a slide, see "Embed and link to Excel content" later in this chapter.

- **Picture** This option pastes an image of the table onto the slide. The table cannot be modified other than by applying image formatting.

- **Keep Text Only** This option inserts unformatted text.

As you point to each option, the table appearance updates to reflect what the table will look like if you choose that option.

Keep Source Formatting

Embed

Effects of different paste options

> **TIP** The Paste Options button appears when pasting a variety of objects. The options on the Paste Options menu vary based on the object being pasted.

If you're accustomed to creating tables in Word by converting text to a table, note that you can't do that on a PowerPoint slide. If a slide contains content you want to display in a tabular format, consider copying the text to a document, converting it to a table, and then copying the table to the slide.

To insert a blank table on a slide

1. Do either of the following to open the Insert Table dialog box:

   - If the slide includes a content placeholder, click the **Insert Table** button in the content placeholder.

   - On any slide, on the **Insert** tab, in the **Tables** group, click the **Table** button, and then click **Insert Table**.

Insert Table

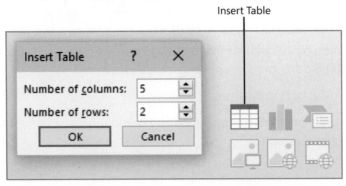

You can insert a table from a content placeholder or the Insert tab

2. In the **Insert Table** dialog box, specify the **Number of columns** and the **Number or rows** you want. Then click **OK**.

Or

1. On the **Insert** menu, in the **Tables** group, click the **Table** button and then point to the cell grid to indicate the size (in rows and columns) of the table you want to create.

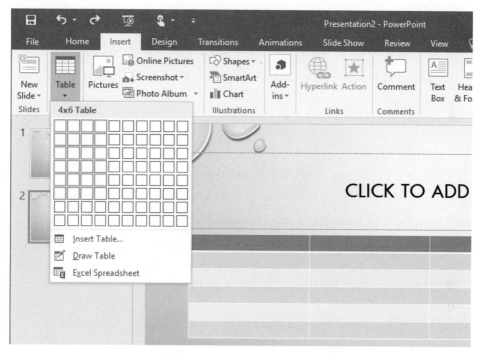

The label above the cell grid indicates the number of columns and rows, as does a red outline around the cells

> **TIP** The maximum table size you can create from the cell grid in PowerPoint 2016 is 10x8. If you need a larger table, use a different method or insert columns and rows after you create the table.

2. Release the mouse button to insert a table of the selected dimensions.

> **TIP** Inserting a table on a slide by clicking the Insert Table icon in a table placeholder or content placeholder inserts the table in that placeholder (and replaces the placeholder). Inserting a table on a slide that doesn't have a related placeholder floats the table on the slide and doesn't remove any of the placeholders.

To insert a table from a Word document on a slide

1. Open the document, and locate the table that you want to copy to the slide.

2. Click the table selector (the four-headed arrow outside the upper-left corner of the table) and then copy the table to the Clipboard by using any of these methods:

   - Press **Ctrl+C**.

   - Right-click the table, and then click **Copy**.

   - On the **Home** tab, in the **Clipboard** group, click the **Copy** button.

3. Switch to PowerPoint and display the slide that you want to insert the table on.

4. Paste the copied table from the Clipboard to the slide by using any of these methods:

   - Press **Ctrl+V**.

   - Right-click the slide, click **Paste Options**, and then click the paste option you want.

   - On the **Home** tab, in the **Clipboard** group, click the **Paste** button.

5. If you don't want the table to match the slide formatting, click the **Paste Options** button that appears in the lower-right corner of the table, and then on the **Paste Options** menu, click the paste option you want.

To insert a table from an Excel worksheet on a slide

1. Open the workbook, and locate the table or data range that you want to copy to the slide.

 TIP Copy and paste methods are described in the preceding procedure.

2. Select the table or data range, and then copy the selection to the Clipboard.

3. Switch to PowerPoint, and display the slide that you want to insert the table on.

4. Paste the copied table from the Clipboard to the slide.

5. If you don't want the table to match the slide formatting, click the **Paste Options** button, and then on the **Paste Options** menu, click the paste option you want.

SEE ALSO For information about embedding linked tables on a slide, see "Embed and link to Excel content" later in this chapter.

To move a table on a slide

1. Click the table frame to select the table.

2. Do either of the following:

   - Point to any outside edge of the table. When the cursor changes to a four-headed arrow, press and hold the mouse button and drag the table to its new location.

   - Press the arrow keys to move the table in small increments, or hold down the Shift key and press the arrow keys to move the table in larger increments.

To enter text in a table cell

1. Do either of the following:

   - Click the cell, and then enter your text.

   - Select text that you want to paste into the table, click the cell you want to paste the text into, and then paste the text. If your original text comes from another table, you can copy and paste multiple cells of content at a time.

To move the cursor to the next table cell

1. Press **Tab**.

   When you press Tab in the last cell in a row, PowerPoint moves to the first cell in the next row. When you press Tab after the last cell in the table, PowerPoint adds a new row to the table and places the cursor in the first cell in that row.

Format tables

When you insert a table on a slide or paste a formatted table from a Word document or Excel workbook, the table takes on the color scheme of the theme that is applied to the presentation. If you insert a blank table, it is formatted to support a heading row and to emphasize (band) every other row to help readers distinguish between separate rows of information. If this isn't the correct formatting for the information you're presenting in the table—for example, if the table headers are in the first column or you want to emphasize columns rather than rows—you can change the formatting to support that.

You work with tables in PowerPoint in much the same way as you work with tables in Word. You can format an entire table or individual cells by using the commands on the Design and Layout tool tabs, which appear when a table is active.

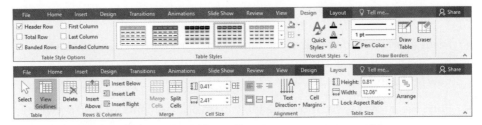

The Design and Layout tool tabs for tables

For example, you can use commands on the Design tool tab to switch to a different table style and apply options that change the text or cell formatting to make key information stand out. If you want, you can also format individual words and individual cells.

ANNUAL SALES REVIEW

Name	Jan	Feb	Mar	Apr	May	Jun
Brock	$ 3,008	$ 5,203	$ 7,854	$ 1,201	$ 3,576	$ 2,123
Charles	$ 4,280	$ 7,501	$ 3,951	$ 1,824	$ 7,644	$ 7,282
Heidi	$ 3,950	$ 6,019	$ 6,678	$ 4,234	$ 4,794	$ 1,800
Helena	$ 1,930	$ 1,602	$ 7,400	$ 6,446	$ 4,457	$ 6,027
Joan	$ 5,656	$ 4,168	$ 2,502	$ 7,927	$ 7,528	$ 3,158
Max	$ 1,082	$ 4,404	$ 5,274	$ 1,903	$ 7,196	$ 4,135
Trinity	$ 8,544	$ 7,295	$ 2,119	$ 6,744	$ 7,220	$ 4,523
	$ 56,881	$ 66,079	$ 68,084	$ 50,155	$ 71,006	$ 72,991

The selected table style options emphasize the header row, total row, and first column, and apply shading to every other row

The available table styles reflect the color scheme of the theme that is applied to the presentation.

You might at times need or want to make part of a table look as though it isn't there. You can do that by removing the fill color and borders from the cells that you want to disappear.

Class	Quarter	
	1	2
Math	95	88
Science	93	95
Art	100	100
Language Arts	97	92
Physical Ed	100	100
Reading	96	92
World History	93	89

You can format a cell in such a way that it appears to not exist

To activate a table for formatting

1. Click anywhere in the table. The Design and Format tool tabs appear on the ribbon.

To lect an entire table

1. Click anywhere in the table. On the **Layout** tool tab, in the **Table** group, click the **Select** button, and then click **Select Table**. The table does not change to indicate that it is selected.

To select rows or columns

1. Do any of the following:

   - Click any cell in the row or column you want to select. On the **Layout** tool tab, in the **Table** group, click the **Select** button, and then click **Select Row** or **Select Column**.

   - Point to the outer edge of a row or column. When the cursor changes to an arrow, click to select the row or column. Drag to select additional contiguous rows or columns.

   - Drag through all the cells of a row or all the cells of a column.

   The selected rows or columns are shaded.

To select multiple contiguous cells

1. Do any of the following:

   - Drag through the cells.

   - Click the first cell, hold down the **Shift** key, and then press the arrow keys to select adjacent cells.

   - Click the first cell, hold down the **Shift** key, and then click the last cell.

   The selected cells are shaded.

To select one cell

1. Click anywhere in the cell. When you select only one cell, the selected cell is not shaded.

To modify table style options

1. Activate the table. On the **Design** tool tab, in the **Table Style Options** group, do any of the following:

   - Clear the **Header Row** check box if the first row of the table doesn't contain column headings.

   - Clear the **Banded Rows** check box to make all rows except the header row the same color.

   - Select the **First Column** or **Last Column** check box to emphasize the content of that column.

   - Select the **Total Row** check box to emphasize the content of the final row of the table.

     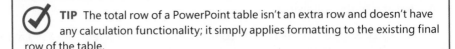 **TIP** The total row of a PowerPoint table isn't an extra row and doesn't have any calculation functionality; it simply applies formatting to the existing final row of the table.

   As you change the table style options, the thumbnails in the Table Style group update to reflect your changes.

To change the table style

1. Activate the table. On the **Design** tool tab, in the **Table Styles** group, click the **More** button to display the Table Styles gallery.

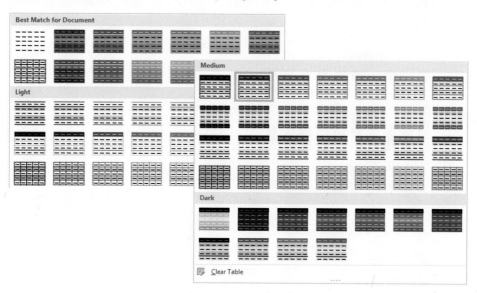

The thumbnails reflect the currently selected table style options

> **TIP** If the Table Styles gallery extends so far that it covers your table and you want to see the style previews, drag the bottom border of the gallery upward to make it shorter.

2. Point to table styles to preview their effects on the table.

3. Click a thumbnail to apply the style.

> **TIP** If you select a table style that doesn't have cell borders, you can temporarily display the cell borders by clicking the View Gridlines button in the Table group on the Layout tool tab.

To fill one or more cells with a specific color

1. Select the cell or cells you want to fill.

2. On the **Design** tool tab, in the **Table Styles** group, click the **Shading** arrow to display the Shading menu.

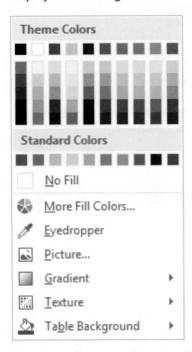

PowerPoint offers more color options than other Office apps

3. Do any of the following:

- In the **Theme Colors** palette, click a color swatch. Colors selected from this palette change with the color scheme.

- In the **Standard Colors** palette, click a color swatch. Colors selected from this palette are the same on all computers.

- On the **Shading** menu, click **More Fill Colors**. On the **Standard** tab of the **Colors** dialog box, click a color on the color wheel; or on the **Custom** tab of the dialog box, select or specify a color. Then click **OK**.

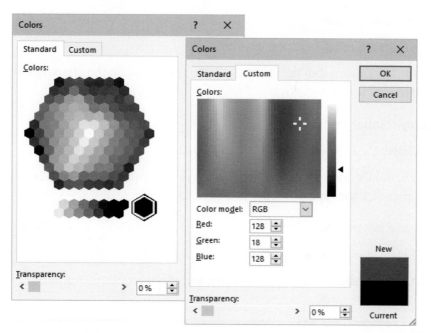

You can choose any color of the rainbow

> **TIP** By default, fill colors are opaque (other cell background formatting doesn't show through). You can make the fill color transparent by setting the Transparency percentage at the bottom of the Colors dialog box. A Transparency setting of 100% makes the fill color invisible, so you'll probably want to start with 50% and adjust it from there.

- On the **Shading** menu, click **Eyedropper**. When the cursor changes to the shape of an eyedropper, click any element in the Slide pane to select that color. The color appears in a Custom Colors section of the menu and you can reuse it from that section.

You also have the option of filling the cell with a picture, gradient, or texture. None of these are particularly suitable fills for most table cells, but you can explore them on your own if you're interested.

> **TIP** When you fill a cell with a specific color, the fill color covers any shading applied by a table style or table style option.

To clear a cell fill color

1. Select the cell or cells you want to clear.

2. On the **Design** tool tab, in the **Table Styles** group, on the **Shading** menu, click **No Fill**.

To apply standard cell borders

1. Select the cell or cells you want to format.

2. On the **Design** tool tab, in the **Table Styles** group, click the **Borders** arrow, and then click the type of border you want to apply.

To remove cell borders

1. Select the cell or cells you want to remove the border from.

2. On the **Design** tool tab, in the **Table Styles** group, on the **Borders** menu, click **No Border**.

 TIP Removing all borders from a cell removes the border on one side of each adjacent cell. You can manually reapply borders to those cells if you want them.

To customize cell borders

1. Select the cell or cells you want to format.

2. On the **Design** tool tab, in the **Draw Borders** group, do any of the following to customize the appearance of the border that you will create:

    • In the **Pen Style** list, click the line or dot or dash pattern you want to use for the border.

    • In the **Pen Weight** list, click the thickness of the border.

    • On the **Pen Color** menu, select the color you want to use for the border.

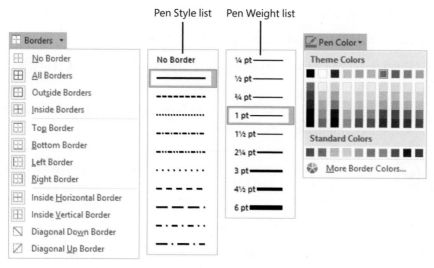

Pen Style list   Pen Weight list

The standard and custom table border tools

3. In the **Table Styles** group, on the **Borders** menu, click the icon representing the side or sides you want to apply the custom border to.

Modify table structure

When you insert a blank table, it has columns of equal width and rows of equal height. You can add (or remove) rows and columns, change the column width to fit the content or balance the table, and merge or split cells to present information in the most precise and easy to understand format.

Merge cells vertically to span rows	Merge cells horizontally to span columns				
	Split cells		Split	cells	horizontally
	vertically				

You can merge and split cells horizontally and vertically

To change the size of a table

1. Activate the table, and then do any of the following:

    -   Drag the sizing handles to change the height, width, or height and width of the table.

    -   On the **Layout** tool tab, in the **Table Size** group, set the **Height** or **Width** to a specific dimension.

    > **TIP** Select the Lock Aspect Ratio check box before changing the table size if you don't want to change the table shape.

To change the width of one or more columns

1. Select the column or columns you want to change, and then do any of the following:

    -   Double-click the right border of a column to size the column to fit its widest content.

    -   On the **Layout** tool tab, in the **Cell Size** group, in the **Width** box, enter a specific dimension, and then press **Enter**.

    -   On the **Layout** tool tab, in the **Cell Size** group, click the arrows to the right of the **Width** box to increase or decrease the width one unit at a time.

    -   On the **Layout** tool tab, in the **Cell Size** group, click **Distribute Columns** to make the columns equal width within the selected space.

    > **TIP** Setting the width of a column to less than is necessary to display the content of a cell wraps the content within the cell.

Or

1. Point to the left or right inner border of any cell. When the cursor changes to a double-headed arrow, drag to the left or right.

To change the height of one or more rows

1. Select the row or rows you want to change, and then do any of the following:

   - On the **Layout** tool tab, in the **Cell Size** group, in the **Height** box, enter a specific dimension, and then press **Enter**.

   - On the **Layout** tool tab, in the **Cell Size** group, click the arrows to the right of the **Height** box to increase or decrease the height one unit at a time.

   - On the **Layout** tool tab, in the **Cell Size** group, click **Distribute Rows** to make the columns equal width within the selected space.

> **TIP** Setting the height of a row to less than is necessary to display its content sets the height to the minimum.

Or

1. Point to the top or bottom inner border of any cell. When the cursor changes to a double-headed arrow, drag up or down.

To add a row to a table

1. Do either of the following:

   - To insert a row at the end of the table, click in the last table cell, and then press **Tab**.

   - To insert a row above or below the active row, on the **Layout** tool tab, in the **Rows & Columns** group, click the **Insert Above** or **Insert Below** button.

To add multiple rows to a table

1. Select the number of rows you want to insert, starting with a row that is adjacent to the insertion location.

2. On the **Layout** tool tab, in the **Rows & Columns** group, click the **Insert Above** or **Insert Below** button.

To add a column to a table

1. Click in the table adjacent to the location where you want to add the column.

2. On the **Layout** tool tab, in the **Rows & Columns** group, click the **Insert Left** or **Insert Right** button.

5

To add multiple columns to a table

1. Select the number of columns you want to insert, starting with a column that is adjacent to the insertion location.

2. On the **Layout** tool tab, in the **Rows & Columns** group, click the **Insert Left** or **Insert Right** button.

To remove one or more rows or columns from a table

1. Do either of the following:

   - Click anywhere in the row or column that you want to remove.

   - Select cells in the rows or columns you want to remove (or select the rows or columns).

2. On the **Layout** tool tab, in the **Rows & Columns** group, click the **Delete** button, and then click **Delete Columns** or **Delete Rows**.

To combine multiple table cells into one cell

1. Select the cells that you want to combine.

2. On the **Layout** tool tab, in the **Merge** group, click the **Merge Cells** button.

Or

1. Activate the table.

2. On the **Design** tool tab, in the **Draw Borders** group, click the **Eraser** button.

3. When the cursor changes to an eraser, click the border that separates the cells you want to merge.

4. When you finish, click the **Eraser** button or press the **Esc** key to return the cursor to turn off the eraser.

To split one table cell into multiple cells

1. Select the cell that you want to split.

2. On the **Layout** tool tab, in the **Merge** group, click the **Split Cells** button.

Or

1. Activate the table.

2. On the **Design** tool tab, in the **Draw Borders** group, click the **Draw Table** button.

3. When the pointer changes to a pencil, drag from the point on one cell border at which you want to start the split down to the point on another cell border at which you want to stop it. A dashed line indicates the split location while you're drawing.

1	
95	——— Drawing a border to split a cell
93	
100	

A dashed line indicates the split location while you're drawing

You must drag from a point on a cell border to another point on a cell border. When you release the cursor, a border of the currently selected line style, width, and color replaces the dashed line.

Embed and link to Excel content

The table capabilities of PowerPoint are perfectly adequate for the display of simple information that is unlikely to change during the useful life of the presentation. However, if your data involves calculations or is likely to require updating, you might want to maintain the information in an Excel worksheet. You can then either embed the worksheet in a slide or link the slide to the worksheet.

Embedded objects and linked objects differ in the following ways:

- An embedded object maintains a direct connection to its original program, known as the *source program*. Be aware that embedding an object increases the presentation's file size, because PowerPoint has to store not only the data itself but also information about how to display the data.

- A linked object is a representation on a slide of information that is still stored in the original document (the source document). Each time you open the presentation, PowerPoint checks the source document and updates the linked content on the slide. Because PowerPoint stores only the data needed to display the information, linking to objects results in a smaller file size than embedding them.

You can open an embedded or linked Excel table in Excel by double-clicking the table. An embedded table opens on the slide. A linked table opens in Excel.

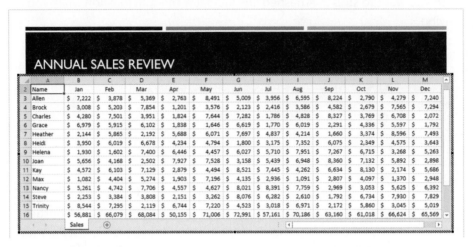

Editing an embedded Excel table

> **IMPORTANT** Always make modifications to the source document, not to the linked object on the slide. Any content or formatting changes you make to the linked object will be overwritten the next time you open the presentation, because PowerPoint will update the linked object to reflect the information in the source document.

Different types of information lend themselves to linking or embedding. For example, suppose you store past sales information and future sales forecasts in Excel worksheets. It would be appropriate to embed the past sales information, because it is unlikely to change. It would be appropriate to link to the future sales forecasts so the information on the slide updates automatically with the linked worksheet.

You can't format linked or embedded table data in the same way that you can format a live table on a slide.

To embed a table from an Excel worksheet on a slide

1. Open the workbook, and locate the table or data range that you want to embed on the slide.

2. Select the table or data range, and then copy the selection to the Clipboard.

3. Switch to PowerPoint, and display the slide that you want to embed the table on.

4. Paste the copied table from the Clipboard to the slide. Click the **Paste Options** button that appears, and then click the **Embed** icon.

 ——— Embed

Embedding the table creates a link to the worksheet

Or

1. Display the slide you want to embed the table on.

2. On the **Insert** tab, in the **Text** group, click the **Object** button.

3. In the **Insert Object** dialog box, click **Create from file**, and then click the **Browse** button.

4. In the **Browse** dialog box, browse to and select the workbook that contains the table you want to embed. Then click **OK** to insert the path in the File box of the Insert Object dialog box.

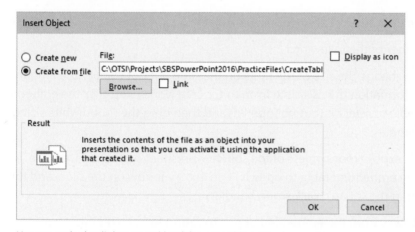

You can embed or link to a workbook by using this method

5. In the **Insert Object** dialog box, click **OK** to embed the workbook and display the most recently active content.

To link to a table in an Excel workbook

1. Display the slide you want to link to the table on.

2. On the **Insert** tab, in the **Text** group, click the **Object** button.

3. In the **Insert Object** dialog box, click **Create from file**, and then click the **Browse** button.

4. In the **Browse** dialog box, browse to and select the workbook that contains the table you want to link to. Then click **OK** to insert the path in the File box of the Insert Object dialog box.

5. In the **Insert Object** dialog box, select the **Link** check box. Then click **OK** to link to the workbook and display a picture of the most recently active content.

To change the embedded or linked content displayed on the slide

1. On the slide, double-click the table.

   An embedded table opens in an Excel window on the slide. A linked table opens in a separate Excel window.

2. Change the active worksheet, resize the window, and scroll the content as necessary to display the same content you want to display on the slide.

3. Click away from the table or close the Excel window.

To resize an embedded Excel worksheet object

1. Do either of the following:

   - To change the size of the table on the slide but not change the amount of information that is visible from the source worksheet, click the embedded table to select it (but not open it) and then drag the round white sizing handles.

   - To expose more or less of the source worksheet on the slide, double-click the embedded table to open it in an Excel window on the slide, and then drag the square black sizing handles.

2. Click away from the embedded object to return to PowerPoint.

Skills review

In this chapter, you learned how to:

- Insert tables
- Format tables
- Modify table structure
- Embed and link to Excel content

Practice tasks

The practice files for these tasks are located in the PowerPoint2016SBS\
Ch05 folder. You can save the results of the tasks in the same folder.

Insert tables

Open the InsertTables presentation, and then perform the following tasks:

1. Display slide **3** (Temperature Range). In the content placeholder, click the **Insert Table** icon, and insert a table that has five columns and three rows.

2. Populate the table with the following information.

	Winter	Spring	Summer	Fall
Minimum	18	41	73	43
Maximum	40	72	105	65

3. Center the table within the content area on the slide.

4. Click away from the table to see the results.

5. Close the presentation, saving your changes if you want to.

Format tables

Open the FormatTables presentation, and then perform the following tasks:

1. Display slide **3** (Temperature Range), and activate the table for formatting.

2. From the **Table Styles** gallery, apply the **Medium Style 2 - Accent 4** table style.

3. Configure the table style options to emphasize the header row and the first column, and to have banded columns (but not banded rows).

4. Remove the shading and borders from the upper-left cell (the cell that doesn't contain any information).

5. Select the cells containing the **Winter**, **Spring**, **Summer**, and **Fall** headings, and fill the cells with the **Orange, Accent 6** shade from the theme colors palette.

6. Select the **Winter**, **Spring**, **Summer**, and **Fall** columns, and center the cell content horizontally.

7. Set the border pen color to **Orange, Accent 3**, and then apply an outside border to the cell that contains the highest temperature.

8. Click away from the table to see the results.

9. Close the presentation, saving your changes if you want to.

Modify table structure

Open the ModifyTables presentation, and then perform the following tasks:

1. Display slide **3** (Temperature Range).

2. In the table, insert a row after the **Minimum** row.

3. Enter the following information in the new row.

Average	29	57	89	54

4. If the cell at the intersection of the **Minimum** row and the **Summer** column has a colored bottom border, remove the bottom border from the cell.

5. Insert a new row above the headings.

6. In the second cell of the new row, enter **Seasonal temperatures (Fahrenheit)**. Notice that the entry wraps within the cell.

7. Select the second through fifth cells of the new row, and merge them. Then center the text vertically and horizontally within the merged cell.

8. Move the table up to again center it in the content area.

9. Click away from the table to see the results.

10. Close the presentation, saving your changes if you want to.

Embed and link to Excel content

Open the LinkTables presentation, and then perform the following tasks:

1. Display slide **9** (Equipment Replacement).

2. Display the **Lease Cost** worksheet of the **NewEquipment** workbook on the slide by linking to it.

3. Resize the linked worksheet object window so that it is just big enough to display the Payment Schedule table.

4. Open the linked worksheet in an Excel window for editing.

5. In cell **B2**, change the interest rate from 5 to **6**, and then press the **Enter** key. Notice that the calculated values change.

6. Select the merged cell that contains the Payment Schedule title, and fill the cell with a color of your choice from the top row of the **Theme Colors** palette.

7. Select cells **A2** through **A8**, and fill the cells with a lighter version of the color you chose in step 5.

8. Close Excel, and redisplay the linked workbook object on the slide in PowerPoint. Notice that the linked table reflects your changes.

9. Close the presentation, saving your changes if you want to.

Part 3

Insert and manage visual elements

Insert and manage simple graphics

6

In this chapter

- Insert, move, and resize pictures
- Edit and format pictures
- Draw and modify shapes
- Capture and insert screen clippings
- Create a photo album

With the ready availability of professionally designed templates, presentations have become more visually sophisticated and appealing. Gone (ideally) are the days of presenters reading a list of bullet points to the audience; successful presentations are likely to have fewer words and more graphic elements. You can use images, diagrams, animations, charts, tables, and other visual elements to graphically reinforce your spoken message (which can be conveniently documented in the speaker notes attached to the slides).

The term *graphics* generally refers to several kinds of visual objects, including photos, "clip art" images, diagrams, charts, and shapes. You can insert all these types of graphics as objects on a slide and then size, move, and copy them. Because elements on a PowerPoint slide float independently, it is simpler to creatively present information on PowerPoint slides than in Word documents.

This chapter guides you through procedures related to inserting, moving, and resizing pictures; editing and formatting pictures; drawing and modifying shapes; capturing and inserting screen clippings; and creating a photo album.

Practice files

For this chapter, use the practice files from the PowerPoint2016SBS\Ch06 folder. For practice file download instructions, see the introduction.

Insert, move, and resize pictures

You can place digital photographs and images created and saved in other programs on slides in your PowerPoint 2016 presentations. Collectively, these types of images are referred to as *pictures*. You can use pictures to make slides more visually interesting, but in a PowerPoint presentation, you're more likely to use pictures to convey information in a way that words cannot.

Pictures can help to illustrate a concept

You can insert a picture onto a slide either from your computer or from an online source, such as the Internet or your cloud storage drive.

> **TIP** Pictures you acquire from the web are often copyrighted, meaning that you cannot use them without the permission of the image's owner. Sometimes owners will grant permission if you give them credit. Professional photographers usually charge a fee to use their work. Always assume that pictures are copyrighted unless the source clearly indicates that they are license free.

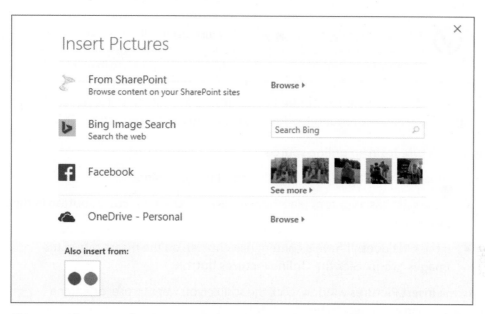

Choose an online storage location or search for an image

After you insert a picture, you can make it larger or smaller and position it anywhere you want on the slide.

Inserting or selecting a picture activates its sizing handles and the Format tool tab in the Picture Tools tab group. This tab contains commands for formatting the appearance of a picture and controlling its position relative to text, images, and other page elements.

To insert a picture from your computer

1. Do either of the following to open the Insert Picture dialog box:

   - If the slide has a content placeholder, click the **Pictures** button in the placeholder.

   - If the slide doesn't have a content placeholder, on the **Insert** tab, in the **Images** group, click the **Pictures** button.

2. In the **Insert Picture** dialog box, browse to and select the picture (or pictures) you want to insert. Then click the **Insert** button.

> **TIP** If a picture might change, you can ensure that the slide is always up to date by clicking the Insert arrow and then clicking Link To File to insert a link to the picture, or by clicking Insert And Link to insert the picture and link it to its graphic file.

The inserted picture is surrounded by a frame to indicate that it is selected. You can use the handles around the frame to size and rotate the picture.

To insert a picture from an online source

1. Do either of the following to open the Insert Pictures window:

   - If the slide has a content placeholder, click the **Online Pictures** button in the placeholder.

   - If the slide doesn't have a content placeholder, on the **Insert tab**, in the **Images group**, click the **Online Pictures button**.

2. In the **Insert Pictures** window, click the source you want to use, or enter a search term in the search box.

3. Browse to and select the picture you want to insert. Then click the **Insert** button.

To select a picture for editing

1. Click the picture once.

To move a picture

1. Point to the image. When the cursor changes to a four-headed arrow, drag the picture to its new location.

> **TIP** As you drag, red dotted lines, called *smart guides*, might appear on the slide to help you align the picture with other elements.

To resize a picture

1. Select the picture, and then do any of the following:

   - To change only the width of the picture, drag the left or right size handle.

   - To change only the height of the picture, drag the top or bottom size handle.

   - To change both the height and the width of the picture without changing its aspect ratio, drag a corner size handle or set the **Height** or **Width** measurement in the **Size** group on the **Format** tool tab, and then press **Enter**.

Graphic formats

Many common graphic formats store graphics as a series of dots, or *pixels*. Each pixel is made up of bits. The number of bits per pixel (bpp) determines the number of distinct colors that can be represented by a pixel.

The mapping of bits to colors isn't 1:1; it's 2^bpp. In other words:

- 1 bpp = 2 colors
- 2 bpp = 4 colors
- 4 bpp = 16 colors
- 8 bpp = 256 colors

- 16 bpp = 65,536 colors
- 32 bpp = 4,294,967,296 colors
- 64 bpp = 18,446,744,073,709,551,616 colors

Image files that you will use in a PowerPoint presentation are usually in one of the following file formats:

- **BMP (bitmap)** There are different qualities of BMPs.

- **GIF (Graphics Interchange Format)** This format is common for images that appear on webpages, because the images can be compressed with no loss of information and groups of them can be animated. GIFs store at most 8 bits per pixel, so they are limited to 256 colors.

- **JPEG (Joint Photographic Experts Group)** This compressed format works well for complex graphics such as scanned photographs. Some information is lost in the compression process, but often the loss is imperceptible to the human eye. Color JPEGs store 24 bits per pixel. Grayscale JPEGs store 8 bits per pixel.

- **PNG (Portable Network Graphic)** This format has the advantages of the GIF format but can store colors with 24, 32, 48, or 64 bits per pixel and grayscales with 1, 2, 4, 8, or 16 bits per pixel. A PNG file can also specify whether each pixel blends with its background color and can contain color correction information so that images look accurate on a broad range of display devices. Graphics saved in this format are smaller, so they display faster.

Of the commonly available file formats, PNG images are usually the best choice because they provide high quality images with a small file size, and support transparency.

6

Edit and format pictures

From time to time in this book, we have alluded to the modern trend away from slides with bullet points and toward presentations that include more graphics. Successful presenters have learned that most people can't listen to a presentation while they are reading slides. So these presenters make sure most of their slides display graphics that represent the point they are making, giving the audience something to look at while they focus on what is being said. PowerPoint gives you the tools you need to create graphic-intensive rather than text-intensive presentations.

After you insert any picture into a presentation, you can modify it by using the commands on the Format tool tab. For example, you can do the following:

- Remove the background by designating either the areas you want to keep or those you want to remove.

- Sharpen or soften the picture, or change its brightness or contrast.

- Enhance the picture's color.

- Make one of the picture's colors transparent.

- Choose an effect, such as Pencil Sketch or Paint Strokes.

- Apply effects such as shadows, reflections, and borders; or apply combinations of these effects.

- Add a border consisting of one or more solid or dashed lines of whatever width and color you choose.

- Rotate the picture to any angle, either by dragging the rotating handle or by choosing a rotating or flipping option.

- Crop away the parts of the picture that you don't want to show on the slide. (The picture itself is not altered—parts of it are simply covered up.)

- Minimize the presentation's file size by specifying the optimum resolution for where or how the presentation will be viewed—for example, on a webpage or printed page. You can also delete cropped areas of a picture to reduce file size.

All these changes are made to the representation of the picture that is on the slide and do not affect the original picture.

To crop a picture

1. Select the picture. On the **Format** tool tab, in the **Size** group, click the **Crop** button to display thick black handles on the sides and in the corners of the picture.

2. Drag the handles to define the area you want to crop to. The areas that will be excluded from the cropped picture are shaded.

Cropping a photo

 TIP When you select a crop handle, be careful to not drag the picture sizing handles instead—they're very close to each other.

3. When you finish defining the area, click away from the picture, or click the **Crop** button again to apply the crop effect.

 TIP To redisplay the uncropped picture at any time, select it and click the Crop button.

Or

1. Select the picture. On the **Format** tool tab, in the **Size** group, click the **Crop** arrow, and then do one of the following:

   - Click **Crop to Shape**, and then click a shape.

   - Click **Aspect Ratio**, and then click an aspect ratio.

   PowerPoint crops the picture to meet your specifications.

You can crop photos to shapes

To frame a picture

1. Select the picture. On the **Format** tool tab, in the **Picture Styles** group, click the **More** button to display the Picture Styles gallery.

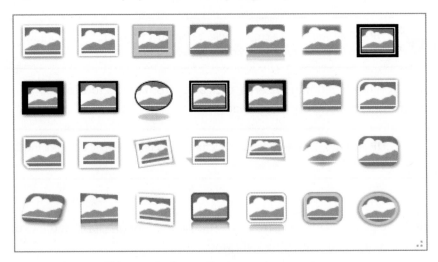

Picture styles can add frames, shadows, reflections, and more

2. Point to each picture style in turn to display a live preview of the frame applied to your picture. Click the picture style you want to apply.

There are a lot of picture styles, so experiment with them to identify those you like

To remove a background from a picture

1. Select the picture. On the **Format** tool tab, in the **Adjust** group, click the **Remove Background** button to display the Background Removal tool tab and apply purple shading to the areas of the picture that the tool thinks you want to remove.

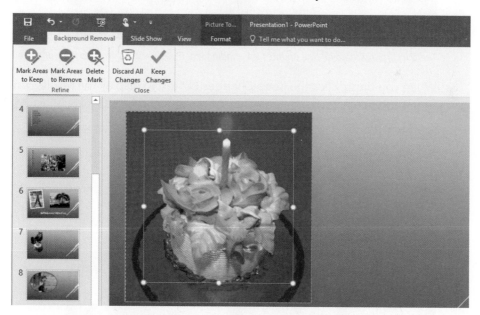

The accuracy of the estimate depends on the intricacy of the background

2. Drag the white handles to define the area that you want to keep. The Background Removal tool updates its shading as you do.

3. On the **Background Removal** tool tab, click **Mark Areas to Keep**, and then click any areas of the photo that are shaded, that you'd like to expose and keep.

4. On the **Background Removal** tool tab, click **Mark Areas to Remove**, and then click any areas of the photo that aren't shaded, that you'd like to remove.

5. Depending on the simplicity of the picture, you might need to make a lot of adjustments or only a few.

The Background removal tool updates the shading when you indicate areas to keep or remove

6. When you finish, click the **Keep Changes** button to display the results. You can return to the Background Removal tool tab at any time to make adjustments.

A floating cake!

To apply an artistic effect to a picture

1. Select the picture. On the **Format** tool tab, in the **Adjust** group, click the **Artistic Effects** button to display the Artistic Effects gallery.

2. Point to each effect to display a live preview of the effect on the selected photo.

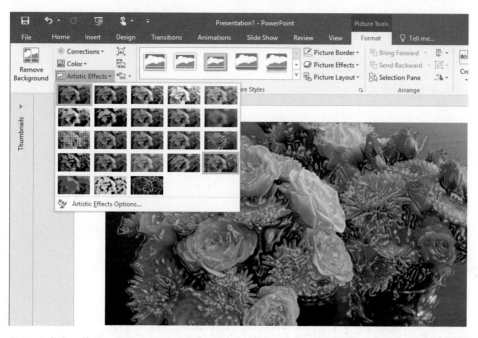

Try out all the effects

3. Click the effect that you want to apply.

Draw and modify shapes

An extensive library of shapes is available in PowerPoint. Shapes can be simple, such as lines, circles, or squares; or more complex, such as stars, hearts, and arrows. Some shapes are three-dimensional (although most are two-dimensional). Some of the shapes have innate meanings or intentions, and others are simply shapes.

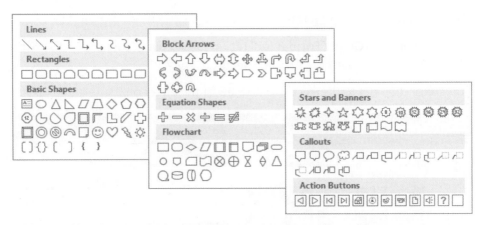

Simple representations of the shapes you can insert on a slide

Pointing to any shape in the gallery displays a ScreenTip that contains the shape name.

Draw and add text to shapes

After you select a shape that you want to add to your slide, you drag to draw it on the slide. Shapes are also text boxes, and you can enter text directly into them. You can format the text in shapes just as you would regular text.

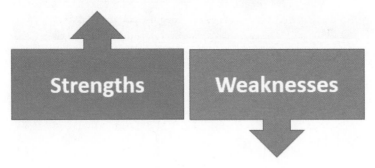

Shapes can help to visually reinforce a concept

With a little imagination, you'll soon discover ways to create images by combining shapes. You can use these images to illustrate a concept on a slide, or you can animate the drawings to convey actions or draw attention to specific elements.

 SEE ALSO For information about animating shapes and text on slides, see "Animate text and pictures on slides" in Chapter 8, "Add sound and movement to slides."

To create a shape on a slide

1. On the **Insert** tab, in the **Illustrations** group, click the **Shapes** button and then, on the **Shapes** menu, click the shape you want to insert.

    TIP If you click a shape button and then change your mind about drawing the shape, you can release the shape by pressing the Esc key.

2. When the cursor changes to a plus sign, do either of the following:

   - Click on the slide to create a shape of the default size.

   - Drag diagonally on the slide to specify the upper-left and lower-right corners of the rectangle that surrounds the shape (the drawing canvas).

    TIP To draw a shape that has the same height and width (such as a circle or square), hold down the Shift key while you drag.

To add text to a shape

1. Select the shape, and then enter the text you want to display on the shape. There is no cursor to indicate the location of the text; simply start typing and it appears on the shape.

6

Locate additional formatting commands

You control the area of the shape that is available for text by formatting the Text Box margins of the shape. This setting is gathered with many others in the Format Shape pane, which you can display by clicking the dialog box launcher (the small diagonal arrow) in the lower-right corner of the Shape Styles, WordArt Styles, or Size group on the Format tool tab.

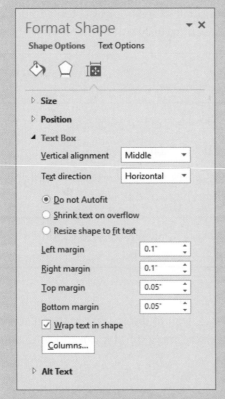

You can display different pages of settings by clicking the text and icons at the top of the pane

In PowerPoint 2016, the most frequently used formatting commands are located on the ribbon. If additional commands are available, the ribbon group includes a dialog box launcher. Clicking the dialog box launcher displays either a dialog box or a control pane.

Move and modify shapes

You can change the size, angles, outline and fill colors, and effects applied to the shape. You can apply different colors to the outline and inside (fill) of a shape.

When you first draw a shape and any time you select it thereafter, it has a set of handles.

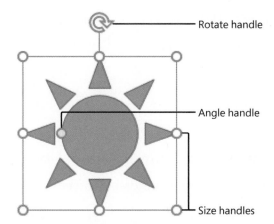

You can easily modify the shape, size, and angle of an image

You can use the handles to manipulate the shape in the following ways:

- Drag the side or corner handles (hollow circles) to change the size or aspect ratio of the shape.

- Drag the angle handles (yellow circles) to change the angles or curves of the text within the shape. Not all shapes have angle handles.

- Drag the rotate handle (circling arrow) to rotate the shape on the slide.

Nine shapes arranged to create a recognizable image

To select a shape for editing

1. Click the shape once.

To select multiple shapes

1. Do either of the following:

   - Click a shape, hold down the **Shift** or **Ctrl** key, and click each other shape.

   - Drag to encompass all the shapes you want to select.

To resize a shape

1. Select the shape, and then do any of the following:

   - To change only the width of the shape, drag the left or right size handle.

   - To change only the height of the shape, drag the top or bottom size handle.

   - To change both the height and the width of the shape, drag a corner size handle.

   - To resize a shape without changing its aspect ratio, hold down the **Shift** key and drag a corner size handle or press an arrow key.

To move a shape on a slide

1. Select the shape that you want to move.

2. Drag the shape or press the arrow keys to move it to the new location.

To rotate or flip a shape

1. Select the shape.

2. On the **Format** tool tab, in the **Arrange** group, click the **Rotate Objects** button.

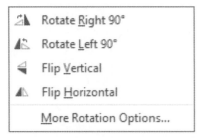

The menu illustrates the rotate and flip options

3. On the **Rotate Objects** menu, click the Rotate or Flip option you want.

> **TIP** You can rotate or flip any type of image. Rotating turns a shape 90 degrees to the right or left; flipping turns a shape 180 degrees horizontally or vertically.

Or

1. Select the shape.

2. Drag the **Rotate** handle in a clockwise or counterclockwise direction until the shape is at the angle of rotation you want.

To change a shape to another shape

1. Select the shape you want to change.

2. On the **Format** tool tab, in the **Insert Shapes** group, click the **Edit Shape** button, click **Change Shape**, and then click the new shape.

   Changing the shape doesn't affect the shape formatting or text.

Format shapes

When a shape is selected, the Format tool tab in the Drawing Tools tab group appears on the ribbon. You can use the commands on the Format tool tab to do the following:

- Replace the shape with another without changing the formatting.

- Change the fill and outline colors of the shape, and the effects applied to the shape.

- Separately, change the fill and outline colors and effects of any text that you add to the shape.

- Arrange, layer, and group multiple shapes on a slide.

Having made changes to one shape, you can easily apply the same attributes to another shape, or you can to apply the attributes to all future shapes you draw on the slides of the active presentation.

6

A happy fan cheering her team to victory!

When you have multiple shapes on a slide, you can group them so that you can copy, move, and format them as a unit. You can change the attributes of an individual shape—for example, its color, size, or location—without ungrouping the shapes.

To format a shape

1. Select the shape that you want to format.

2. On the **Format** tool tab, in the **Shape Styles** groups, click the **More** button to display the Shape Styles gallery.

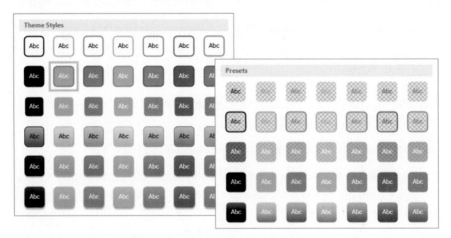

The shape style color options reflect the current color scheme

3. Point to thumbnails to display live previews of their effects, and then select a style thumbnail to apply the selected style.

To format text on a shape

1. Select the shape.

2. On the **Format** tool tab, in the **WordArt Styles** group, modify the style, text fill, text outline, or text effects.

Or

1. Select the text on the shape.

2. Do either of the following:

   - On the **Format** tool tab, in the **WordArt Styles** group, modify the style, text fill, text outline, or text effects.

   - On the **Home** tab, in the **Font** and **Paragraph** groups, use the standard text formatting commands.

To copy formatting from one shape to another

1. Select the formatting source shape.

2. On the **Home** tab, in the **Clipboard** group, click the **Format Painter** button.

3. Click the shape you want to copy the formatting to.

To set formatting as the default for the active presentation

1. Right-click the formatting source shape, and then click **Set as Default Shape**.

> **TIP** The Set As Default Shape command doesn't actually set a default shape; it sets only the default shape formatting.

To group shapes together as one object

1. Select all the shapes on a slide that you want grouped together.

2. On the **Format** tool tab, in the **Arrange** group, click the **Group** button (when you point to this button, the ScreenTip that appears says Group Objects) and then, in the list, click **Group**.

Grouped objects have a common set of handles

To move an entire group

1. Point to any shape in the group.

2. When the pointer changes to a four-headed arrow, drag the group to the new location.

To ungroup shapes

1. Select the group.

2. On the **Format** tool tab, in the **Arrange** group, click the **Group** button, and then click **Ungroup**.

To regroup shapes

1. Select any one shape from the former group.

2. On the **Format** tool tab, in the **Arrange** group, on the **Group** menu, click **Regroup**.

Connect shapes

If you want to show a relationship between two shapes, you can connect them with a line by joining special handles called *connection points*.

To connect shapes, follow these steps:

1. On the **Insert** tab, in the **Illustrations** group, click the **Shapes** button. In the **Lines** area of the **Shapes** gallery, click a **Connector** shape.

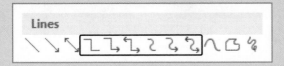

You can identify connectors by the word Connector in their names

2. Point to the first shape that you want to connect.

3. When a set of small black connection points appears, point to a connection point, press and hold the mouse button, and then drag to the other shape (don't release the mouse button).

4. When connection points appear on the other shape, point to a connection point, and release the mouse button.

When you move a shape, the connector line adapts to the change

TROUBLESHOOTING The connector has green handles when the shapes are connected. If a handle is white, drag it to a connection point.

After you draw a connector, you can adjust its shape by dragging a yellow handle and format it by changing its color and weight. If you move a connected shape, the connector moves with it, maintaining the relationship between the shapes.

6

Capture and insert screen clippings

Many people rely on the web as a source of information. At times, there might be information that you want to include in a PowerPoint presentation. For example, you might display an image of a page of a client's website in a sales presentation. PowerPoint 2016 provides a screen-clipping tool that you can use to easily capture an image of anything that is visible on your computer screen. After you capture the image, you can edit it just as you can other graphics.

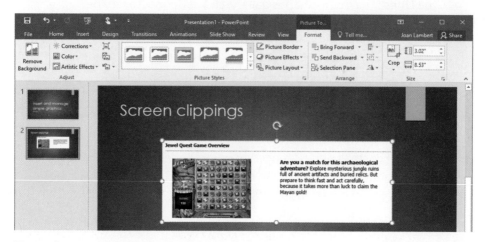

You can format a screen clipping just as you can any other image

> **TIP** You aren't limited to capturing screen clippings with the Office tools; you can also use the Windows Snipping Tool (available in the Windows Accessories folder) to capture an image and add it to your Screenshot list.

To insert an image of an on-screen window

1. Display the window that you want to capture and size it to display its contents as you want to show them.

2. Switch to PowerPoint and display the slide you want to insert the screen content on.

3. On the **Insert** tab, in the **Images** group, click **Screenshot**. The Screenshot menu displays thumbnails of all the windows on your screen that are currently available to insert.

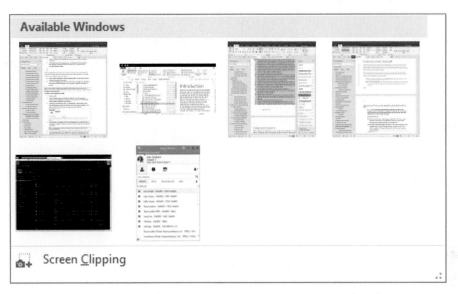

Some open windows aren't available from this menu and must be captured as clippings

> **IMPORTANT** At the time of this writing, the Screenshot menu displays only desktop app windows; it doesn't display Store app windows.

4. On the **Screenshot** menu, click the window you want to insert an image of on the slide.

5. Resize the inserted image to suit your needs.

To capture a screen clipping from PowerPoint

1. Display the content that you want to capture.

2. Switch to PowerPoint and display the slide you want to insert the screen content on.

3. On the **Insert** tab, in the **Images** group, click **Screenshot**.

4. On the **Screenshot** menu, click **Screen Clipping**. The PowerPoint menu minimizes to the taskbar, and a translucent white layer covers the entire display.

> **TIP** If you change your mind about capturing the screen clipping, press the Esc key to remove the white layer.

5. When the cursor changes to a plus sign, point to the upper-left corner of the area you want to capture, and then drag down and to the right to define the screen clipping borders.

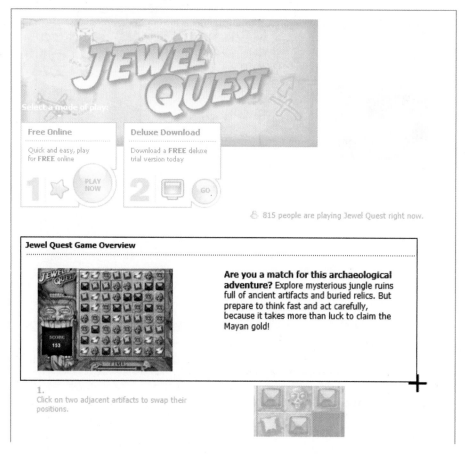

The screen clears from the area you select

When you release the mouse button, PowerPoint captures the clipping, restores the window, and inserts the clipping in the center of the slide.

 SEE ALSO For information about formatting pictures, see "Insert, move, and resize pictures" and "Edit and format pictures" earlier in this chapter.

Create a photo album

When you want to display a dynamic array of pictures in a presentation, you can use a photo album template to do the initial layout and then customize the album by adding frames of different shapes, in addition to captions.

A PowerPoint photo album

The first step in creating a photo album is to choose the pictures you want to include. After you know the album contents, you can configure the album options.

When creating a photo album, you have several choices. The primary choice is the slide layout. You can choose from seven layouts that display one, two, or four pictures per slide. The pictures can optionally have titles. The default layout is Fit To Slide, which creates one slide per photo. The photo album uses the layout you select on all pages of the album.

A basic preview of the selected layout is available in the Photo Album dialog box while you're creating the album. When you choose a layout, a slide number appears next to the first picture that will be on that slide. If you want to group pictures differently, you can reorder the photos before creating the album.

You can insert a text box on a photo album page, where it takes the place of a picture. You can use the text boxes to display comments about the pictures on that page, or you can leave them blank to control the layout. The total number of text boxes and pictures on a slide is the same as the layout that you choose. (In other words, if you choose a four-picture layout, the slide can display any combination of pictures and text boxes for a total of four objects.)

When you choose any layout other than Fit To Slide, you can opt to display captions below all the pictures. It isn't necessary to specify the captions when you select the photos for the album; if you choose the option to have captions, PowerPoint creates placeholders for them.

You can choose from these seven picture frame styles:

- Rectangle
- Rounded Rectangle
- Simple Frame, White
- Simple Frame, Black
- Compound Frame, Black
- Center Shadow Rectangle
- Soft Edge Rectangle

PowerPoint applies the same frame to all the pictures in the album.

You can choose a theme for the album when you're creating it, but it's easier to create the album and then apply the theme separately, because you can't preview the theme in the Photo Album dialog box.

You can also choose to render all the pictures in the album in black and white rather than their native colors. You can make these changes when creating the album, or you can create an album and then edit its settings to make changes.

> **TIP** To integrate the slide layouts from a photo album template into a more traditional presentation, create the photo album and then import its slides into the other presentation by clicking Reuse Slides at the bottom of the New Slide gallery. For information about reusing slides, see the "Copy and import slides and content" section of "Add and remove slides" in Chapter 3, "Create and manage slides."

To create a photo album

1. Start PowerPoint and display any blank or existing presentation. (PowerPoint creates the photo album as an entirely separate file.)

2. On the **Insert** tab, in the **Images** group, click the **Photo Album** button to open the Photo Album dialog box.

3. In the **Insert picture from** area, click **File/Disk** to open the Insert New Pictures dialog box.

4. Browse to the folder that contains the pictures you want to use, and select the photos. Then click **Insert** to add the selected files to the Pictures In Album list in the Photo Album dialog box.

> ✓ **TIP** If you want to include all the pictures in a folder in your photo album, browse to the folder, click one picture, and press Ctrl+A to select all the folder contents. Then click Insert to add all the files to the photo album.

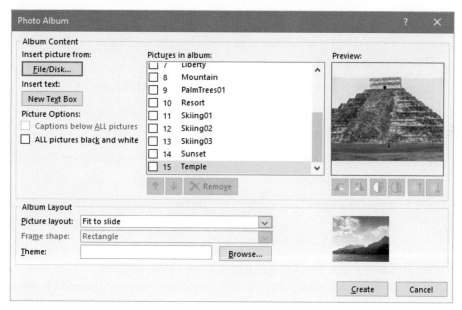

Default photo album settings

5. Next, configure the album layout. In the **Picture layout** list, click the layout you want to use. A generic preview of the layout appears to the right of the list. The numbers preceding the photo file names change to reflect the slide number the photo appears on.

The numbers change to show which pictures will be on each slide

6. Now confirm the picture order and slide content. Do any of the following in the **Pictures in album** list:

   - To preview a picture, click its file name (not its check box).

   - To move a picture to an earlier position, select its check box, and then click the **Move Up** button.

   - To move a picture to a later position, select its check box, and then click the **Move Down** button.

   - To rotate or adjust the coloring of a picture, select its check box, and then click the buttons below the preview to rotate it, or to increase or decrease the contrast or brightness.

   - To insert a blank text box in a picture position, click the picture that you want to precede the text box, and then click the **New Text Box** button.

   - To remove a photo from the album, select its check box, and then click the **Remove** button.

7. Next, if the picture layout is set to something other than Fit To Slide, choose the picture frame. In the **Frame shape** list, click the frame you want to use.

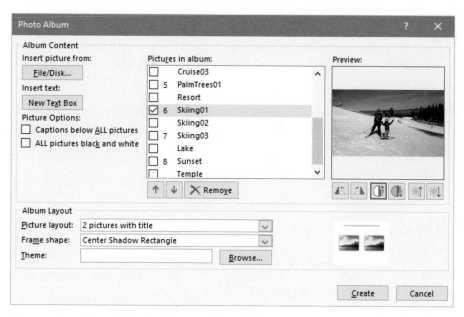

The generic preview updates to reflect your frame choice

8. Finally, do any of the following:

    •   If you want to display captions below the photos, select the **Captions below ALL pictures** check box.

    •   If you want to display grayscale versions of the photos, select the **ALL pictures black and white** check box.

    •   If you know the theme you want to apply to the photo album, click the **Browse** button to the right of the **Theme** box, and then double-click the theme you want to use.

9. To create the photo album, click **Create**.

10. Review the photo album, and do any of the following:

    •   Change the photo album title from the generic *Photo Album* to something more meaningful.

    •   If you added titles, captions, or text boxes, insert appropriate content in the placeholders.

    •   If you didn't choose a theme, or don't like the theme you chose, choose an appropriate theme from the **Themes** gallery on the **Design** tab.

11. Save the photo album.

To edit photo album settings

1. On the **Insert** tab, in the **Images** group, click the **Photo Album** arrow, and then click **Edit Photo Album** to open the Photo Album dialog box with all the current settings.

2. Add, remove, and modify photos; change the photo order; insert or remove text boxes; change the picture layout or frame; add or remove captions; or make any other changes you want.

3. When you finish, click the **Update** button to apply your changes.

Skills review

In this chapter, you learned how to:

- Insert, move, and resize pictures

- Edit and format pictures

- Draw and modify shapes

- Capture and insert screen clippings

- Create a photo album

Practice tasks

The practice files for these tasks are located in the PowerPoint2016SBS\
Ch06 folder. You can save the results of the tasks in the same folder.

Insert, move, and resize pictures

Open the InsertPictures presentation, and then perform the following tasks:

1. Display slide **5**.

2. In the content placeholder, click the **Pictures** icon. Browse to the practice file folder, and insert the **Flowers** picture.

3. From the **Size** group on the **Format** pane, resize the picture to a width of **4"**. Ensure that the aspect ratio doesn't change.

4. Move the picture on the slide to identify locations in which the smart guides appear—for example, the edges of the content space, and below the slide title. Align the picture with the upper-right corner of the content area as defined by the smart guides.

5. On the **Insert** tab, in the **Images** group, click **Online Pictures**. In the **Insert Pictures** window that opens, enter the word **flowers** in the **Bing** search box, and then press **Enter**.

6. Review the search results and locate a picture that you like. Insert the picture onto the slide.

7. Resize the picture to a width of **4"**, and align it with the right side of the content area, near the bottom of the slide (a smart guide might not appear at the bottom of the slide). Note that the pictures overlap near the center of the slide.

8. Close the presentation, saving your changes if you want to.

Edit and format pictures

Open the EditPictures presentation, and then perform the following tasks:

1. Display slide **5**.

2. Select the picture that is located on the right side of the slide.

3. On the **Format** tool tab, in the **Adjust** group, click **Corrections**, and then point to the thumbnails to identify one that will brighten the picture to make it similar to the picture on the left. Click that thumbnail to apply the correction.

4. Click the **Crop** arrow, point to **Aspect Ratio**, and then click **1:1**. Adjust the picture so the flowers are in the center, and then complete the cropping process.

5. Display the **Picture Styles** gallery, and point to the thumbnails in the gallery to find one that you like. Click the thumbnail to apply the picture style.

6. Select the picture that is located on the left side of the slide.

7. Remove the neutral background from the selected picture.

8. Close the presentation, saving your changes if you want to.

Draw and modify shapes

Open the DrawShapes presentation, and then perform the following tasks:

1. Display slide **5**.

2. Draw a **5-Point Star** shape (in the **Stars and Banners** category of the **Shapes** gallery) near the center of the slide.

3. Draw a small arrow (in the **Block Arrows** category of the **Shapes** gallery) to the right of the star.

4. Drag a copy of the arrow to the left of the star, and align it with the right arrow. Then flip the left arrow so that it points away from the star.

5. Adjacent to the left arrow, add a scroll shape, and then adjacent to the right arrow, add a heart shape.

6. Paste a copy of the heart shape on top of the original, and make the second heart smaller than the first.

7. In the star, enter the word **ME**. Then increase the font size to make it prominent.

8. Repeat task 7 to add the word **Education** to the scroll shape and **Family** to the heart shape. Then resize the shapes as necessary to make all the words fit on one line.

9. Select the scroll, star, and heart shapes (don't select the text), and apply the style **Intense Effect – Light Blue, Accent 6**.

10. Suppose you have completed your education and entered the workforce. Change the scroll shape to the **Up Arrow** (in the **Block Arrows** category) to reflect your new status.

11. In the up arrow shape, change the word *Education* to **Job**. Then adjust the size and position of the shape so that it balances with the other shapes on the slide, using the smart guides to help align the shapes.

12. Group all the shapes together as one object, and apply a purple outline.

13. Move the entire group until the shapes are centered and balanced with the slide title.

14. Change the fill color of the left and right arrows to Purple.

15. Close the presentation, saving your changes if you want to.

Capture and insert screen clippings

Open the InsertScreens presentation, and then perform the following tasks:

1. Display slide **4**.

2. Open a web browser window and locate a webpage that has information about tablets.

3. Return to PowerPoint. Then capture and insert a screen clipping of part of the webpage.

4. Close the presentation, saving your changes if you want to.

Create a photo album

Start PowerPoint, and then perform the following tasks:

1. From the **Insert** tab, create a new photo album. Select photos from the practice file folder, or select your own photos.

2. While creating the album, do the following:

    *   Experiment with the different picture layouts and frame shapes.

    *   Change the order of the pictures in the album.

    *   Insert text boxes to make spaces between photos.

    *   Apply a theme.

3. After you create the album, experiment with the changes you can make from within PowerPoint. For example:

    *   Replace placeholder text.

    *   Change the theme.

    *   Resize pictures.

4. If you want to, click the **Edit photo album** command to return to the Photo Album dialog box and make additional changes.

5. Save your photo album as **MyPhotoAlbum**, and then close it.

Create and manage business graphics

PowerPoint presentations frequently include slides that describe processes, show hierarchical relationships, and convey specific information based on data. Diagrams and charts are useful in conveying these types of information.

PowerPoint 2016 includes a powerful diagramming feature called *SmartArt* that you can use to create diagrams directly on slides. By using these dynamic diagram templates, you can produce eye-catching and interesting visual representations of information. SmartArt graphics can illustrate many different types of concepts. Although they consist of arrangements of shapes, SmartArt graphics are merely visual containers for information stored as bulleted lists. You can also incorporate pictures and other images.

You'll often find it helpful to reinforce the argument you are making in a presentation by providing facts and figures. When it's more important for your audience to understand trends than identify precise values, you can use a chart to present numerical information in visual ways. You can create a chart directly on a slide or import a completed chart from another app. The chart takes on the design elements of the presentation template and blends in with the rest of the presentation content.

This chapter guides you through procedures related to creating, modifying, and formatting diagrams and charts.

In this chapter

- Create diagrams
- Modify diagrams
- Format diagrams
- Create charts
- Modify charts
- Format charts

Practice files

For this chapter, use the practice files from the PowerPoint2016SBS\Ch07 folder. For practice file download instructions, see the introduction.

Create diagrams

Sometimes the concepts you want to convey to an audience are best presented in diagrams. You can easily create a dynamic, visually appealing diagram by using SmartArt graphics, which visually express information in predefined sets of shapes.

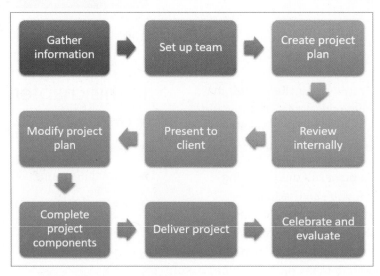

SmartArt can add visual interest to a slide

You can use SmartArt graphics to easily create sophisticated diagrams that illustrate the following concepts:

- **List** These diagrams visually represent lists of related or independent information—for example, a list of items needed to complete a task, including pictures of the items.

- **Process** These diagrams visually describe the ordered set of steps that are required to complete a task—for example, the steps for getting a project approved.

- **Cycle** These diagrams represent a circular sequence of steps, tasks, or events, or the relationship of a set of steps, tasks, or events to a central, core element—for example, the looping process for continually improving a product based on customer feedback.

- **Hierarchy** These diagrams illustrate the structure of an organization or entity—for example, the top-level management structure of a company.

- **Relationship** These diagrams show convergent, divergent, overlapping, merging, or containment elements—for example, how using similar methods to organize your email, calendar, and contacts can improve your productivity.

- **Matrix** These diagrams show the relationship of components to a whole—for example, the product teams in a department.

- **Pyramid** These diagrams illustrate proportional or interconnected relationships—for example, the amount of time that should ideally be spent on different phases of a project.

7

The layout of content in a SmartArt diagram is controlled by a behind-the-scenes bulleted list. When creating a SmartArt diagram in PowerPoint, you choose a layout first, and then populate the associated list in a window called the *Text pane*, or you can convert an existing bulleted list directly to a SmartArt layout.

 TIP Although other Office 2016 apps support the creation of SmartArt, only PowerPoint enables you to convert an existing list to a SmartArt diagram.

The dialog box from which you choose the SmartArt graphic layout displays monochromatic and generically colored representations of the layouts. The actual colors of the SmartArt diagram are based on the color scheme of the presentation, and you can choose from several different color patterns. The categories in the left pane of the dialog box are not mutually exclusive, so some diagrams appear in more than one category.

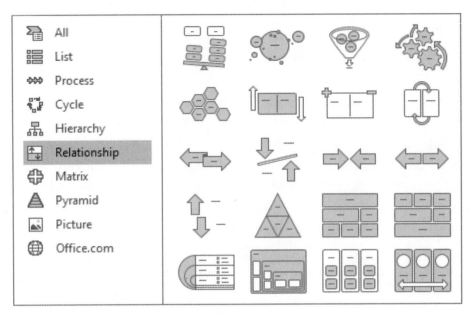

PowerPoint 2016 includes about 200 SmartArt templates

> **TIP** After you create a SmartArt diagram, you can change its content, layout, and colors. For information about changing the diagram colors, see "Modify diagrams" later in this chapter.

Clicking a layout in the Choose A SmartArt Graphic dialog box displays a color mockup of the diagram and information about any restrictions on the number of entries or list levels that the layout supports.

> **TIP** You can find the layout information in the Text pane after you create the diagram. Sometimes the Text pane displays the layout name and description at the bottom; other times, only the layout name is displayed. If the description isn't displayed in the Text pane, you can point to the layout name to display its description in a ScreenTip.

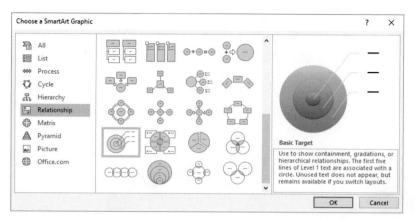

The detailed description of the selected SmartArt diagram can help you choose the right diagram for your needs

After you choose a layout, PowerPoint inserts the basic diagram on the slide and displays the Text pane containing placeholder information. Most diagram layouts adapt when you enter more or less information than is required by the original diagram.

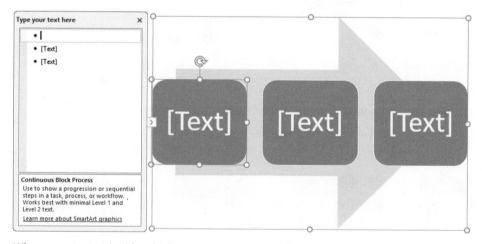

When you enter text in either the Text pane or the selected shape, that text also appears in the other location

You can insert and modify text either directly in the diagram shapes or in the associated Text pane. (You can hide the Text pane when you're not using it, and redisplay it if you need it.) The Text pane might display only a single-level bulleted list, or it might display a multilevel list if the diagram layout supports multiple levels. You can expand the diagram either by adding more list items or by adding more shapes. Some diagram layouts support a specific number of entries, and others can be expanded significantly.

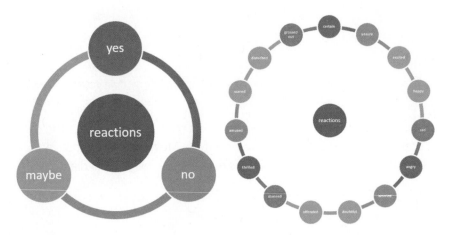

The number of items displayed by a diagram can be expanded or reduced to convey the precise meaning you want to convey

In layouts that support additional entries, the diagram shapes change to accommodate the content. Within a diagram, the shape size and font size always stay consistent. If a text entry is too long to fit a shape, the text size changes in all the shapes.

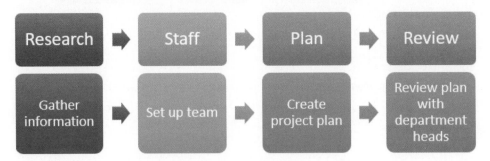

SmartArt diagrams automatically adjust text and shape size

After you create a diagram and add the text you want to display in it, you can move and size it to fit the space, and format it to achieve professional-looking results.

Picture diagrams

Most SmartArt graphics present text information in shapes, but some can display pictures instead of, or in addition to, text. Most SmartArt graphic categories include some picture options, but picture diagrams are also available in their own category to help you locate them if you specifically want to create a diagram that includes pictures.

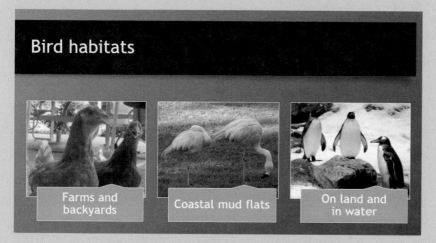

Diagrams that include spaces for pictures have "Picture" in the layout name

You can insert pictures into a SmartArt graphic from the same sources that you can insert them directly onto a slide: your computer or a connected storage location, a SharePoint library, a Facebook photo album, a OneDrive or OneDrive for Business storage folder, or the Internet. As always, take care when reusing pictures that you find on the Internet to ensure that you don't violate someone's copyright.

When you insert or select a picture in a SmartArt graphic, the SmartArt Tools tab group and the Picture Tools tab group are active. You can edit pictures that you insert in diagrams the same way you edit those you insert directly onto slides.

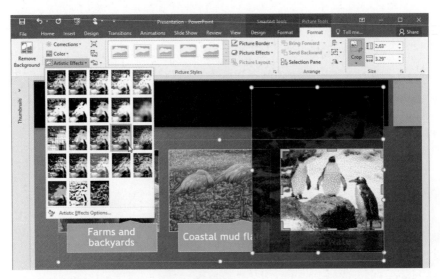

You can magnify the picture within the diagram space, remove the picture background, or apply an artistic effect

To convert bulleted list items to a diagram

1. Click anywhere in the placeholder containing the bullet points you want to convert.

2. Right-click anywhere in the selected placeholder, and point to **Convert to SmartArt**.

3. Do either of the following:

   - If the diagram layout you want appears in the gallery, click its thumbnail. (You can pause over a thumbnail to display a live preview of the bulleted list converted to that layout.)

   - If the layout you want is not displayed, click **More SmartArt Graphics**. Then in the **Choose a SmartArt Graphic** dialog box, click the layout you want, and click **OK**.

4. Adjust the size, position, and look of the diagram in the usual way.

To create a diagram on a slide

1. Do any of the following to open the **Choose a SmartArt Graphic** dialog box:

    - In a content placeholder, click the **Insert a SmartArt Graphic** button.

    - On the **Insert** tab, in the **Illustrations** group, click the **SmartArt** button.

    - Press **Alt+N+M**.

2. In the left pane, select a type of diagram. Then in the center pane, select a diagram layout thumbnail to view an example, along with a description of what the diagram best conveys, in the right pane.

3. Click **OK** to insert the selected diagram at the cursor.

To enter text into diagram shapes

1. If the **Text** pane isn't open, select the diagram, and then do either of the following:

    - Click the chevron on the left side of the diagram frame to open the Text pane.

    - On the **Design** tool tab for SmartArt (not the regular presentation window Design tab), in the **Create Graphic** group, click the **Text Pane** button.

2. In the **Text** pane, select the first placeholder, and enter the text you want to display in the corresponding shape. Notice that the content you enter in the bulleted list appears immediately in the corresponding diagram shape. Then do any of the following:

    - Press the **Down Arrow** key to move to the next placeholder.

    - At the beginning of a list item, press **Tab** to indent the list item one level further than its predecessor and demote the corresponding diagram shape.

    - At the beginning of an indented list item, press **Backspace** or **Shift+Tab** to decrease the indent level and promote the corresponding diagram shape.

    - At the end of a list item, press **Enter** to add a list item at the same level to the bulleted list and add a shape to the diagram.

    - Press **Delete** to remove an unused list item.

7

3. Repeat step 2 until you've entered all the diagram content.

You can enter and review text, and change shape hierarchy, in the Text pane

> **TIP** For a clean look, don't use ending punctuation for the text that appears in the SmartArt graphic shapes.

4. In the **Text** pane, click the **Close** button (the **X**).

To replace a picture placeholder in a diagram

1. In the **Text** pane or in a diagram shape, click the **Insert Picture** icon to open the Insert Pictures window.

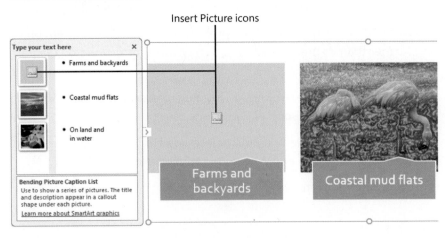

You can insert pictures from any usual source into a picture diagram

2. In the **Insert Pictures** window, which displays the locations from which you can insert pictures into the diagram, click the source you want to use, or enter a term in the search box and then click the **Search** button.

The Insert Pictures window provides access to local and online resources

> **TIP** The From A File and Bing Image Search options are available to all PowerPoint users; other locations in the Insert Pictures window are services you have connected Office to that store pictures. You can review and modify connection options in the Connected Services area of the Account page of the Backstage view. For more information, see "Manage Office and app settings" in Chapter 1, "PowerPoint 2016 basics."

3. Browse to (or search for) and select the picture you want to use. Then click the **Insert** button to replace the picture placeholder.

Modify diagrams

If the diagram layout you originally selected doesn't precisely meet your needs, you can easily change to a different layout. Most layouts preserve information that doesn't fit, but some don't; a message at the bottom of the Text pane provides information so you can make an informed decision.

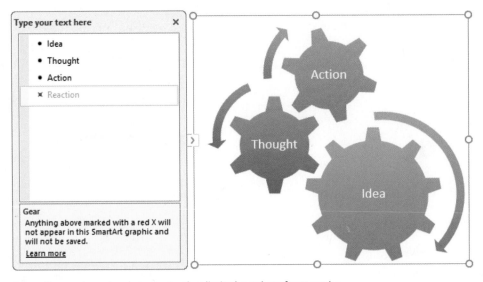

Some diagram layouts can support only a limited number of text entries

When a SmartArt graphic is active, the SmartArt Tools tab group on the ribbon includes two tabs: Design and Format.

The Design tool tab for SmartArt graphics

You can make many changes directly on the diagram canvas, but if you prefer, you can also make changes from the ribbon. From the Design tool tab, you can make changes such as the following:

- Add, move, and change the hierarchy of shapes.

- Change to a different layout.

- Change the color scheme of the diagram.

- Change the effects applied to the diagram shapes.

- Reset the diagram to its default settings.

To change a SmartArt graphic to a different layout

1. Select the diagram.

2. On the **Design** tool tab, in the **Layouts** group, click the **More** button to expand the **Layouts** gallery. This view of the gallery displays only the available diagram layouts for the currently selected diagram layout category.

3. In the **Layouts** gallery, do either of the following:

   - Click a thumbnail to change the diagram to the new layout in the same category.

   - At the bottom of the gallery, click **More Layouts** to display the Choose A SmartArt Graphic dialog box. Locate and select the layout you want to apply, and then click **OK**.

To add a shape to a diagram

1. Select the diagram, and do either of the following:

   - Open the **Text** pane. At the end of a list item, press **Enter** to add an item to the bulleted list and a shape to the diagram.

   - On the **Design** tool tab, in the **Create Graphic** group, click the **Add Shape** button.

To remove a shape from a diagram

1. Do either of the following:

   - In the diagram, select the shape that you want to delete.

   - In the **Text** pane, select the list item that represents the shape you want to delete.

2. Press the **Delete** key.

To move a shape in a SmartArt graphic

1. In the diagram, select the shape that you want to move.

2. On the **Design** tool tab, in the **Create Graphic** group, click the **Move Up** or **Move Down** button to change the order within the current hierarchy and update the list in the Text pane.

Or

1. In the **Text** pane, select the list item that represents the shape you want to move.

2. Using standard cut and paste techniques, move the item within the list and move the shape in the diagram.

To change the hierarchy of shapes in a SmartArt graphic

 IMPORTANT You can promote and demote shapes only in SmartArt layouts that support multiple levels of content.

1. In the diagram, select the shape that you want to move.

2. On the **Design** tool tab, in the **Create Graphic** group, click the **Promote** or **Demote** button to change the hierarchy level of the shape and update the list in the Text pane.

Or

1. In the **Text** pane, click at the beginning of the list item that represents the shape you want to move.

2. To demote the shape, do either of the following:

   - Press **Tab**.

   - On the **Design** tool tab, in the **Create Graphic** group, click the **Demote** button.

3. To promote the shape, do either of the following:

- Press **Shift+Tab**.

- On the **Design** tool tab, in the **Create Graphic** group, click the **Promote** button.

Format diagrams

You can format the shapes and lines that make up a diagram, and you can format the text within the shapes.

The Format tool tab for SmartArt graphics

From the Format tool tab, you can make changes such as the following:

- Change a shape or size of one or more individual shapes. For example, you could emphasize a specific stage of a process by changing the shape that represents it from a rectangle to an oval, or by making that shape larger than the others in the diagram.

- Apply a built-in shape style to quickly format the shape fill, outline, and visual effects.

- Apply fill, colors, and effects to specific shapes.

- Apply WordArt text effects to the text in a shape.

- Position and resize the SmartArt graphic.

Additional tool tabs are available when you select specific diagram components, such as pictures. You can format those components by using the commands on the tool tab just as you would in any other setting.

7

To change the color scheme of a SmartArt graphic

1. On the **Design** tool tab, in the **SmartArt Styles** group, click the **Change Colors** button to display the SmartArt coloring options in the current color scheme.

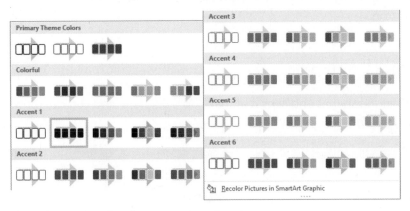

The options are based on the presentation color scheme

2. Point to any color set to display a live preview of that option. Click the color set that you want to apply to the diagram.

To select multiple shapes

1. Click one shape, and then hold down the **Shift** key and click the other shapes.

To apply shape styles to SmartArt graphic shapes

1. Select the diagram to format all the shapes, or select one or more individual shapes that you want to format.

2. On the **Format** tool tab, in the **Shape Styles** group, click the **More** button to expand the Shape Styles gallery.

3. In the **Shape Styles** gallery, point to any thumbnail in the **Theme Styles** or **Presets** area to display a live preview of that style. Click the shape style you want to apply.

To change the colors or visual effects of shapes

1. Select the diagram to format all the shapes, or select one or more individual shapes that you want to format.

2. On the **Format** tool tab, in the **Shape Styles** group, do any of the following:

    -   On the **Shape Fill** menu, select the color, picture, gradient, or texture for the inside of the shape, or click **No Fill**.

    -   On the **Shape Outline** menu, select the color, weight, and form for the shape outline, or click **No Outline**.

    -   On the **Shape Effects** menu, click **Preset**, **Shadow**, **Reflection**, **Glow**, **Soft Edges**, **Bevel**, or **3-D Rotation**, and then select the visual effect for the shape.

To change the shape of individual diagram shapes

1. Select one or more individual shapes.

2. On the **Format** tool tab, in the **Shapes** group, click **Change Shape**, and then click the shape you want to apply.

> **TIP** The Change Shape command is unavailable when the entire SmartArt graphic is selected.

To change the size of individual diagram shapes

1. Select one or more individual shapes, and then do any of the following:

    -   On the **Format** tool tab, in the **Shapes** group, click **Larger** or **Smaller**.

    -   Drag the sizing handles of any selected shape to change the height, width, or both of all the shapes.

    -   On the **Format** tool tab, in the **Size** group, set the **Height** and **Width**.

> **TIP** The Larger and Smaller commands are unavailable when the entire SmartArt graphic is selected. The Height and Width commands are available, but control the size of the diagram canvas (the space allocated to the diagram). Changing the canvas size can also change the size of all the diagram shapes.

7

To apply WordArt text effects to the text in shapes

1. Select the diagram to format the text in all the shapes, or select one or more individual shapes that you want to format.

2. On the **Format** tool tab, in the **WordArt Styles** group, click the **More** button to display the WordArt Styles gallery.

3. In the **WordArt Styles** gallery, point to any thumbnail to display a live preview of the effect.

4. Click a thumbnail to apply the effect to the selected shape or shapes.

 TIP For a custom WordArt effect, you can select the text fill color, text outline color, and text effect individually from the corresponding menus in the WordArt Styles group.

To reset a SmartArt graphic to its default formatting

1. Select the diagram or click anywhere in the diagram.

2. On the **Design** tool tab, in the **Reset** group, click the **Reset Graphic** button.

 TIP You can use the Reset Graphic command only to reset the entire SmartArt graphic, not to reset individual shapes.

Create charts

You can easily add a chart to a slide to help identify trends that might not be obvious from looking at numbers. PowerPoint 2016 has 15 chart categories, including Combo charts, which display multiple data series independently on a common axis.

The most frequently used chart categories include:

- **Column** These charts show how values change over time.
- **Line** These charts show erratic changes in values over time.
- **Pie** These charts show how parts relate to the whole.
- **Bar** These charts show the values of several items at one point in time.

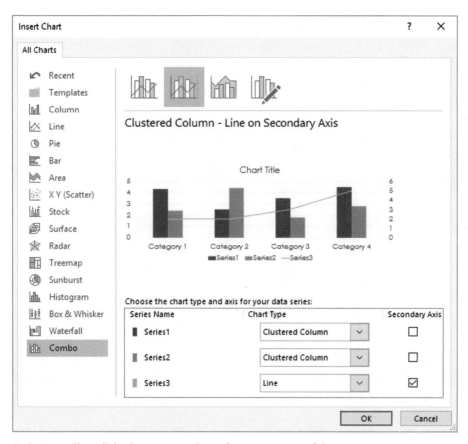

In the Insert Chart dialog box, you can choose from many types of charts

Some chart categories include two-dimensional and three-dimensional variations. The Treemap, Sunburst, Histogram, Box & Whisker, and Waterfall categories are new to the Microsoft Office apps in Office 2016.

>
>
> **SEE ALSO** For information about creating pie charts, see the sidebar "Pie charts" later in this chapter.

When you create a chart in PowerPoint, you specify the chart type, and then Power-Point opens a linked Microsoft Excel worksheet that contains sample data that is appropriate to the selected chart type. You replace the sample data in the worksheet with your own data, and the chart on the slide adapts to display your data.

IMPORTANT The procedures in this chapter assume that you have Excel 2016 installed on your computer. If you don't have that app, the procedures won't work as described.

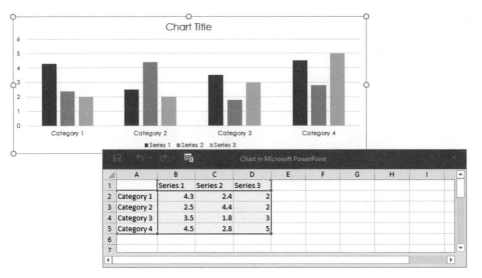

The worksheet title bar identifies it as specific to the chart

You can enter the data directly into the linked worksheet, or you can copy and paste it from an existing Microsoft Access table, Word table, or Excel worksheet.

After you plot the data in the chart, you can move and size the chart to fit the space available on the slide, and add and remove chart elements to most clearly define the chart content for the audience. You can edit the data in the worksheet at any time—both the values and the column and row headings. PowerPoint replots the chart to reflect your changes.

When a chart is active on a slide, you can work with the chart and its components by using commands from the Design and Format tool tabs that are available on the ribbon, and the Chart Elements, Chart Styles, and Chart Filters panes that open when you click the buttons to the right of the chart.

 TIP The Chart Filters button appears only if it is appropriate for the currently selected chart type.

If you decide that the type of chart you initially selected doesn't adequately depict your data, you can change the type at any time.

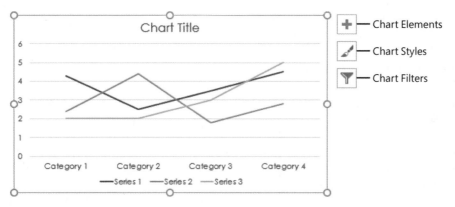

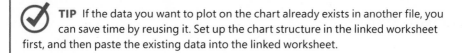

Manage a chart from the ribbon or from option panes

To create a chart on a slide

1. Do either of the following to open the Insert Chart dialog box:

   - In a content placeholder, click the **Insert Chart** button.

   - On the **Insert** tab, in the **Illustrations** group, click the **Chart** button.

2. In the left pane of the **Insert Chart** dialog box, click a chart category to display the chart variations in the right pane.

3. In the right pane, click the chart type that you want to create, and then click **OK** to insert a sample chart and open its associated Excel worksheet containing the plotted data.

4. In the linked Excel worksheet, enter the values to be plotted, following the pattern of the sample data.

   > **TIP** If the data you want to plot on the chart already exists in another file, you can save time by reusing it. Set up the chart structure in the linked worksheet first, and then paste the existing data into the linked worksheet.

5. If the chart data range defined by the colored outlines doesn't automatically expand to include new data, drag the blue handle in the lower-right corner of the range to expand it.

6. Close the Excel window.

7

To insert a chart from Excel onto a slide

1. In the source workbook, click the chart border to select it.

2. Copy the chart to the Clipboard.

3. Switch to PowerPoint, display the slide, and then paste the chart from the Clipboard.

> ✓ **TIP** You can also import data into your chart from a text file, webpage, or other external source, such as Microsoft SQL Server. To import data, first display the associated Excel worksheet. Then on the Excel Data tab, in the Get External Data group, click the button for your data source, and navigate to the source. For more information, refer to Excel Help.

To change the type of a selected chart

1. On the **Design** tool tab, in the **Type** group, click the **Change Chart Type** button.

2. In the **Change Chart Typ**e dialog box, click a category on the left, click a chart type at the top, and then click **OK**.

> ✓ **TIP** When you click a chart type in the top row, the dialog box displays a preview of that chart type as applied to the current data. You can point to the preview to display a larger version.

Modify charts

You can modify a chart by changing the data or elements that it displays.

Manage chart data

The Excel worksheet is composed of rows and columns of cells that contain values, which in charting terminology are called *data points*. Collectively, a set of data points is called a *data series*. Each worksheet cell is identified by an address consisting of its column letter and row number—for example, A2. A range of cells is identified by the address of the cell in the upper-left corner and the address of the cell in the lower-right corner, separated by a colon—for example, A2:D5.

By default, a chart is plotted based on the series of data points in the columns of the attached worksheet, and these series are identified in the legend. You can easily switch the chart to base it on the series in the rows instead, or you can select specific cells of the worksheet data to include in the chart.

You can edit the chart data at any time, either in the linked worksheet window or in Excel. The ribbon is available only when you open the worksheet in Excel.

To select a chart for editing

1. Point to a blank area of the chart, outside of the plot area.

2. When the *Chart Area* ScreenTip appears, click once.

To open the linked chart data worksheet in PowerPoint

1. Do either of the following:

   • Right-click the chart, and then click **Edit Data**.

   • Select the chart. Then on the **Design** tool tab, in the **Data** group, click the **Edit Data** button.

    TIP The chart must be active (surrounded by a frame) when you make changes to the data in the worksheet; otherwise, the chart won't automatically update.

To open the linked chart data worksheet in Excel

1. Select the chart.

2. On the **Design** tool tab, in the **Data** group, click the **Edit Data** arrow, and then click **Edit Data in Excel**.

 TIP If you open the worksheet in the linked window and then need access to commands on the ribbon, you can open the worksheet in Excel by clicking the Edit Data In Microsoft Excel button on the Quick Access Toolbar of the linked window.

To switch the data across the category and series axes

1. Open the linked chart data worksheet.

2. In PowerPoint, on the **Design** tool tab, in the **Data** group, click the **Switch Row/Column** button.

   IMPORTANT The Switch Row/Column button is active only when the linked worksheet is open.

7

To select worksheet data for editing

1. Do any of the following:

   - To select a cell, click it.

   - To select a column, click the column header (the letter at the top of the column).

   - To select a row, click the row header (the number at the left end of the row).

   - To select multiple cells, columns, or rows, do either of the following:

     - Select the first element, and then hold down the **Shift** key as you select subsequent elements.

     - Drag through adjacent cells, columns, or rows.

   - To select an entire worksheet, click the **Select All** button (the triangle in the upper-left corner of the worksheet, at the intersection of the row and column headers).

To change the area of a worksheet that is included in the chart

1. Drag the blue handle in the lower-right corner of the range to expand or contract it.

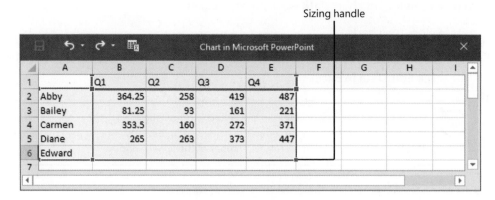

Different colors identify the series, categories, and values

To filter the chart to display only specific data

1. Select the chart, and then click the **Chart Filters** button to display the Chart Filters pane. The Chart Filters pane lists all the series and categories in the data set.

 TIP Chart Filters appears only if it is appropriate for this type of chart.

2. Point to any series or category to emphasize it.

3. Clear the check boxes of the series or categories you do not want to plot on the chart.

 TIP To clear all the check boxes in a group at once, clear the Select All check box.

7

4. At the bottom of the **Chart Filters** pane, click **Apply** to replot the data.

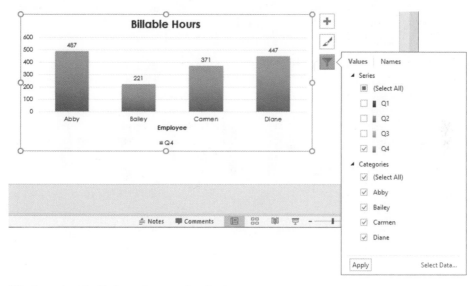

Filtering a chart to display only one series of values

5. Click the **Chart Filters** button to close the Chart Filters pane.

 SEE ALSO For information about working with the other two buttons to the right of the chart, see "Format charts" later in this chapter.

Modify the display of chart elements

Each data point in a data series is represented graphically in the chart by a data marker. The data is plotted against an x-axis—which is referred to as the *horizontal axis* or *category axis*—and a y-axis—which is referred to as the *vertical axis* or *value axis*. (Three-dimensional charts also have a z-axis—which is referred to as the *depth axis* or *series axis*.)

The primary components of a chart on a slide are the following:

- **Chart area** This is the entire area within the chart frame.

- **Plot area** This is the rectangular area bordered by the axes.

- **Data markers** These are the graphical representations of the values, or data points, of each data series in the linked worksheet.

You can add chart elements to the chart components to help explain the data.

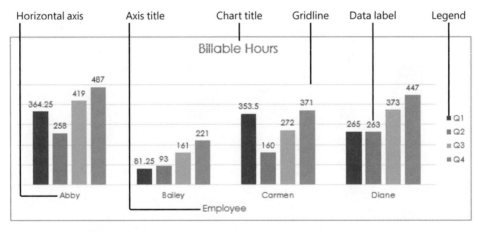

Some default and optional chart elements

The available chart elements include the following:

- **Axes** These elements control the display of the category and value axis labels, not the display of the data.

- **Axis titles** These identify the categories, values, or series along each axis.

- **Chart title** A title by which you identify the chart. The chart title can appear above the chart or overlaid across the center of the chart.

- **Data labels** These identify the exact values represented by the data markers on the chart. They can be displayed inside or outside of the data markers.

- **Data table** This table provides details of the plotted data points in table format, essentially mimicking the worksheet. A data table can incorporate a legend.

- **Error bars** These indicators mark a fixed amount or percentage of deviation from the plotted value for one or more series.

- **Gridlines** Major and minor horizontal and vertical gridlines identify measurement points along each axis and help to visually quantify the data points.

- **Legend** This listing correlates the data marker color and name of each data series. The legend can be displayed on any side of the plot area.

- **Lines** On charts that plot data that doesn't touch the category axis (such as an area chart or line chart), these lines drop from the plotted points to the corresponding value on the category axis.

- **Trendline** This line marks a value that is calculated on all the series values in a category. It most commonly marks the average of the values but can also be based on other equations.

- **Up/down bars** These bars indicate the difference between the high and low values for a category of data in a series.

All of the chart elements are optional. Some chart types don't support all of the elements. For example, a pie chart doesn't display axes or gridlines.

Each chart type has a set of Quick Layouts that you can use to display or position specific sets of chart elements.

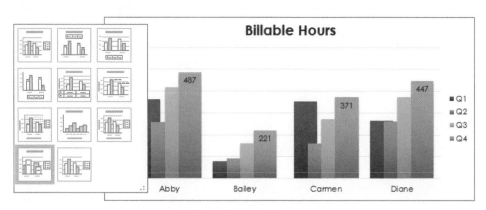

Apply a Quick Layout to quickly change multiple chart elements

The Quick Layouts are preset combinations of the available chart elements. When the preset layouts don't produce the chart you want, you can create a custom layout by mixing and matching different chart elements. You can control the display of chart elements from the Add Chart Element menu on the Design tool tab, and from the Chart Elements pane that opens when you click the button to the right of the chart.

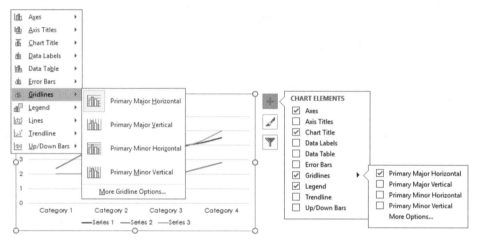

The menu and pane include only chart elements that apply to the current chart type

You can apply the same chart elements from both locations. The Add Chart Element menu provides a bit more visual guidance than the Chart Elements pane, but is further from the chart.

> **TIP** You can use standard techniques to add pictures, shapes, and independent text boxes to slides to enhance charts.

You can adjust a chart layout by adding, deleting, moving, and sizing chart elements. To perform any of those tasks, you must first select the element. The following table describes some of the options available for common chart elements.

Chart element	Options
Axes	Primary Horizontal, Primary Vertical, or both
Axis Titles	Primary Horizontal, Primary Vertical, or both
Chart Title	Above Chart or Centered Overlay
Data Labels	Center, Inside End, Inside Base, Outside End, or Data Callout
Data Table	With Legend Keys or No Legend Keys
Error Bars	Standard Error, Percentage, or Deviation
Gridlines	Primary Major Horizontal, Primary Major Vertical, Primary Minor Horizontal, Primary Minor Vertical, or any combination of the four options
Legend	Right, Top, Left, or Bottom
Lines	Drop Lines or High-Low Lines
Trendline	Linear, Exponential, Linear Forecast, or Moving Average
Up/Down Bars	(on or off)

7

To apply a preset layout to a chart

1. Select the chart. On the **Design** tool tab, in the **Chart Layouts** gallery, click the **Quick Layout** button, and then click the layout you want.

To display the Add Chart Element menu

1. Select the chart. On the **Design** tool tab, in the **Chart Layouts** group, click the **Add Chart Element** button.

To open the Chart Elements pane

1. Select the chart, and then click the **Chart Elements** button that appears to the right of the chart.

To specify which chart elements to display on the chart

1. Select the chart, and then display the **Add Chart Element** menu.

2. On the **Add Chart Element** menu, click the chart element, and then click one or more options to select or clear them.

Or

1. Select the chart, and then open the **Chart Elements** pane.

2. In the **Chart Elements** pane, do either of the following:

   - Clear the check box for the chart elements you want to remove from the chart.

   - Select the check box for the chart elements you want to display on the chart. Click the arrow that appears to the right of the element to open the display options menu for that element, and then click the option you want.

To change the size of a selected chart or chart element

1. Point to any sizing handle (the hollow dots around the chart frame), and when the pointer changes to a double-headed arrow, drag in the direction you want the chart to grow or shrink.

> **TIP** If an element cannot be resized, it doesn't have sizing handles when selected.

To change the position of a selected chart element

1. Point to the border around the element, away from any handles, and when the four-headed arrow appears, drag the chart to the new location.

> **TIP** Some elements cannot be moved, even if the four-headed arrow appears.

To rotate a three-dimensional chart layout

1. Right-click the chart, and then click **3-D Rotation**.

2. In the **3-D Rotation** area of the **Effects** page of the **Format Chart Area** pane, set the angle of rotation for each axis.

Pie charts

Unlike column, bar, and line charts, which plot at least two series of data points, pie charts plot only one series, with each data point, or *slice*, reflecting a fraction of the whole series. If you plot a multiseries chart and then change the chart type to a pie chart, PowerPoint hides all but the first series, retaining the hidden information in case you change back to a chart type capable of showing more than one series. You can switch to a different series by clicking the Chart Filters button to the right of the chart, selecting the series you want in the Series area of the Chart Filters pane, and clicking Apply.

When you plot a pie chart, you can use an effective formatting option that is not available with multiseries chart types. To draw attention to individual data points, you can "explode" the pie by dragging individual slides away from the center. Or you can double-click a slice to select it and open the Format Data Point pane, where you can set a precise Angle Of First Slice and Point Explosion percentage. For a really dynamic effect, you can animate the slices so that they move when you advance slide content while delivering the presentation.

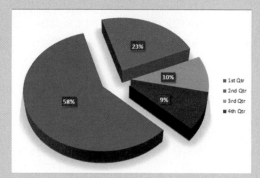

An exploded pie chart

TIP You can draw attention to the series in any chart by animating them. Start by animating the entire chart; for example, you might apply the Pulse effect. Then in the Effect Options list, click By Series. Alternatively, you can animate each category or even individual data points. For information about animation, see Chapter 8, "Add sound and movement to slides."

Format charts

You can quickly format a chart and its individual parts by applying fills, outlines, and effects to the following components:

- **Chart area** You can specify the background fill, the border color and style, effects such as shadows and edges, the 3-D format and rotation, and the size and position. You can also attach text to be displayed when someone points to the chart.

- **Plot area** You can specify the background fill, the border color and style, effects such as shadows and edges, and the 3-D format and rotation.

- **Data markers** You can specify the background fill, the border color and style, effects such as shadows and edges, and the 3-D format. You can also precisely determine the gap between data points.

- **Legend** You can specify the background fill, the border color and style, and effects such as shadows and edges. You can also specify the legend's position and whether it can overlap the chart.

- **Axes** You can specify the background fill, the line color and style, effects such as shadows and edges, and the 3-D format and rotation. For the category axis, you can also specify the scale, add or remove tick marks, adjust the label position, and determine the starting and maximum values. You can set the number format (such as currency or percentage), and set the axis label alignment.

- **Gridlines** You can set the line color, line style, and effects such as shadows and edges.

- **Data table** You can specify the background fill, the border color and style, effects such as shadows and edges, and the 3-D format. You can also set table borders.

- **Titles** You can specify the background fill, the border color and style, effects such as shadows and edges, and the 3-D format. You can also set the title's alignment, direction, and angle of rotation.

If you don't want to spend a lot of time formatting individual chart elements, you can apply a predefined chart style to create a sophisticated appearance with a minimum of effort. Chart styles affect only the formatting of the chart components and elements; they don't change the presence or location of the chart elements.

The Chart Styles pane has two pages: Style and Color. From the Style page, you can preview and apply the chart styles. From the Color page, you can change the colors that are used in the chart without affecting other presentation elements.

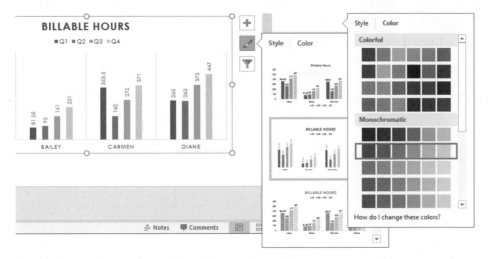

You can change the chart colors without changing the template

You can apply these same styles and colors from the Chart Styles group on the Design tool tab. From the Format tool tab, you can apply shape styles and WordArt styles to chart elements.

You can fine-tune the formatting of a selected chart element in its Format pane. Each type of element has a specific Format pane. Most Format panes have settings that are divided into multiple pages such as Fill & Line, Effects, Size & Position, and an Options page that is specific to the selected chart element. You can display different options by clicking the elements in the pane header.

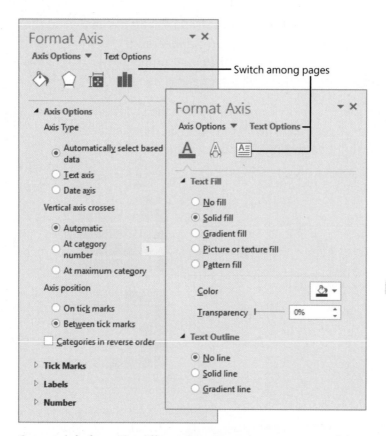

Commands for formatting different elements are on separate pages of the pane

To apply a chart style to a chart

1. Select the chart, and then do either of the following:

   - On the **Design** tool tab, in the **Chart Styles** gallery, click the style you want.

   - Click the **Chart Styles** button, and then on the **Style** page of the **Chart Styles** pane, click the style you want.

To change the colors of chart elements without changing the template colors

1. Select the chart, and then do either of the following:

   - On the **Design** tool tab, in the **Chart Styles** gallery, click the **Change Colors** button, and then click the color set you want.

   - Click the **Chart Styles** button, and then on the **Color** page of the **Chart Styles** pane, click the style you want.

To select a chart component for formatting

1. Do either of the following:

   - On the chart, click the element once.

   - If the element is difficult to identify or click, on the **Format** tool tab, in the **Current Selection** group, display the **Chart Elements** list, and then click the component you want to select.

   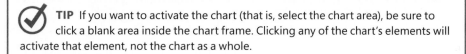

   > **TIP** If you want to activate the chart (that is, select the chart area), be sure to click a blank area inside the chart frame. Clicking any of the chart's elements will activate that element, not the chart as a whole.

To apply a preset style to a selected chart component

1. On the **Format** tool tab, in the **Shape Styles** gallery, click the style you want.

To apply a fill color, outline color, or effect to a selected chart component

1. On the **Format** tool tab, in the **Shape Styles** group, click the **Shape Fill**, **Shape Outline**, or **Shape Effects** button, and then click the option you want.

To apply a WordArt style to the text in a selected chart

1. On the **Format** tool tab, in the **WordArt Styles** gallery, click the style you want.

To apply WordArt style components to a selected chart component

1. In the **WordArt Styles** group, click the **Text Fill**, **Text Outline**, or **Text Effects** button, and then click the option you want.

To open the Format pane for a chart element

1. Do any of the following:

   - Double-click the chart element.

   - Right-click the element, and then click **Format Element**.

   - At the top of an open **Format** pane, click the downward-pointing triangle to the right of the **Options** label, and then click an element to display that Format pane.

Or

1. If you have trouble double-clicking a smaller chart element, on the **Format** tool tab, in the **Current Selection** group, display the **Chart Elements** list, and then click the element you want to select.

 TIP To display the Format Major Gridlines pane, right-click any gridline, and then click Format Gridlines. To display the Format Data Table pane, right-click the selected data table, and then click Format Data Table.

Skills review

In this chapter, you learned how to:

- Create diagrams
- Modify diagrams
- Format diagrams
- Create charts
- Modify charts
- Format charts

Custom chart templates

If you make extensive modifications to the design of a chart, you might want to save it as a template. Then when you want to plot similar data in the future, you can avoid having to repeat all the changes by applying the template as a custom chart type.

To save a customized chart as a template, follow these steps:

1. Select the chart (not a chart element).

2. Right-click the chart, and then click **Save as Template** to open the Save Chart Template dialog box displaying the contents of your Charts folder.

   TIP The default Charts folder is the *AppData\Roaming\Microsoft\Templates\Charts* subfolder of your user profile folder.

3. Enter a name for the chart template in the **File name** box, and then click **Save**.

You can work with custom chart templates in the following ways:

- To locate a custom chart type, display the Chart Type or Change Chart Type dialog box, and then click Templates.

- To delete a custom chart type, display the Templates folder in the Chart Type or Change Chart Type dialog box. In the lower-left corner, click Manage Templates. Then in the File Explorer window that opens, right-click the template and click Delete.

7

Practice tasks

The practice files for these tasks are located in the PowerPoint2016SBS\
Ch07 folder. You can save the results of the tasks in the same folder.

Create diagrams

Open the CreateDiagrams presentation, and then perform the following tasks:

1. Display slide **2**, and then do the following:

   a. Select the bulleted list items on the slide. Right-click the selection, and then click **Convert to SmartArt**.

   b. On the **Convert to SmartArt** submenu, point to each of the layout thumbnails to preview the selected list in that layout. Notice that some of the layouts display all the list items, and others don't.

   c. Click the layout that you think best presents the information, to create the SmartArt Graphic with that layout.

2. Display slide **3**, and then do the following:

   a. Create a new SmartArt Graphic on the slide, using the **Hexagon Radial** layout in the **Cycle** category.

   b. If the **Text** pane for the SmartArt graphic isn't already open, open it. Notice that the Text pane displays two levels of bullets. The first-level bullet populates the center hexagon and the second-level bullets populate the six surrounding hexagons.

   c. In the **Text** pane, select the first bullet and then enter **My Health**. Notice that the words appear in the center hexagon.

   d. In the **Text** pane, replace the first three second-level list item placeholders with **Physical**, **Mental**, and **Emotional**. Notice that the words appear in the outer hexagon shapes.

   e. In the diagram, enter **Financial**, **Social**, and **Spiritual** in the three empty outer hexagon shapes.

3. Display slide **4**, and then do the following:

   a. Select the **Picture Frame** diagram on the slide, and then open its **Text** pane.

   b. For each shape, insert the picture that corresponds with the file name in the **Text** pane.

   c. Use the tools on the **Pictures** tool tab to brighten the **Flowers03** picture so that it matches the others.

   d. Experiment with any other changes you want to make to the pictures.

4. Save and close the presentation.

Modify diagrams

Open the ModifyDiagrams presentation, and then perform the following tasks:

1. Display slide **2**, and then do the following:

   a. Select the **Basic Process** diagram on the slide.

   b. On the **Design** tool tab, expand the **Layouts** gallery to display all the layouts in the Process category.

   c. Point to thumbnails that interest you to preview the diagram in those layouts. Apply the **Segmented Process** layout.

   d. Expand the **Layouts** gallery again, and then click **More Layouts** to open the Choose A SmartArt Graphic dialog box.

   e. Apply a layout from a category other than Process, and then consider whether and how it changes the information that is conveyed by the diagram.

2. Display slide **3**, and then do the following:

   a. Select the **Balance** diagram on the slide. If the **Text** pane doesn't automatically open, open it.

   b. In the **Text** pane, click at the end of the word *Family*, and then press **Enter** to create a new second-level bullet and add a corresponding shape to the diagram. Notice that with three shapes on each side, the scale moves to show that the two sides are balanced.

    c.   In the new shape, enter **Sports**.

    d.   In the diagram, click the **Job** shape to select it.

    e.   From the **Design** tool tab, add a shape to the **Work** side of the diagram. In the new shape, enter **Household management**. Notice that the scale tips to show that there are more shapes on the **Work** side.

    f.   In the **Text** pane, move the **Troop leader** and **Coach** shapes from the **Work** side of the diagram to the **Life** side. Notice that when there is more content than the shape supports, the unused content is dimmed and preceded by an X.

    g.   Experiment with any other modifications you'd like to make to the diagram.

3.   Save and close the presentation.

Format diagrams

Open the FormatDiagrams presentation, and then perform the following tasks:

1.   Display slide **2**, and select the **Pyramid** diagram.

2.   On the **Design** tool tab, expand the **Change Colors** menu.

3.   Preview different color schemes, and then apply the **Colorful Range – Accent Colors 2 to 3** color scheme.

4.   Expand the **SmartArt Styles** gallery, and preview different styles. Then from the **3-D** section, apply the **Inset** style.

5.   In the pyramid, select the shape that represents the food group you like best.

6.   On the **Format** tool tab, expand the **WordArt Styles** gallery. Apply a WordArt style that you like to the text in the selected shape.

7.   In the pyramid, select the shape that represents the food group you like least.

8.   On the **Format** tool tab, expand the **Shape Styles** gallery. Apply one of the **Transparent – Colored Outline** styles to the selected shape.

9.   Reset the SmartArt graphic to its default formatting. Then undo the action to reinstate your formatting changes.

10.   Save and close the presentation.

Create charts

Open the CreateCharts presentation, and then perform the following tasks:

1. Display slide **2**.

2. Insert a chart, using the **3-D Clustered Column** chart type (fourth from the left in the **Column** category).

3. In the linked chart data worksheet, select and delete all the sample data, leaving only the colors that identify the series, categories, and values.

4. In cell **B1**, enter **March**. Then press the **Tab** key to enter the heading on the chart and move to the next cell of the worksheet.

5. In cells **C1** through **E1**, enter **June**, **September**, and **December**.

> ✓ **TIP** If you were entering a sequential list of months, you could enter *January* and then drag the fill handle in the lower-right corner of the cell to the right to fill subsequent cells in the same row with the names of the months.

   When you enter *December*, notice that it is outside of the colored guides and does not appear on the chart in the presentation. You will fix this in the next set of practice tasks.

6. In cells **A2** through **A4**, enter **Minimum**, **Average**, and **Maximum**, pressing the **Enter** key between entries.

> ✓ **TIP** Press Enter to move down in the column (or to the beginning of a data entry series) or Shift+Enter to move up. Press Tab to move to the right in the same row or Shift+Tab to move to the left.

7. In cell **B2**, enter **37**, and press **Tab**. Notice that a corresponding column appears in the chart.

8. In cells **C2** through **E2**, enter **54**, **53**, and **29**, pressing **Tab** to move from cell to cell. After you enter the last number, press **Enter** to move to cell **B3**.

9. Enter the following data into the chart worksheet, noticing as you enter data that the chart columns and scale change to reflect the data.

	B	C	D	E
3	47	67	66	35
4	56	80	70	41

10. Close the **Chart in Microsoft PowerPoint** window.

   Notice that the temperatures on the chart are grouped by category rather than by month, and the December temperatures are missing. You will fix these issues in the next set of practice tasks.

11. Open the **Temperatures** workbook from the practice file folder. Select the chart that is on the worksheet, and copy it to the Clipboard.

12. Return to the **CreateCharts** presentation, and display slide **3**. Paste the chart from the Clipboard onto the slide. Notice that the chart takes on the color scheme of the presentation.

   The chart type used for this data, Stacked Column, sums the minimum, average, and maximum temperatures for each month.

13. Change the chart type of the new chart to **Line with Markers** (the fourth chart from the left in the **Line** category) to display the three temperature series individually.

14. Save and close the presentation. Then close the workbook.

Modify charts

Open the ModifyCharts presentation, and then perform the following tasks:

1. Select the chart, and open the linked chart data worksheet in PowerPoint.

2. In the worksheet, drag the blue handle so that the colored cells include only those that contain content (A1:E4). Notice that the December data appears in the chart.

3. In the presentation, select the chart. Then switch the data across the category and series axes to display the temperatures in groups by month.

4. In the worksheet, change the text in cells **B1:E1** to **Spring, Summer, Fall**, and **Winter**. Then close the linked chart data worksheet.

5. Open the **Chart Filters** pane, and then do the following:

   - Point to each item in the **Series** and **Category** areas of the pane to highlight those values on the chart.

   - Clear all the check boxes in the **Series** area, and then select only the **Average** check box.

   - Click **Apply** to modify the chart.

6. Repeat step 5 to display only the **Minimum** and **Maximum** series values.

7. From the **Quick Layout** gallery on the **Design** tool tab, apply **Layout 9** to the chart. Notice that this adds a chart title, axis titles, and a legend to the chart area.

8. Add the following elements to the chart:

   - Primary Minor Horizontal gridlines

   - Data labels

 TIP You can add data labels to the chart only from the Chart Elements pane, not from the Add Chart Elements menu.

9. Remove the horizontal **Axis Title** placeholder from the chart.

10. Replace the vertical **Axis Title** placeholder with **Degrees Fahrenheit**.

11. Replace the **Chart Title** placeholder with **Regional Averages**.

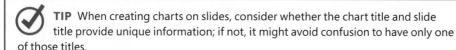 **TIP** When creating charts on slides, consider whether the chart title and slide title provide unique information; if not, it might avoid confusion to have only one of those titles.

12. Select the legend. Drag its top border to align with the top horizontal gridline, and its bottom border to align with the bottom horizontal gridline. Notice that the legend entries move to fill the space.

13. Drag the chart title to the right so that it right-aligns with the legend. Then click outside the chart to view the results.

14. Experiment with any other chart modification procedures that interest you. Then save and close the presentation.

Format charts

Open the FormatCharts presentation, and then perform the following tasks:

1. Display slide **2**, and select the chart.

2. From the **Chart Styles** gallery on the **Design** tool tab, apply **Style 8** to the chart. Notice that the legend changes location.

3. Change the colors of the chart elements to the **Color 14** color set without affecting the presentation theme.

4. Select the legend. From the **Shape Styles** gallery on the **Format** tool tab, apply a **Moderate Effect** of your choice. Then change the font size to **16** points.

5. Select the chart title. From the **WordArt Styles** gallery, apply a WordArt style of your choice. Then change the fill and outline colors, and add a shadow effect if the WordArt style doesn't already have one.

6. Select the plot area (not the chart area), and double-click it to display its Format pane. In the **Format Plot Area** pane, explore the various options that are available for formatting this component.

7. At the top of the pane, click the downward-pointing arrow next to **Plot Area Options**, and select another chart component or element to display its Format pane.

8. Experiment with any other chart formatting procedures that interest you. Then save and close the presentation.

Add sound and movement to slides

8

A PowerPoint presentation might be designed to provide ancillary information for a live presentation, or to stand alone as an information source. Regardless of the method of delivery, a presentation has no value if it doesn't keep the attention of the audience. An element that can make the difference between an adequate presentation and a great presentation is the judicious use of animated content, sound, and videos. By incorporating these dynamic effects, you can grab and keep the attention of your audience. You can emphasize key points, control the focus of the discussion, and entertain in ways that will make your message memorable.

With PowerPoint 2016, you have so many opportunities to add pizzazz to your slides that it is easy to end up with a presentation that looks more like an amateur experiment than a professional slide show. When you first start adding animations, sound, and videos to your slides, it is best to err on the conservative side. As you gain more experience, you'll learn how to mix and match effects to get the results you want for a particular audience.

This chapter guides you through procedures related to animating text and pictures on slides, customizing animation effects, adding audio and video content to slides, compressing media to decrease file size, and adding and managing slide transitions.

In this chapter

- Animate text and pictures on slides
- Customize animation effects
- Add audio content to slides
- Add video content to slides
- Compress media to decrease file size
- Add and manage slide transitions

Practice files

For this chapter, use the practice files from the PowerPoint2016SBS\Ch08 folder. For practice file download instructions, see the introduction.

Animate text and pictures on slides

In the context of PowerPoint, *animation* refers to the movement of an element on a slide. When used appropriately, animated slide elements can both capture the audience's attention and effectively convey information. You can animate any individual objects on a slide, including text containers, pictures, and shapes. (You can't animate objects that are part of the slide background or slide master, other than as part of the transition between slides.)

 SEE ALSO For information about the movement that occurs between slides, see "Add and manage slide transitions" later in this chapter.

Thoughtfully designed animations can be very informative, particularly for audience members who are more receptive to visual input than to auditory input. Animations have the added benefit of providing a consistent message with or without a presenter to discuss or externally illustrate a process.

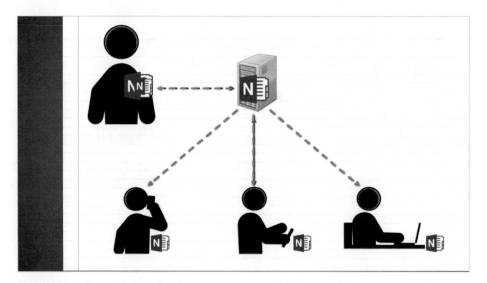

The elements of a multipart animation

You can configure four types of animations: the appearance, movement, emphasis, and disappearance of objects on the slide. There are multiple options within these four categories. The options are categorized as Basic, Subtle, Moderate, and Exciting (although you might have a different concept of "exciting" than the PowerPoint developer who categorized the effects). A few more animation effects are available for text than for other slide objects.

Here's a breakdown of the animation effects that are available in PowerPoint 2016:

- **Entrance animations** An object with an animated entrance is not visible when the slide first appears. (It is visible during the development process, but not when you present the slide show.) It then appears on the slide in the manner specified by the entrance effect. Some entrance effects are available in the Animation gallery. They're illustrated in green, and their icons provide some idea of the movement associated with the effect.

Have fun experimenting with the different effects

Clicking More Entrance Effects at the bottom of the Animation menu opens a dialog box that displays all the available entrance animations by category to help you choose an appropriate effect.

8

Basic		Moderate	
★ Appear	★ Blinds	★ Basic Zoom	★ Center Revolve
★ Box	★ Checkerboard	★ Compress	★ Float Down
★ Circle	★ Diamond	★ Float Up	★ Grow & Turn
★ Dissolve In	★ Fly In	★ Rise Up	★ Spinner
★ Peek In	★ Plus	★ Stretch	
★ Random Bars	★ Split	**Exciting**	
★ Strips	★ Wedge	★ Basic Swivel	★ Boomerang
★ Wheel	★ Wipe	★ Bounce	★ Credits
Subtle		★ Curve Up	★ Drop
★ Expand	★ Fade	★ Flip	★ Float
★ Swivel	★ Zoom	★ Pinwheel	★ Spiral In
		★ Whip	

The entrance animation effects available for text

■ **Emphasis animations** These effects animate an object that is already visible on the slide to draw attention to it, without changing its location. The emphasis effects that are available in the Animation gallery are illustrated in yellow.

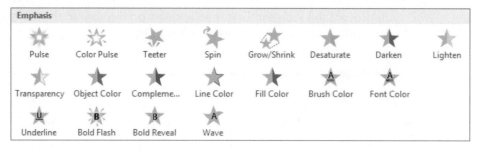

Effects range from subtle to bold

Clicking More Emphasis Effects at the bottom of the Animation menu opens a dialog box that displays all the available emphasis animations by category.

Basic
★ Fill Color   **A** Font Color
★ Grow/Shrink   ★ Line Color
★ Spin   ★ Transparency

Subtle
B Bold Flash   ★ Brush Color
★ Complementary Color   ★ Complementary Color 2
★ Contrasting Color   ★ Darken
★ Desaturate   ★ Lighten
★ Object Color   ★ Pulse
B Underline

Moderate
★ Color Pulse   ★ Grow With Color
★ Shimmer   ★ Teeter

Exciting
★ Blink   **B** Bold Reveal
★ Wave

The emphasis animations available for text and images

- **Motion Path animations** These effects move an object along a path that you specify, over a period of time that you specify. A few simple motion paths are available from the Animation gallery, but a surprisingly large variety is available from the dialog box that opens when you click More Motion Paths at the bottom of the Animation menu.

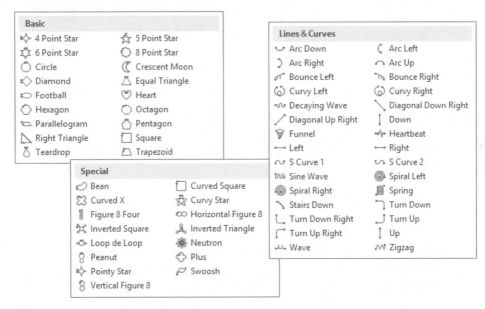

The motion path animations available for text

- **Exit animations** These effects take an existing object through a process that results in the object no longer being visible on the slide. The exit effects that are available in the Animation gallery are illustrated in red.

Choose an effect that suits the style of your presentation

Additional exit effects are available from the Change Exit Effect dialog box.

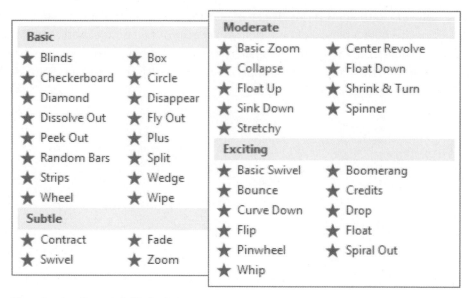

The exit animations available for text

Animations can be very simple, or very complex. Many animations have options that you can configure, such as the direction, speed, size, or color. For example, when you configure an entrance effect for a bulleted list, you can specify whether to have the entire list enter the slide at the same time, or to have only one bulleted item enter at a time. After you choose an effect, the applicable options are available on the Effect Options menu.

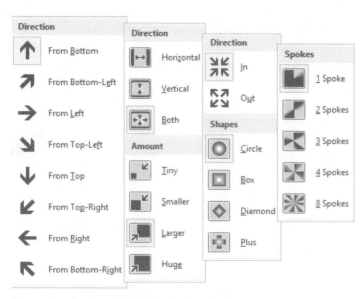

Some animations have options, and others don't

You can apply multiple animation effects (for example, an entrance effect and an emphasis effect) to a single object. As you assign animations to slide objects, numbers appear on the objects to specify the order of the animation effects. The numbers are visible only when the Animation tab is active.

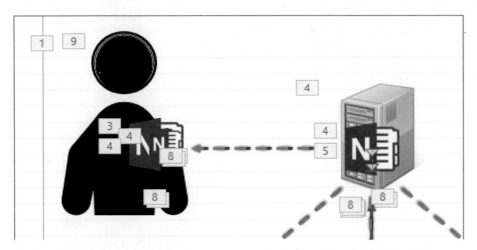

Each number represents one animation

As you build an animated slide, you can add and animate individual elements, or you can add all the elements to the slide first, and then animate them. Regardless of the process you choose, position the objects on the slide as follows:

- **Entrance effects** Position the object where you want it to end up after it enters the slide.

- **Emphasis effects** Position the object where it will be before and after the effect.

- **Exit effects** Position the object where it will be before it leaves the slide.

After all the elements are in place, animate them in the order you want the animations to occur. (If you're animating multiple objects, it might be helpful to write out a description of the process before starting.) If you animate something out of order, don't worry—you can reorder the animations from within the Animation Pane.

8

Animate this

Animations can greatly enrich presentation content. However, incorporating a "dazzling" array of animation effects into a presentation can be distracting or confusing to the audience. Ensure that the time you put into creating an animation has value to you and to your audience members.

Consider using animations to provide subliminal information—for example, in a multipart presentation, use one consistent entrance effect for the part opener titles to draw the attention of the audience members and cue them to a change of subject.

An excellent use of animation is to create "build slides" that add information in layers and essentially culminate in a review slide. Simple examples of build slides include:

- A bulleted list that adds one item to the list at a time. For greater impact, display an image related to the current list item, and replace the image as each new list item appears.

- A pie chart that displays each chart wedge individually, and finishes with the complete pie. Make this even more informative by displaying a detailed breakdown of the chart data for each category as you display its chart wedge.

You could achieve these effects by creating series of separate slides, but it's much simpler to animate the list or chart object.

A more difficult but often worthwhile use of slide object animation is to provide a visual image of a process as you describe it. You can narrate the animation in person or, if you're going to distribute the presentation electronically, you can record the narration and synchronize the animations with the relevant wording.

To animate an object on a slide

1. Display the slide in the **Slide** pane, and select the object that you want to animate, or its container. (For example, if you want to animate the entrance of a bulleted list, select the text box that contains the bulleted list.)

2. On the **Animations** tab, in the **Animation** group, click the **More** button to display the **Animation** menu and gallery.

 TIP If the menu expands to cover the slide content, you can drag the handle in the lower-right corner of the menu to resize it.

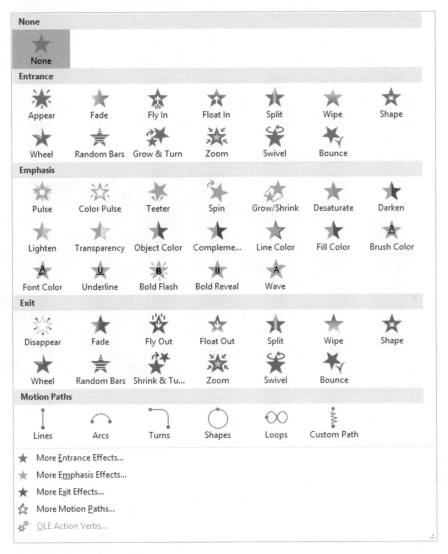

The Animation gallery and menu

3. Do either of the following:

- In the **Animation** gallery, click the icon that represents the animation you want to apply.

- On the **Animation** menu, click the **More** command for the type of animation you want to apply, and then in the **Change *Type* Effect** dialog box, click the animation you want.

PowerPoint displays a live preview of the selected animation effect and adds an animation number adjacent to the object. A star appears next to the slide thumbnail to indicate that the slide contains either an animation or a transition.

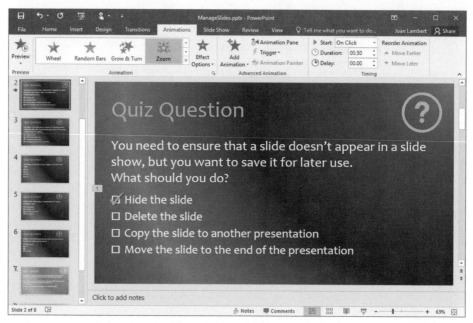

In the Thumbnails pane, the star below the slide number indicates the presence of movement on the slide

> **TIP** When you apply an animation, PowerPoint automatically previews (plays) the animation. If this is distracting to you, you can turn off this feature by clicking the Preview arrow (in the Preview group on the Animations tab) and then clicking AutoPreview to remove the check mark that indicates the option is turned on.

To select an applied animation

1. On the slide or in the **Animation Pane**, click the animation number.

To display or hide the Animation Pane

1. On the **Animations** tab, in the **Advanced Animation** group, click the **Animation Pane** button.

 TIP You can expand and collapse sets of animation effects in the Animation Pane to help you focus on those you want to work with.

To configure animation options

1. Apply the animation, or select a previously applied animation.

2. On the **Animations** tab, in the **Animation** group, click the **Effect Options** button. (If the button is unavailable, the animation has no configurable options.)

    The Effect Options menu has one titled section for each option that you can configure.

3. On the **Effect Options** menu, click one option in each section.

To apply multiple animation effects to one object

1. Apply the first animation effect and configure any options.

2. Select the object (not the animation). The existing animation information is highlighted on the Animations tab and in the Animation Pane.

3. On the **Animations** tab, in the **Advanced Animation** group, click the **Add Animation** button. In the **Add Animation** gallery, click the additional animation you want to apply.

To copy a set of animation effects from one object to another object

1. Select the source object.

2. On the **Animations** tab, in the **Advanced Animation** group, click the **Animation Painter** button.

3. Point to the object you want to format. When a paintbrush appears to the right of the cursor, click the object to apply the formatting.

8

> **TIP** The Animation Painter is similar to the Format Painter. If you click the Animation Painter button one time, you can copy the formatting to one other object. If you double-click the Animation Painter button, you can copy the formatting to many other objects, until you click the button again or press Esc to deactivate it.

To preview animations

1. Do any of the following:

   - To preview all animations on a slide in order, on the **Animations** tab, in the **Preview** group, click the **Preview** button.

   - To preview a specific animation and those that follow, in the **Animation Pane**, click the first animation, and then click the **Play From** button.

   - To preview one animation, select the animation on the slide and then, in the **Animation Pane**, click the **Play Selected** button.

To remove animation effects from slide objects

1. Do either of the following in the **Animation Pane**:

   - To remove one animation, right-click the animation, and then click **Remove**.

   - To remove all animations, click any animation, press **Ctrl+A** to select all the animations, and then press **Delete**.

Customize animation effects

Many presentations don't require much in the way of animation, and you might find that transitions and ready-made animation effects will meet all your animation needs. However, for those occasions when you want a presentation with pizzazz, you can customize the animation effects.

> **TIP** Animations can be useful for self-running presentations, where there is no presenter to lead the audience from one concept to another.

After you apply an animation effect, you can fine-tune its action in the following ways:

- Specify the direction, shape, or sequence of the animation. (The options vary depending on the type of animation you apply.)

- Specify what action will trigger the animation. For example, you can specify that clicking a different object on the slide will animate the selected object.

- As an alternative to clicking the mouse button to build animated slides, have PowerPoint build the slide for you.

- Control the implementation speed (duration) of each animation, or delay an animation effect.

- Change the order of the animation effects.

Entrance and exit effects cause objects to appear and disappear when you're previewing or presenting a slide. However, all the objects are visible while you're working in the Slide pane. A very helpful tool when managing multiple animated objects on a slide is the Animation Pane. Each numbered animation on the slide has a corresponding entry in the Animation Pane that provides information and options for managing the animations.

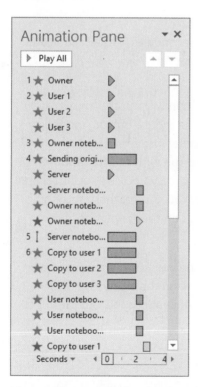

Manage all aspects of animations from the Animation Pane

The color coding of the Entrance, Emphasis, and Exit effects is visible in the Animation Pane, and a timeline is available at the bottom of the pane. The visual indicators to the right of each object name represent the type, starting point, and duration of each animation event, as follows:

- The indicator color represents the animation type (green for Entrance, yellow for Emphasis, blue for Motion Path, and red for Exit).

- The left side of the indicator aligns with the animation starting point. If the left sides of two indicators align, those animations start at the same time. If the left side of an indicator aligns with the right side of the previous indicator, the animations run in order.

- The width of the indicator is the animation duration as it relates to the timeline at the bottom of the Animation Pane.

- The right side of the indicator is either triangular or square. A square indicates that the animation has a fixed duration; a triangular edge indicates that the duration is set to Auto.

Each animation is an individual event. By default, each animation starts immediately "on click," meaning when you switch to the slide, click the mouse button, tap the screen, or press an arrow key—any action that would otherwise move to the next slide. You can change the animation "trigger" either to run with or after another event, to run it after a certain length of time, or to run it when you click a specific screen element or reach a bookmark in an audio or video clip. You control these settings either from the Advanced Animation and Timing groups on the Animations tab, or from the Animation Pane.

Clicking an animation in the Animation Pane selects the animation and displays an arrow to the right of the animation timing indicators. Clicking the arrow displays a menu of actions. Some of these actions are available from the Animations tab, but the effect options available from this menu are more complex than those on the Effect Options menu in the Animation group.

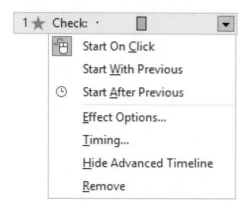

You can configure these actions from the Animation Pane to customize an animation

Clicking Effect Options on the shortcut menu provides access to an effect-specific dialog box where you can refine that type of animation in the following ways:

- Specify whether the animation should be accompanied by a sound effect.

- Dim or hide the element after the animation, or have it change to a specific color.

- If the animation is applied to text, animate all the text at once or animate it word by word or letter by letter.

- Repeat an animation and specify what triggers its action.

- If a slide has more than one level of bullet points, animate different levels separately.

- If an object has text, animate the object and the text together (the default) or separately, or animate one but not the other.

The dialog box title is the animation type, and the options available in the dialog box are specific to that type of animation.

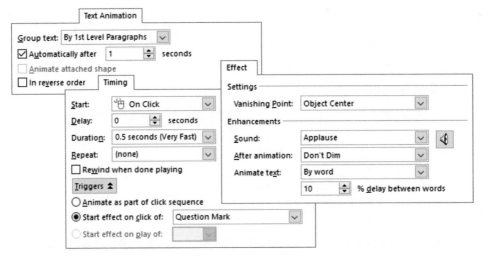

Some of the settings available through the Animation Pane Effect Options menu

To open the effect-specific dialog box for an animation

1. Do either of the following in the **Animation Pane**:

   - Point to the animation, click the arrow, and then click **Effect Options**.

   - Double-click the animation.

To change the order of animation effects on a slide

1. On the slide or in the **Animation Pane**, select the animation you want to reorder.

2. On the **Animations** tab, in the **Timing** group, click **Move Earlier** or **Move Later**.

Or

1. In the **Animation Pane**, select the animation or animations that you want to move.

2. Drag the selection to the new position in the **Animation Pane**. The animation numbers change to reflect the new positions.

 TIP After reordering animations, it's a good idea to preview the animations to ensure that the actions happen in a logical order.

To set the trigger for a selected animation

 TIP Many of the following settings can be configured on the Animations tab, in the Animation Pane, or in the effect-specific options dialog box. We've provided one path to the setting, but use the interface that you're most comfortable with.

1. Do any of the following in the **Timing** group on the **Animations** tab:

   - To start the animation manually, click the **Start** list, and then click **On Click**.

   - To start the animation based on the previous animation, click the **Start** list, and then click **With Previous** or **After Previous**.

   - To start the animation a specific period of time after the trigger, specify the **Delay** in seconds.

Or

1. Do either of the following in the **Advanced Animation** group on the **Animations** tab:

   - To start the animation when you click an object on the slide, click the **Trigger** button, click **On Click of**, and then click a trigger object on the slide.

   - To start the animation at a specific point during the playback of an audio clip or video clip, in the **Trigger** list, click **On Bookmark**, and then click a bookmark that you've set in an audio or video clip.

     SEE ALSO For information about setting bookmarks, see the sidebar "Bookmark points of interest in media clips" later in this chapter.

Or

1. In the **Animation Pane**, drag the colored indicator bar to the starting point you want.

To set the duration of a selected animation

1. Do either of the following:

   - On the **Animations** tab, in the **Timing** group, specify the **Duration** in seconds.

   - In the **Animation Pane**, drag the right side of the colored indicator bar to set the duration in accordance with the timeline at the bottom of the pane.

To add a sound effect to an animation

1. In the **Animation Pane**, double-click the animation to open the animation-specific effect options dialog box.

2. On the **Effect** tab, click the **Sound** list, and then click the sound effect you want to assign to the animation.

3. Click the speaker icon to the right of the **Sound** list to display the volume slider, and set the volume level of the sound effect.

4. Click **OK** to close the dialog box.

Bookmark points of interest in media clips

Bookmarks are a useful new feature for PowerPoint users who incorporate audio, video, and animation into presentations. You can insert bookmarks into audio and video clips to identify locations either that you want to be able to quickly get to or that you want to use as triggers for other events.

For example, you could create an animation that visually describes a process, and record a narration that verbally describes the process. Instead of setting up a series of timing points to synchronize the narration and animation, you could insert bookmarks at key points in the narrative audio clip that trigger specific segments of the animation to play.

As another example, you could embed a video on a slide, and record audio comments about certain parts of the video. Then you can insert bookmarks at those points of the video to trigger the playback of the relevant audio comments.

When you insert bookmarks in audio and video clips within PowerPoint, those bookmarks exist only in PowerPoint and don't affect the original recording.

To insert a bookmark in an audio or video clip, follow these steps:

1. Display the slide in Normal view and select the audio or video clip to display the Audio Tools or Video Tools tab group.

2. Play the clip by clicking the **Play** button on the playback toolbar or in the **Preview** group on the **Playback** tool tab.

3. At the point that you want to insert a bookmark, click the **Add Bookmark** button in the **Bookmarks** group on the **Playback** tool tab.

4. To insert additional bookmarks, repeat steps 2 and 3.

Bookmarks in audio or video clips are indicated by circles on the playback toolbar. Pointing to a bookmark on the toolbar displays a ScreenTip that includes the bookmark name. You can select a bookmark as the starting point for an animation, from the Trigger list on the Animations tab.

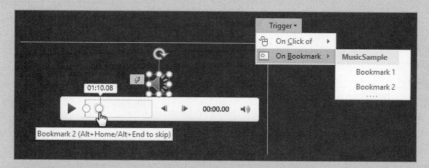

Adding a bookmark to a media clip makes it available as a trigger

If you create a bookmark but then don't need it, you can remove it by selecting it and then clicking the Remove Bookmark button in the Bookmarks group on the Playback tool tab.

Add audio content to slides

You can enhance presentations by adding sound to slide transitions, to animated content, to an individual slide, or to the presentation as a whole. For example, you could run a presentation that provides basic information and icebreakers during the time leading up to your actual presentation. You can add a pleasant royalty-free soundtrack that loops while the presentation plays, to avoid the discomfort of a room full of people who don't want to break the silence.

If you plan to distribute a presentation electronically for people to watch on their own, you might want to add audio narration to an animation, or provide narration for the entire presentation.

> **SEE ALSO** For information about adding sound effects to animations, see "Customize animation effects" earlier in this chapter; and to slide transitions, see "Add and manage slide transitions" later in this chapter.

You can add prerecorded audio content to a presentation, or record your own content directly within PowerPoint. PowerPoint supports the most common audio formats—MP3, MP4, Windows audio (.wav) and Windows Media audio (.wma), and more specialized formats such as ADTS, AU, FLAC, MIDI, and MKA audio.

> **TIP** The Insert Online Audio feature that was present in earlier versions of PowerPoint is not available in PowerPoint 2016. However, you can download royalty-free audio music and sound effects from many online sources. Some of these require that you credit the website as the source, so be sure to read the website fine print. When you locate an audio clip that you want to use, you can download it to your computer and follow the instructions in this topic to use it in a PowerPoint presentation.

When you add audio to a slide (rather than to an animation or transition), the audio icon (shaped like a speaker) and an accompanying trigger icon appear on the slide, and the trigger event appears in the Animation Pane.

The trigger is created and added to the Animation Pane automatically

When the audio icon is selected, the Audio Tools tab group, which includes the Format and Playback tool tabs, appears on the ribbon, and audio playback controls appear on the slide.

The playback controls are simple but provide sufficient options

You can start audio content on a slide automatically or from the playback controls. The playback controls are visible only when the audio icon is selected. The icon isn't obtrusive, but you can disguise or hide it if you want to.

You can change the size or angle of the audio icon by using the sizing handles or rotation handle

8

You can customize the audio content by using commands on the Playback tool tab, as follows:

- Edit the audio content so that only part of it plays.

- Make the sound gradually increase and decrease in volume.

- Adjust the volume or mute the sound.

- Specify whether the audio content plays:

  - Automatically when the slide appears.

  - Only if you click its icon.

- Make the audio object invisible while the presentation is displayed in Reading view or Slide Show view.

- Specify that the audio content should play continuously until you stop it.

- Ensure that the audio content starts from the beginning each time it is played.

To insert an audio clip onto a slide

1. Save the audio clip on your computer or on a network-connected location.

2. On the **Insert** tab, in the **Media** group, click the **Audio** button, and then click **Audio on My PC** to open the Insert Audio dialog box.

3. In the **Insert Audio** dialog box, browse to and select the audio file, and then click the **Insert** button.

Or

1. In File Explorer, open the folder that contains the audio file.

2. Arrange the File Explorer and PowerPoint windows on your screen so that both are visible.

3. Drag the audio file from File Explorer to the slide.

To record audio directly onto a slide

1. On the **Insert** tab, in the **Media** group, click the **Audio** button, and then click **Record Audio** to open the Record Sound dialog box.

2. In the **Name** box, enter a name to uniquely identify the recording. Then click the **Record** button (labeled with a red circle).

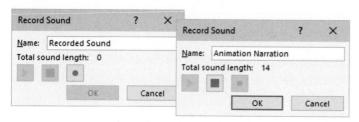

The Record Sound dialog box

3. Speak or otherwise provide the audio that you want to record. When you finish, click the **Stop** button (labeled with a blue square). The audio icon and an accompanying trigger icon appear in the center of the slide, and the trigger event appears in the Animation Pane.

> ✅ **TIP** If you record multiple clips, the audio icons stack up in the same location on the slide. It might be necessary to move one or more out of the way to get to an earlier clip.

8

To restrict the playback of an audio clip to a specific segment

1. Select the audio icon. On the **Playback** tool tab, in the **Editing** group, click the **Trim Audio** button to open the Trim Audio dialog box.

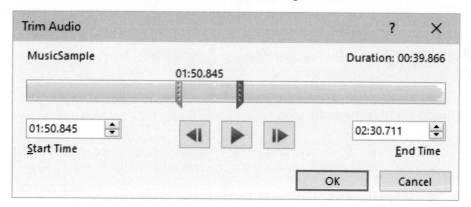

You can trim audio from the beginning and end of the clip, but not from the middle

2. In the **Trim Audio** dialog box, do any of the following:

   • Click the **Play** button to play the clip, and then click the **Pause** button to pause when you locate a point that you want to mark.

   • Drag the green **Start** marker to specify a playback starting point other than the beginning of the clip. (If you drag the marker near the point at which you paused the playback, the marker snaps to that location.)

- Drag the red **End** marker to specify a playback end point other than the end of the clip.

- Select the **Start** or **End** marker, and then click the **Previous Frame** or **Next Frame** button to move the selected marker back or forward 0.1 seconds (one-tenth of a second).

3. When you finish, click **OK** to close the Trim Audio dialog box.

> **TIP** Trimming the audio affects only the playback of the audio on the slide, not the original audio clip. You can re-trim or restore the audio clip at any time. For information about discarding trimmed content, see "Compress media to decrease file size" later in this chapter.

To fade into or out of an audio clip

1. Select the audio icon. On the **Playback** tool tab, in the **Editing** group, do the following:

   - In the **Fade In** box, specify the length of time over which you want to increase the audio to full volume.

   - In the **Fade Out** box, specify the number of seconds at the end of the audio clip over which you want to decrease the audio volume.

   > **TIP** The Fade In and Fade Out times can be specified precisely down to a hundredth of a second.

To modify or hide the audio icon

1. Select the audio icon, and then do any of the following:

   - Drag the sizing handles to make the icon larger or smaller.

   - Drag the icon to a different location on the slide, or to a location slightly off the slide but still on the development canvas.

   - Use the commands on the **Format** tool tab to change the icon's appearance.

   - Replace the default icon with a different image (such as a picture or logo).

To manually start audio playback

1. Do any of the following:

   - In Normal view, Reading view, or Slide Show view, point to the audio icon. When the playback controls appear, click the **Play** button.

   - In Normal view, click the audio icon, and then click the **Play** button on the playback toolbar or in the **Preview** group on the **Playback** tool tab.

   - In Slide Show view, after the audio icon has had focus, press **Alt+P**.

 TIP To play sounds and other audio content, you must have a sound card and speakers installed.

To automatically start audio playback

1. On the **Playback** tool tab, in the **Audio Options** group, in the **Start** list, click **Automatically**. Then select the **Loop until Stopped** check box.

 TIP If your presentation might be viewed by people using assistive technologies such as screen readers or text-to-speech tools, you should avoid starting audio clips or files automatically. Instead, allow the user to play the audio content after the tool has finished communicating the slide content.

To prevent an audio clip from stopping when the slide changes

1. On the **Playback** tool tab, do either of the following:

   - To play to the end of the audio and then stop, in the **Audio Options** group, select the **Play Across Slides** check box.

   - To loop the audio until the end of the slide show regardless of other audio tracks, in the **Audio Styles** group, click the **Play in Background** button.

8

To loop (repeat) an audio clip

1. On the **Playback** tool tab, in the **Audio Options** group, select the **Loop until Stopped** check box.

> ✅ **TIP** To automatically start and continuously play an audio clip through an entire slide show, configure the settings as follows: On the Playback tool tab, in the Audio Options group, change the Start setting to Automatically. Then select the Play Across Slides, Loop Until Stopped, and Hide During Show check boxes.

Add video content to slides

Sometimes the best way to ensure that your audience understands your message is to show a video. For example, if your company has developed a short advertising video, it makes more sense to include the video in a presentation about marketing plans than to try to describe it by using bullet points or even pictures. To save you the trouble of switching between PowerPoint and a video player, you can embed a video recording directly onto a slide, and then play the video as part of presenting the slide show. This is a much smoother way of presenting information from multiple sources than switching between them.

You can insert a video onto a slide from your computer or a connected local storage device, from your Facebook account, from YouTube, or from a website that provides an "embed code" (basically, an address that you can link to).

> ✅ **TIP** If a publicly posted video clip has an "embed code" available, you can link to the online video rather than embedding it in the slide show. PowerPoint uses the embed code to locate and play the video. As long as the video remains available in its original location (and you have an active Internet connection), you will be able to access and play the video from the slide at any time.

After you insert the video, you can format its representation on the slide in all the ways that you can other imagery. You can move and resize it, display it in a frame of your choice, and even adjust the brightness or color contrast.

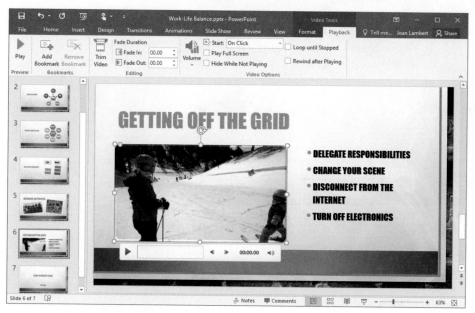

You can resize the video frame

> **TIP** The changes that you make to an image on a slide also affect the video playback. So, for example, if you change the aspect ratio of the video representation on the slide, imagery in the video might appear to be skewed.

When working with local videos that you embed rather than online videos that you link to, you can fade into and out from the video playback, and manage the content of the video by trimming it to play only a specific portion. You can insert bookmarks to use as triggers for other events (for example, you might display a list of selling points as each is presented in the advertising video).

Set your start and end times to focus on the specific content you want to highlight

When you're previewing or presenting a slide show, you can play (and pause) embedded audio or video, move around within the recording, and control the volume by using the controls that appear when the audio icon or video placeholder image is active. When playing back a video, you can display it at the embedded size or full screen.

Many of the processes for managing video clips are the same as those for managing audio clips:

- Restricting the playback of a video clip to a specific segment

- Fading into or out of a video clip

- Manually or automatically starting video playback

- Preventing a video clip from stopping when the slide changes

- Looping a video clip

 SEE ALSO For additional information related to the preceding processes, see "Add audio content to slides" earlier in this chapter.

To insert a video clip onto a slide

1. On a slide that includes a content placeholder, click the **Insert Video** button in the content placeholder to display the Insert Video window that contains links to all the video sources you've configured Office to connect to.

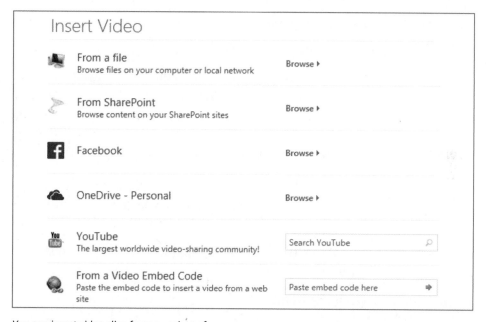

You can insert video clips from a variety of sources

2. In the **Insert Video** window, click the source of the video that you want to insert, and then follow the process to insert a video from the selected source.

Or

1. On any slide, on the **Insert** tab, in the **Media** group, click the **Insert Video** button, and then do either of the following:

   - Click **Online Video** to open the Insert Video window. In the **Insert Video** window, click the source of the video that you want to insert, and then follow the process to insert a video from the selected source.

   - Click **Video on My PC** to open the Insert Video dialog box. In the **Insert Video** dialog box, browse to and select the video file, and then click the **Insert** button.

To select an embedded video

1. Click the video image one time. Selection handles appear around the video image, the playback toolbar appears below it, and the Video Tools tab group appears on the ribbon.

To move the video image on the slide

1. Select the video, and then do either of the following:

   - Drag the video to the new location. Smart guides might appear on the slide to help you align the video with other objects.

   - Press the arrow keys to move the video by small amounts.

To resize the video image on the slide and retain its aspect ratio

1. Do either of the following:

   - Drag any corner handle. Smart guides appear on the slide to help you align the video with other objects.

   - On the **Format** tool tab, in the **Size** group, set a specific **Video Height** or **Video Width**, and then press **Enter** to change both settings.

To format the video image on the slide

1. Select the video, and then apply formatting from the **Format** tool tab just as you would for a picture.

> **SEE ALSO** For information about formatting pictures, see "Edit and format pictures" in Chapter 6, "Insert and manage simple graphics."

To configure an embedded video to play back at full screen size

1. Select the video.

2. On the **Playback** tool tab, in the **Video Options** group, select the **Play Full Screen** check box.

To set the relative volume of a video soundtrack

1. Select the video.

2. On the **Playback** tool tab, in the **Video Options** group, click the **Volume** button.

3. In the **Volume** list, click **Low**, **Medium**, **High**, or **Mute**.

Compress media to decrease file size

Trimming an audio or video clip affects only the playback of the media on the slide, not the original media clip. The original media clip is stored in its entirety as part of the presentation, and you can re-trim or restore the media clip at any time.

You can decrease the size of a PowerPoint file that contains trimmed media clips by discarding the unused portions of the clips. PowerPoint 2016 offers three compression configurations designed to balance size and quality.

 Presentation Quality
Save space while maintaining overall audio and video quality.

 Internet Quality
Quality will be comparable to media which is streamed over the Internet.

 Low Quality
Use when space is limited, such as when sending presentations via e-mail.

Choose the size and quality that best fits your needs

When you save and close the file after compressing the media, the trimmed portions of the videos are discarded and no longer available. You can reverse the compression operation until you save and close the file.

Hyperlink to additional resources

Presentations often include URLs of websites that provide additional information related to the presentation topic. When a presentation will be viewed electronically, the URLs can be formatted as hyperlinks so that the websites can be accessed directly from the presentation. Hyperlinks can also provide access to information that might be on a hidden slide in the presentation, or in a separate file.

TIP If you use Microsoft Outlook, you can also use a hyperlink to open an email message window so that people viewing the presentation can easily contact you.

Hyperlinks are most frequently in text format, but you can attach a hyperlink to any object—for example, an image such as a shape, logo, or picture. Clicking the hyperlinked object then takes you directly to the linked location. Editing the object does not disrupt the hyperlink; however, deleting the object also deletes the hyperlink.

The simplest method of creating a hyperlink is to enter a URL in a text box and then press the Enter key. PowerPoint automatically inserts the hyperlink and formats the URL so that people recognize it as a hyperlink.

If you want the same hyperlink to appear on every slide in a presentation, attach the hyperlink to text or an object on the presentation's master layout. For information about slide masters, see "Customize slide masters and layouts" in Chapter 12, "Create custom presentation elements."

To attach a hyperlink to an object, follow these steps:

1. Select the object that you want to hyperlink from.

2. Open the **Insert Hyperlink** box by doing either of the following:

   - On the **Insert** tab, in the **Links** group, click **Hyperlink**.

   - Press **Ctrl+K**.

3. In the **Link to** list, click the type of target you're linking to. Often this is a webpage or another place in the file.

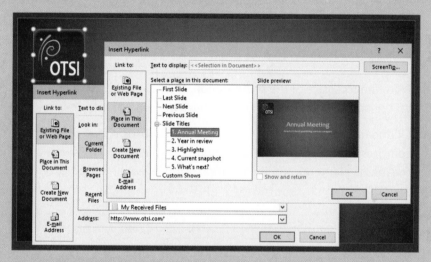

You can link to internal, local, and online locations

4. If you're linking to a webpage, enter the URL in the **Address** box. If you're linking to a slide or heading in the current file, click it in the **Select a place in this document** pane. Then click **OK**.

To compress media files

1. Save the PowerPoint presentation, and then display the **Info** page of the Backstage view.

Media size   File size

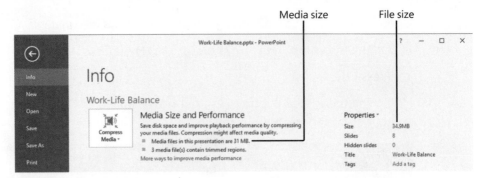

Info page of the Backstage view

2. Note the total size of the presentation, the size of the media files in the presentation, and the number of files that have been trimmed.

3. On the **Info** page, click the **Compress Media** button, and then click the level of compression you want. In the Compress Media window, PowerPoint itemizes the media elements and their compression levels, and reports the total space savings.

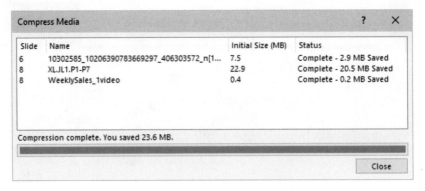

Compressing media files can make a big difference in file size

4. In the **Compress Media** window, click the **Close** button. In the Media Size And Performance area of the Info page, the Compress Media button is active to indicate that media has been compressed, and specifics about the compression are available.

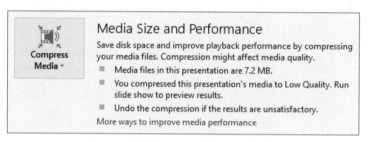

You can undo the compression if you don't like the results

5. Play the presentation to assess the quality, and then save the file if the quality is acceptable.

To reverse the compression of media files

1. On the **Info** page, click the **Compress Media** button, and then click **Undo**. PowerPoint immediately reverts to the uncompressed files.

Add and manage slide transitions

When you deliver a presentation, you can manually specify when to display the next slide, or you can have PowerPoint move automatically to the next slide after a specific amount of time. Rather than simply replacing one slide with the next, you can use *transitions* to control the way each slide appears on the screen.

PowerPoint 2016 has 48 basic transition effects divided into three categories: Subtle, Exciting, and Dynamic Content. Many of these have multiple options, such as the direction or specific form of the content in the effect.

8

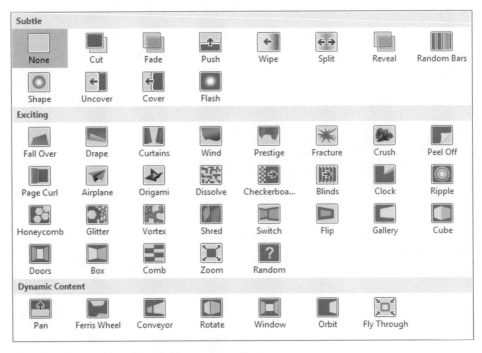

PowerPoint has a wide variety of slide transition effects

As with animations, take care when using transitions to not overdo it. That being said, transitions can be a useful way of visually drawing the audience's attention to the display of a new slide. The effects in the Subtle category are designed to make the incoming slide content available to the audience members with the least amount of movement.

Here are some ideas about other ways to use transitions:

- In a multisection presentation, use one transition on all the slides, and then use a different transition at the beginning of each new section of the presentation to signal a change in topic.

- Use a more dramatic slide transition to get the audience's attention at a specific point in a presentation.

You apply and manage transition effects by using the commands on the Transitions tab of the ribbon. The basic transition effects are available from the Transition To This Slide gallery. If you apply a transition that has additional options, the Effect Options button becomes active and you can choose an option from the list. You can specify the duration of the transition effect, or add a sound effect if you want to.

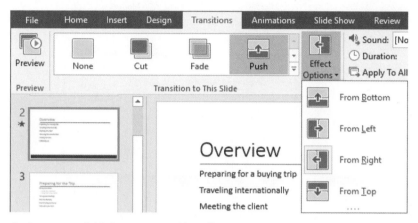

Options are available for many transition effects

 TIP You can add a sound effect even when the Transition is set to None. If you do, the sound effect plays during the normal slide replacement.

You can apply a transition effect or configure effect options for one slide at a time, for a group of slides, or for an entire presentation by first selecting the slide or slides you want to work with. (You can also apply and configure a transition effect on one slide and then apply that effect to all slides.) When you apply a transition effect or select an effect option, PowerPoint immediately demonstrates it.

As mentioned in "Animate text and pictures on slides" earlier in this chapter, PowerPoint displays a star next to the slide thumbnail to indicate that a slide has an animation or transition. (There is no indication on the slide itself.) In the Thumbnails pane or in Slide Sorter view, you can click the star to preview the animated slide elements beginning with the transition.

Every transition effect has a default duration of between 0.1 seconds and 6 seconds based on the complexity of the effect; most are from 1 to 2 seconds. You can change the duration of an effect so that the animation completes in less or more time. The duration is specified in seconds and can be from a minimum of .01 seconds to a maximum of 59 seconds.

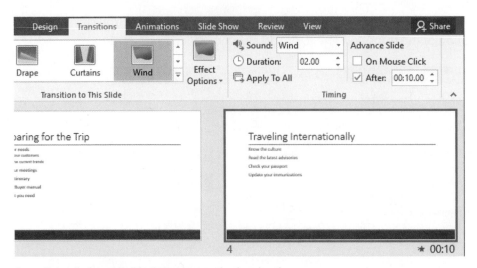

PowerPoint displays the slide timing next to the thumbnail

When you configure a transition, it affects the entrance of the slide. You can't specifically configure an exit transition, but some of the transitions have an effect on the exit of the preceding slide. You can, however, configure whether the move to the next slide is manually initiated or happens automatically after the slide has been displayed for a specific length of time (which can be from 0.01 seconds to just under 24 minutes).

> **SEE ALSO** For more information about slide timings, see "Rehearse a presentation and set slide timings" in Chapter 10, "Prepare and deliver presentations."

To select slides to apply or configure transitions

1. Do either of the following:

   - Display the presentation in Normal view, and select one or more slides in the **Thumbnails** pane.

   - Display the presentation in Slide Sorter view, and select one or more slides in the **Slides** pane.

> **TIP** To select multiple contiguous slides, click the first slide, hold down the Shift key, and then click the last slide. To select multiple noncontiguous slides, click the first slide, hold down the Ctrl key, and then click each additional slide.

To apply a transition to one or more slides

1. Select the slide or slides you want to apply the transition to.

2. On the **Transitions** tab, in the **Transition to This Slide** gallery, click the transition effect you want to apply.

To apply a transition to all slides in a presentation

1. Select all the slides, apply the transition, and then configure the transition and timing options.

Or

1. Apply the transition to one slide, and then configure transition and timing options.

2. On the **Transitions** tab, in the **Timing** group, click the **Apply To All** button.

To modify a transition

1. On the **Transitions** tab, in the **Transition to This Slide** group, click the **Effect Options** button, and then click the option you want. PowerPoint previews the modified transition effect.

To add a sound effect to a transition

1. On the **Transitions** tab, in the **Timing** group, click the **Sound** arrow, and then click the sound you want to play. PowerPoint doesn't automatically play the sound when you select it; only when you preview the transition.

> **TIP** If you want to use a sound file of your own, click Other Sound... at the bottom of the Sound list. In the Add Audio dialog box that opens, browse to and select the audio file you want to use, and then click OK. The audio file must be in the .wav file format.

2. If you want the sound to repeat until another sound effect plays, select the sound effect and then, in the **Sound** list, click **Loop Until Next Sound**.

3. If you loop the sound effect and want it to stop when you move to the next slide, do either of the following on the next slide:

   • In the **Sound** list, click **[Stop Previous Sound]**.

   • In the **Sound** list, click any sound effect other than the one on the preceding slide.

To specify the duration of a transition

1. On the **Transitions** tab, in the **Timing** group, enter or set the duration in seconds in the **Duration** box.

To preview slide transitions

1. To preview one slide transition, do any of following:

   - Display the slide in Normal view. On the **Transitions** tab, in the **Preview** group, click the **Preview** button.

   - Display the slide in Normal view. In the **Thumbnails** pane, click the star next to the slide number.

   - Display the presentation in Slide Sorter view, and then click the star next to the slide number.

Or

1. To preview multiple slide transitions, select the first slide that you want to preview, and then do either of the following:

   - On the **Slide Show** tab, in the **Start Slide Show** group, click the **From Current Slide** button.

   - Press **Shift+F5**.

2. Advance through the slide show to preview each slide transition as the slide appears.

Or

1. To preview all slide transitions, do any of the following to start the slide show from the beginning, and then advance through the slide show to preview each slide transition as the slide appears:

   - On the Quick Access Toolbar, click the **Start From Beginning** button.

   - On the **Slide Show** tab, in the **Start Slide Show** group, click the **From Beginning** button.

   - Press **F5**.

To remove slide transitions

1. Display or select the slides you want to remove the transitions from.

2. On the **Transitions** tab, in the **Transition to This Slide** gallery, in the **Subtle** section, click **None**.

Skills review

In this chapter, you learned how to:

- Animate text and pictures on slides

- Customize animation effects

- Add audio content to slides

- Add video content to slides

- Compress media to decrease file size

- Add and manage slide transitions

8

Practice tasks

The practice files for these tasks are located in the PowerPoint2016SBS \Ch08 folder. You can save the results of the tasks in the same folder.

Animate text and pictures on slides

Open the AnimateSlides presentation, and then perform the following tasks:

1. On slide **1**, apply the **Shape** entrance animation to the slide title and then to the subtitle. Notice that the animation numbers 1 and 2 appear to the left of the animated objects.

2. Display slide **2**, and apply the **Shape** entrance animation to the left content placeholder. Notice that boxes containing the numbers 1 through 3 appear to the left of the bullet points to indicate the order of their animations.

3. Repeat task 2 for the placeholder on the right.

4. Preview all the animations on slide **2**.

5. Display slide **3**. Apply the **Shape** entrance animation to the frog photo, and then add the **Pulse** emphasis animation.

6. Copy the animations from the frog photo to the crow photo and to the cat photo.

7. Preview the animations on the slide, and then preview the entire presentation.

8. Return to Normal view.

9. Save and close the presentation.

Customize animation effects

Open the CustomizeAnimations presentation, and then perform the following tasks:

1. On slide **1**, apply the **Diamond** entrance effect to the slide title. Set the direction to **Out**.

2. Copy the animation from the slide title to the subtitle. Then change the timing of the subtitle animation to **After Previous**.

3. Switch to Reading view, and preview the animation effects on slide **1**.

4. Switch back to Normal view, display slide **2**, and then click anywhere in the bulleted list on the left.

5. Display the **Animation Pane**. Right-click animation **1**, and then click **Effect Options** to open the Circle dialog box.

6. In the **Circle** dialog box, do the following:

    - Apply the **Chime** sound.

    - Dim the text color to **Red** after the animation.

    - Animate the text by letter.

    - Set the duration to **3 seconds (Slow)**.

7. Watch the effects of your changes to the animation effects.

    The Shape animation doesn't work very well with the selected effect options, so let's adjust them.

8. On the slide, click the left content placeholder. Notice that in the Animation Pane, all the animations for the bullet points in the placeholder are selected.

9. Apply the **Float In** entrance animation to the entire placeholder, and then display the effect options.

10. In the **Float Up** dialog box, do the following:

    - Apply the **Chime** sound.

    - Dim the text color to **Red** after the animation.

    - Animate text by letter.

    - Set the duration to **1 seconds (Fast)**.

11. Preview the animations, and make any additional adjustments you want to your custom animation effects.

12. Copy the animation effects of the bullet points on the left to those on the right.

13. Switch to Reading view, and then click the **Next** button to display the animated bullet points on slide 2.

14. When all the bullet points are visible and dimmed to red, press the **Esc** key to return to Normal view.

15. Save and close the presentation.

Add audio content to slides

Open the AddAudio presentation, display slide 1, and then perform the following tasks:

1. On the **Insert** tab, in the **Media** group, click the **Audio** button, and then click **Audio on My PC** to open the Insert Audio dialog box.

2. In the **Insert Audio** dialog box, browse to the practice file folder, and double-click the **SoundTrack** file to insert the audio clip on the slide.

3. On the **Playback** tool tab, in the **Audio Options** group, change the **Start** setting to **Automatically**. Then select the **Play Across Slides**, **Loop until Stopped**, and **Hide During Show** check boxes.

4. Switch to Reading view, and listen to the audio file as the presentation moves from slide to slide.

5. Press **Esc** to stop the presentation and return to Normal view.

6. Save and close the presentation.

Add video content to slides

Open the AddVideo presentation, and then perform the following tasks:

1. In the left content placeholder, insert the **Butterfly** video from the practice file folder.

2. On the playback toolbar, click the **Play/Pause** button, and then watch the video.

3. Insert the **Wildlife** video from the practice file folder into the content placeholder on the right, and then play the video.

4. With the **Wildlife** video selected, open the **Trim Video** dialog box, and drag the green start marker until it sits at about the **00:17.020** mark. Then, frame-by-frame, adjust the starting point until the first marmot frame comes into view at about the **00:17.292** mark.

5. Drag the red stop marker until it sits at about the **00:20.900** mark. Then, frame-by-frame, adjust the ending point until the last marmot frame comes into view at about the **00:20.790** mark.

6. Play the trimmed video, and then click **OK** to close the Trim Video dialog box.

7. Change the height of the **Butterfly** video representation to **3**".

8. Change the height of the **Wildlife** video representation to **3**", and then crop it to a width of **4**".

9. Drag the video representations until they are evenly spaced on the slide and center-aligned with each other.

10. Apply the **Reflected Bevel, Black** (in the **Intense** area of the **Video Styles** gallery) video style to both video objects.

11. Set up the **Butterfly** video to play back on mute, to start automatically, and to loop until stopped.

12. Set up the **Wildlife** video to play back on mute, to start on click, and to loop until stopped.

13. Preview and pause the **Butterfly** video. Then preview and pause the **Wildlife** video.

14. Return to Normal view.

15. Save and close the presentation.

Compress media to decrease file size

There are no practice tasks for this topic.

Add and manage slide transitions

Open the AddTransitions presentation, and then perform the following tasks:

1. Display slide **2** in Normal view.

2. Apply the **Cover** transition effect (from the **Subtle** category) to the slide.

3. Configure the transition effect options so that the transition starts from the upper-left corner of the slide.

4. Apply the configured slide transition to all slides in the presentation.

5. In the **Thumbnails** pane, display the effect of the **Cover** transition from slide **2** to slide **3**.

6. Remove the transition from slide **1**.

7. Preview the slide show and notice the transitions. When you exit the slide show, switch to Slide Sorter view.

8. Select all the slides that have transitions (slides **2** through **7**), add the **Wind** sound effect to the transition, and then set the duration of the transition effect to **1.75** seconds.

9. Preview the transition effect on one slide.

10. Save and close the presentation.

Part 4

Finalize presentations

Review presentations

9

After you complete the content of a presentation, you can add notes to the slides, either to prompt you while presenting the presentation or to include in handouts that you will provide to the audience.

When the slide and note content is complete, you can do several things to prepare the presentation for electronic or print delivery. You can configure the slides to display at a specific screen aspect ratio or to print at a specific paper size. You can run an inspection tool to check for comments, notes, hidden content, file properties, and other elements that you might want to remove. You can run other inspection tools to identify presentation elements that aren't compatible with earlier versions of PowerPoint, or that won't be available to apps that are scanning the content. Then you can print the presentation for a final review, or print handouts for the audience. Handouts can include slide images, speaker notes, and space for audience members to write their own notes.

This chapter guides you through procedures related to adding notes to slides, configuring slides for presentation or printing, inspecting and finalizing presentations, and printing presentations and handouts.

In this chapter

- Add notes to slides
- Configure slides for presentation or printing
- Inspect and finalize presentations
- Print presentations and handouts

Practice files

For this chapter, use the practice files from the PowerPoint2016SBS\Ch09 folder. For practice file download instructions, see the introduction.

Add notes to slides

Each slide in a PowerPoint presentation has a corresponding notes page in which you can enter notes that relate to the slide's content. You can print the notes to help you rehearse your content, display the notes to guide your speaking points as you deliver your presentation to a live audience, or print them with slides as part of a handout that you provide to the audience. If you want to keep the notes for your own reference, you can make a copy of the presentation to provide to other people and remove the notes from it as part of the inspection process.

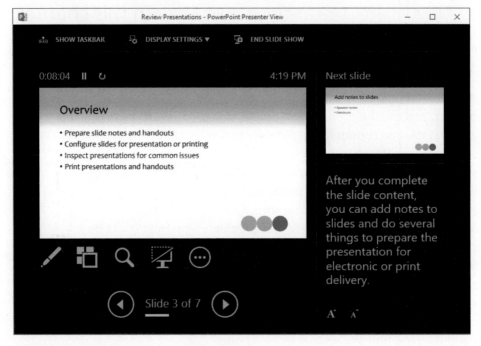

Slide notes are available to you in Presenter view

SEE ALSO For information about removing notes, see "Inspect and finalize presentations" later in this chapter. For information about printing handouts, see "Print presentations and handouts" later in this chapter.

Slide notes can be as basic or as detailed as you like. You can create simple notes when working in Normal view, or more detailed notes in Notes Page view.

In Normal view, you can open the Notes pane and enter text in it. The benefit of working in this view is that the current slide content and surrounding slide thumbnails are available for reference while you enter the notes.

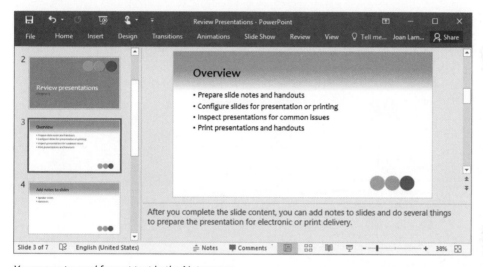

You can enter and format text in the Notes pane

If you need more working space, you can close the Thumbnails pane or resize the Notes pane. If you need significantly more working space, or want to include content such as pictures or diagrams, you can do so in Notes Page view.

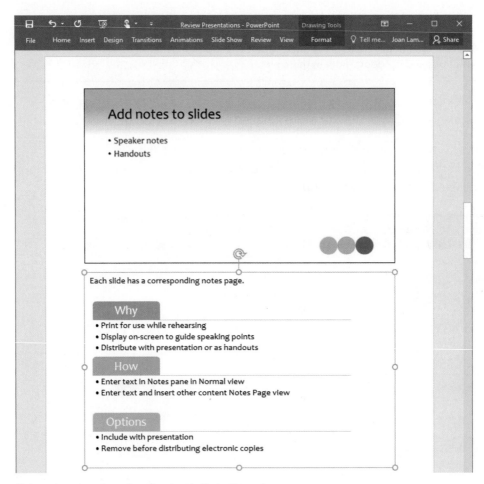

You can insert content other than text in Notes Page view

Notes Page view displays a large note pane below an image of the slide. Here are some important things to know about Notes Page view:

- You can't edit the slide content in Notes Page view.

- Content such as images and SmartArt graphics that you insert into the note pane in Notes Page view isn't visible in the Notes pane in Normal view, or in Presenter view. It is visible only in Notes Page view and when you print the notes.

- The appearance of content on the slides and in the notes in Normal view is governed by the slide master. The appearance of content in Notes Page view and in printed notes pages is governed by the notes master. The appearance of content in printed handouts is governed by the handout master. The colors and fonts of the masters are independent of each other. If you want the colors and fonts of two or more of these content types to match, you must set them for all the masters that are in use.

> **SEE ALSO** For information about switching among content development views, see "Display different views of presentations" in Chapter 2, "Create and manage presentations." For information about Presenter view, see "Present slide shows" in Chapter 10, "Prepare and deliver presentations."

To open and close the Notes pane in Normal view

1. On the status bar, click the **Notes** button.

To enter notes in the Notes pane

1. Click in the **Notes** pane, and then enter text.

To format text in the Notes pane

1. Select the text, and then do any of the following:

   - Apply formatting from the Mini Toolbar that appears immediately after you select the text.

   - Apply formatting from the **Font** and **Paragraph** groups on the **Formatting** tab.

   - Apply formatting by using keyboard shortcuts, such as **Ctrl+B**, **Ctrl+I**, or **Ctrl+U**.

   > **SEE ALSO** For information about keyboard shortcuts, see "Keyboard shortcuts" at the end of this book.

To resize the Notes pane

1. Point to the top border of the pane.

2. When the cursor changes to a double-headed arrow, drag the border up or down.

9

To enter notes in Notes Page view

1. Click in the area below the slide image to activate the text box.

2. Do either of the following:

   - Enter text in the text box.

   - Insert objects such as tables, pictures, shapes, SmartArt graphics, and charts by using the commands on the **Insert** tab. When you create the objects, they will float on the notes page. Resize and move the objects as necessary to align them with note text.

> ⊙ **SEE ALSO** For information about tables, see Chapter 5, "Present text in tables." For information about pictures and shapes, see Chapter 6, "Insert and manage simple graphics." For information about SmartArt graphics and charts, see Chapter 7, "Create and manage business graphics."

Configure slides for presentation or printing

In the old days, presentations were delivered by speakers with few supporting materials. Little by little, "visual aids" such as white board drawings or flip charts on easels were added. Eventually, savvy speakers began accompanying their presentations with 35mm slides or transparencies projected onto screens. To accommodate these speakers, early versions of PowerPoint included output formats optimized for slides of various sizes, including 35mm slides and the acetate sheets used with overhead projectors.

Technology has evolved to the point where most presentations are now delivered electronically. When you create a new presentation based on the Blank Presentation template or any of the PowerPoint design templates, the slides are sized for a wide-screen monitor because the likelihood is that you will be delivering the presentation with a portable computer and a projection device designed for this format. With the default Widescreen setting, slides are oriented horizontally with a width-to-height ratio of 16:9 and actual dimensions of 13.333 inches by 7.5 inches.

If you find it necessary to change the slide size of a presentation to best fit the display you're presenting it on, you can easily do so. Remember, though, that you'll need to carefully review the slides to ensure that your original content still fits. When you decrease the height or width of slides, PowerPoint prompts you to specify whether you want to maximize the size of the slide content or scale it down to ensure that it fits.

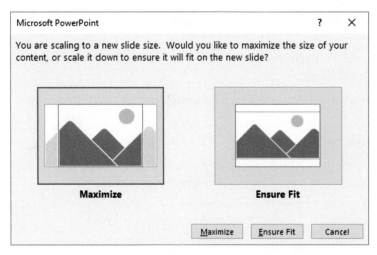

You can scale content to maintain the aspect ratio when you change the slide size

The content scaling option affects only the "live" slide content. Regardless of your content scaling choice, changing the slide size will compress or stretch images that are part of the slide layout, such as background images or logos. You can correct the problem by changing the Scale Width setting for the affected images on the slide layouts.

> **TIP** It is a lot more efficient to set the slide size of the presentation before you begin developing your content, so that you can select and place text and image elements appropriately. When you change the slide size, you have to check the content of each slide and adjust it as necessary so that it still appears as you want it. If your slides contain a lot of content or any images, this can be a tedious undertaking.

If the Widescreen and Standard formats don't suit your needs—for example, if you want to size the slides to match a specific paper size for printing purposes—you can click Custom Slide Size at the bottom of the Slide Size menu and select from the following slide sizes in the Slide Size dialog box:

- **On-screen Show (4:3)** For an electronic slide show on screens of various aspects: 4:3 (the Standard format), 16:9 (the Widescreen format), or 16:10.

- **Letter Paper (8.5x11 in)** For a presentation that will be printed on 8.5-by-11-inch US letter-size paper.

- **Ledger Paper (11x17 in)** For a presentation that will be printed on 11-by-17-inch legal-size paper.

9

- **A3 Paper, A4 Paper, B4 (ISO) Paper, B5 (ISO) Paper** For presentations that will be printed on paper of various international sizes.

- **35mm Slides** For 35mm slides that will be placed in a slide carousel and displayed through a slide projector.

- **Overhead** For transparencies that will be displayed through an overhead projector.

- **Banner** For webpage banner images.

- **Custom** For slides that are a nonstandard size. You can set the slide width, height, and orientation in the Slide Size dialog box.

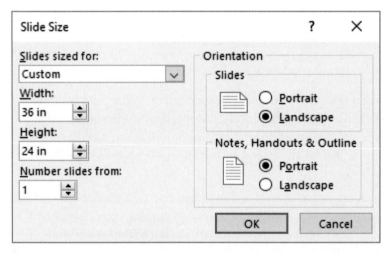

Choose a standard or custom slide size

> **TIP** In the Slide Size dialog box, you can specify a width and height of up to 56 inches. You can also change the slide orientation to Portrait, so that it is taller than it is wide. These options are particularly useful if you're using PowerPoint to lay out elements for a printed presentation such as a yard sign or poster.

To set the slide size to a standard screen aspect ratio

1. On the **Design** tab, in the **Customize** group, click the **Slide Size** button, and then do any of the following:

   - To set the slide aspect ratio to 4:3, click **Standard (4:3)**.

   - To set the slide aspect ratio to 16:9, click **Widescreen (16:9)**.

   - To configure the slides for a nonstandard screen aspect ratio or paper size, click **Custom Slide Size**.

2. If your selection decreases the slide height or width, PowerPoint prompts you to specify how you want to adjust the slide content. In the **Microsoft PowerPoint** dialog box, click **Maximize** to keep text and images as large as possible, or **Ensure Fit** to scale all the slide content.

To set the slide size to a standard paper size or screen aspect ratio

1. On the **Design** tab, in the **Customize** group, click the **Slide Size** button, and then click **Custom Slide Size**.

2. In the **Slide Size** dialog box, do the following:

    a. In the **Slides sized for** list, click the paper size or screen aspect ratio you want.

    b. In the **Slides** area of the **Orientation** section, click **Portrait** or **Landscape** to indicate the slide orientation you want.

    c. Click **OK**.

3. If your selection decreases the slide height or width, PowerPoint prompts you to specify how you want to adjust the slide content. In the **Microsoft PowerPoint** dialog box, click **Maximize** to keep text and images as large as possible, or **Ensure Fit** to scale all the slide content.

To set a custom slide size

1. On the **Design** tab, in the **Customize** group, click the **Slide Size** button, and then click **Custom Slide Size**.

2. In the **Slide Size** dialog box, do the following:

    a. In the **Slides sized for** list, click **Custom**.

    b. Set the **Width** and **Height** as you want them. If the width is less than the height, the slide orientation sets itself to Portrait; if the width is greater than the height, the slide orientation sets itself to Landscape.

    c. If you want to switch the Width and Height measurements, click the other orientation in the **Slides** area of the **Orientation** section.

    d. Click **OK**.

3. If your selection decreases the slide height or width, PowerPoint prompts you to specify how you want to adjust the slide content. In the **Microsoft PowerPoint** dialog box, click **Maximize** to keep text and images as large as possible, or **Ensure Fit** to scale all the slide content.

9

To scale slide layout images

1. Display the presentation in Slide Master view and locate a slide layout that includes an image that has been unevenly scaled.

2. Click the image to select it. Then on the **Format** tool tab, click the **Size** dialog box launcher to display the Size & Properties page of the Format Picture pane.

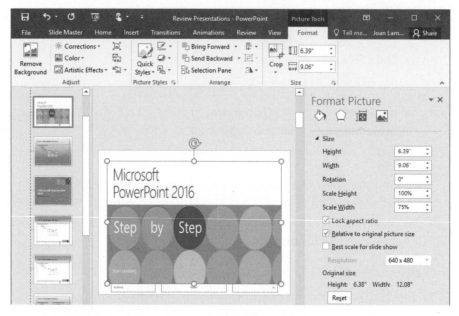

You must scale background images separately from slide content

3. Review the **Scale Height** and **Scale Width** settings. Change the larger number to match the smaller number, and then reposition the image as necessary to fit the new slide size.

Inspect and finalize presentations

These days, many presentations are delivered electronically as email attachments or from a website. As you develop a presentation, it can accumulate information that you might not want in the final version, such as the names of people who worked on the presentation, comments that reviewers have added to the file, or hidden text about status and assumptions. If your presentation file will never leave your computer, you don't have to worry that it might contain something that shouldn't be available to other people. However, if you plan to share the presentation file with other people, you might want to remove this information before you distribute the presentation.

To automate the process of finding and removing all extraneous and confidential information, PowerPoint provides a tool called the *Document Inspector*. When inspecting a presentation, the Document Inspector looks for the following elements:

- Comments, ink annotations, and slide notes
- Embedded content and content that isn't visible on the slide because it has been hidden from the Selection pane or is outside of the slide area
- Automatically generated or manually created properties that are saved with the presentation
- Content add-ins, task pane add-ins, macros, formats, ActiveX controls, and custom XML data saved with the presentation

After you run the Document Inspector, it displays a summary of its search results. You have the option of removing all the items found in each category. You can't review the items individually from the Document Inspector—if you want to do so, you must close the Document Inspector and manually locate the items. After removing items by using either method, you can reinspect the presentation.

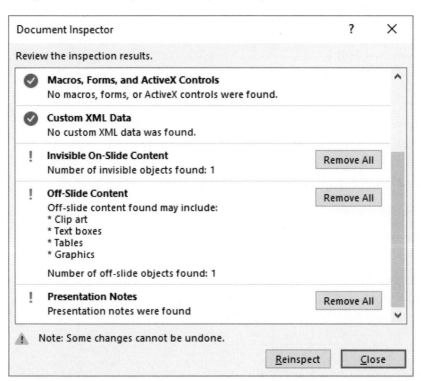

The Document Inspector has identified hidden slide content, off-slide content, and slide notes in the presentation

Many of the elements the Document Inspector looks for are harmless, and you might intend to leave them where they are. For example, you might have a title box that is formatted as invisible or positioned outside of the slide area so it provides a slide title for the outline and ScreenTips, but doesn't display the title on the slide. The job of the Document Inspector is to identify that these elements exist; it's then up to you to determine whether you want to keep or remove them.

PowerPoint includes two other tools that you can use to check presentations for issues:

■ The Accessibility Checker scans the presentation for content and formatting that might be difficult to view or that might not be compatible with assistive technologies. It reports its findings and offers suggestions for fixing any potential issues.

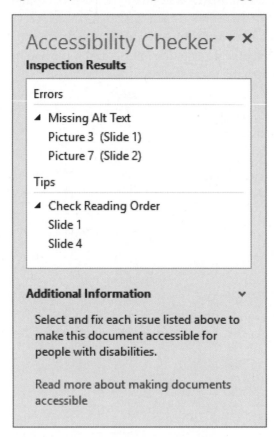

The Accessibility Checker reports problems and provides tips for improving the accessibility of the presentation

- The Compatibility Checker scans the presentation for content that is supported by PowerPoint 2016 but not by earlier versions of PowerPoint. These are most commonly related to images, shapes, SmartArt graphics, effects, animations, transitions, and embedded media.

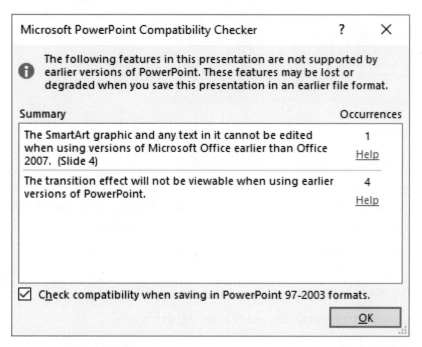

The Compatibility Checker reports the number, and sometimes location, of each problem

You access all three of these inspection tools from the Inspect Presentation area of the Info page of the Backstage view.

After you optimize a presentation for the delivery method and audience, you can mark it as final to indicate that changes shouldn't be made to it. Marking a presentation as final makes it read-only and deactivates most of the ribbon commands; anyone who wants to edit the presentation must acknowledge and dismiss the Marked As Final status.

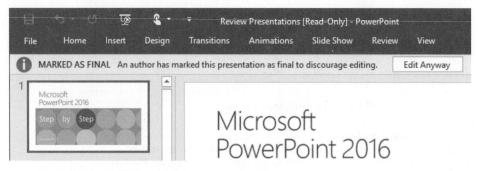

The information bar discourages people from making casual changes

To inspect a presentation for common issues

1. Display the **Info** page of the Backstage view.

2. In the **Inspect Presentation** area on the left side of the **Info** page, click the **Check for Issues** button, and then click **Inspect Document** to open the Document Inspector dialog box, which lists the items that will be checked.

3. If PowerPoint prompts you to save changes to the file, click **Yes**.

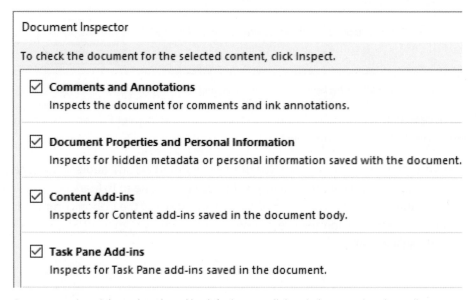

Some categories might not be selected by default, so scroll the window to review them all

4. Clear the check boxes for any of the elements that you don't want to check for, and then click **Inspect** to display the Document Inspector report.

5. Review the results, and then click the **Remove All** button for any category of information that you want to remove.

 TIP You can choose to retain content identified by the Document Inspector if you know that it is appropriate for distribution.

6. In the **Document Inspector** dialog box, click **Reinspect**, and then click **Inspect** to verify the removal of the properties and other data you selected.

7. When you're satisfied with the results, close the **Document Inspector** dialog box.

To inspect a presentation for accessibility issues

1. On the **Info** page of the Backstage view, click the **Check for Issues** button, and then click **Check Accessibility** to run the Accessibility Checker.

2. In the **Accessibility Checker** pane, review the inspection results and make any changes you want to the presentation.

3. When you are done, do either of the following:

   • Click the **X** in the upper-right corner of the **Accessibility Checker** pane to close the pane.

   • Leave the pane open to continue checking for accessibility issues as you work with the presentation.

To check a presentation for compatibility with earlier versions of PowerPoint

1. On the **Info** page of the Backstage view, click the **Check for Issues** button, and then click **Check Compatibility** to run the Compatibility Checker.

2. In the **Microsoft PowerPoint Compatibility Checker** dialog box, review the results, make any changes you want, and then click **OK**.

 TIP By default, PowerPoint checks for compatibility whenever you save a presentation in the .ppt file format. If you don't want PowerPoint to do this, clear the Check Compatibility When Saving In PowerPoint 97-2003 Formats check box in the Microsoft PowerPoint Compatibility Checker dialog box.

9

To mark a presentation as final

1. On the **Info** page of the Backstage view, in the **Protect Presentation** area, click the **Protect Presentation** button, click **Mark as Final**, and then click **OK** in the message box that appears.

2. A message tells you that the presentation has been marked as final, the status property has been set to Final, and typing, editing commands, and proofing marks are turned off. In the message box, click **OK**.

   The presentation title bar changes to indicate that the presentation is read-only, and the Protect Presentation area indicates that the file has been marked as final.

The title bar and Info page change to indicate the Final status

3. Click the **Return** button (the arrow above the Backstage view page tabs) to return to the presentation. Notice that only the ribbon tabs are visible; the commands are hidden.

4. Click the **Insert** tab to temporarily expand it, and notice that all the buttons are inactive (dimmed). Then click away from the tab to contract it. PowerPoint displays an information bar, notifying you that the presentation has been marked as final.

To make changes to a presentation that has been marked as final

1. On the information bar, click the **Edit Anyway** button to remove the Final designation and read-only protection from the file.

Print presentations and handouts

Throughout most of this book, I discuss the creation of a presentation for on-screen delivery in the form of a slide show. PowerPoint also offers the ability to print a presentation, either in the form of slides, or as handouts that include slides and notes. You can print a presentation for the purpose of review or for distribution to other people.

When printing a presentation, you can choose from several slide or handout layouts. You can preview the presentation as it will appear when printed, and configure the print settings to meet your requirements. You perform all these tasks on the Print page of the Backstage view.

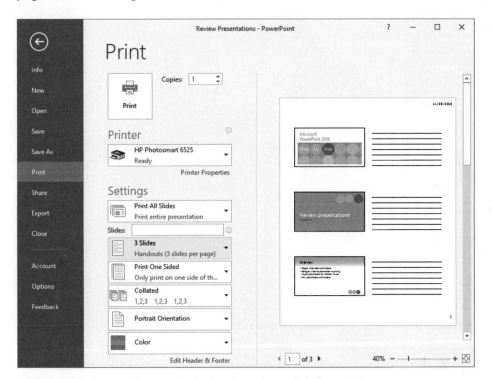

9

Preview various forms of the presentation in color or grayscale before printing

The process of selecting a printer and configuring the print settings is quite straightforward. Here's what you need to know about printing in PowerPoint that's different from other apps:

- You can print the entire presentation or only selected slides.

- You can print from one to nine slides per page, or you can print handouts that include slides and slide notes or note-taking space. If you need only the text of the slides, you can print an outline of the presentation without the images.

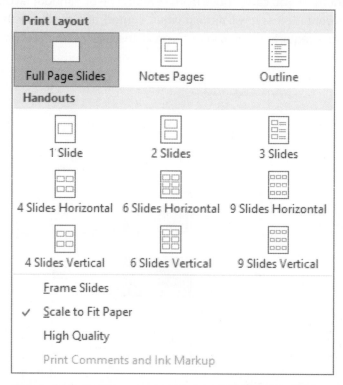

You can choose the slides you want to print, and the number of slides per page

 TIP For information about coordinating the appearance of content on slides, notes pages, and handouts, see "Add notes to slides" earlier in this chapter.

- You can add a narrow frame around each slide to set it off on the page.

- If the presentation contains comments, or slides have ink markup, you can print that with the presentation.

> **SEE ALSO** For information about adding comments to slides, see "Add and review comments" in Chapter 13, "Save and share presentations." For information about marking up slides, see "Present slide shows" in Chapter 10, "Prepare and deliver presentations."

■ The preview area displays the presentation content in color only when you select a printer that supports color.

■ You can select Color, Grayscale, or Pure Black And White for the preview and output. If the selected printer isn't a color printer, selecting Color displays the presentation as it will appear if PowerPoint sends the presentation to the printer in color format rather than as grayscale or black and white.

Some elements print in shades of gray even when you select the Pure Black And White option. The following table identifies the way specific objects print when you select the Grayscale or Pure Black And White options.

Object	Grayscale	Pure Black And White
Text	Black	Black
Bitmaps	Grayscale	Grayscale
Charts	Grayscale	Grayscale
Clip art	Grayscale	Grayscale
Embossing	Grayscale	Hidden
Fills	Grayscale	White
Frames	Black	Black
Lines	Black	Black
Object shadows	Grayscale	Black
Pattern fills	Grayscale	White
Slide backgrounds	White	White
Text shadows	Grayscale	Hidden

If you want to supplement the information on the printouts, you can add headers and footers that display the date and time, page numbers, or any other information that you want to print on each page.

9

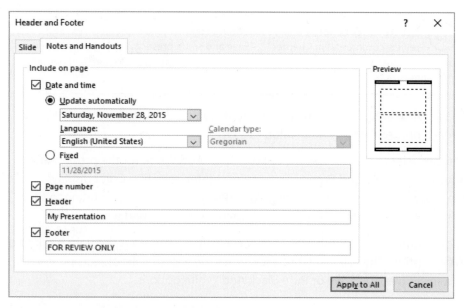

Selections on this tab affect only the printout, not the slides

Instead of printing the handouts with the print settings, you have an option to export the presentation content to a Microsoft Word document in which you could theoretically do additional page development.

To select the slide or slides to print

1. If you want to print only one slide, display that slide. If you want to print specific slides, select those slides in the **Thumbnails** pane of Normal view or in Slide Sorter view.

2. Display the **Print** page of the Backstage view.

3. In the **Settings** area, expand the first list, and then in the **Slides** section, do one of the following:

   - To select the entire presentation, click **Print All Slides**.

   - To select only the currently selected slides, click **Print Selection**.

   - To select only the currently displayed slide, click **Print Current Slide**.

   - To select specific slides by entering a custom range, click **Custom Range**, and then in the **Slides** box, enter individual slide numbers separated by commas, ranges separated by hyphens, or both. (For example, entering *2,5,12-15* in the Slides box prints slides 2, 5, 12, 13, 14, and 15.)

To select the print format

1. In the **Settings** area of the **Print** page of the Backstage view, expand the second menu, and then do any of the following:

    -   To print one slide per page with no additional content, click **Full Page Slides**.

    -   To print one slide per page with the slide notes below the slide, click **Notes Pages**.

    -   To print a text outline of the slide content, click **Outline**.

    -   To print handouts, in the **Handouts** section of the menu, click the thumbnail that indicates the number of slides you want to print on each page and the order of the slides. *Horizontal* orders the slides from left to right and then top to bottom; *Vertical* orders the slides from top to bottom and then left to right. If in doubt, click one of the options to preview it.

2. To add or remove the frame around each slide image, click **Frame Slides**. A check mark indicates that the option is turned on.

> **TIP** The *Handouts* options automatically frame each slide image.

9

To print double-sided pages

1. In the **Settings** area of the **Print** page of the Backstage view, expand the third menu, and then click the **Print on Both Sides** thumbnail that indicates the way you want to flip the pages.

> **TIP** To choose the correct page-flipping option, imagine that you're turning the page over. To keep the tops of both pages on the same edge of a sheet of paper, flip portrait-oriented content on the long edge and landscape-oriented content on the short edge.

To preview the printouts

1. The preview area displays only the slides you've selected to print, in the selected layout. To preview the printout content, do any of the following:

    -   To move to the next or previous page of the printout, click the **Next Page** or **Previous Page** button below the lower-left corner of the preview.

- To move to a specific page of the printout, enter the page number in the box below the lower-left corner of the preview, and then press **Enter**.

- To scroll through the pages that will be printed, drag the scroll bar, or click above or below the scroll box.

- To display the page at the largest size that fits in the preview pane, click the **Zoom to Page** button in the lower-right corner of the **Print** page.

- To change the page magnification, drag the **Zoom** slider, or click the **Zoom In** or **Zoom Out** button.

To specify the print colors

1. On the **Print** page of the Backstage view, in the **Printer** list, click the printer you intend to use, so that PowerPoint knows whether the printer supports color.

2. In the **Settings** area, click **Color**, and then do any of the following:

    - To transmit the color settings when printing, click **Color**.

    - To convert colors to shades of gray, click **Grayscale**.

    - To convert colors other than those in bitmaps, charts, and clip art images to black or white, click **Pure Black and White**.

 SEE ALSO See the table earlier in this chapter for information about color conversion when printing in grayscale or pure black and white.

To add headers or footers to printouts

1. Do either of the following to display the Notes And Handouts page of the Header And Footer dialog box:

    - Display the **Print** page of the Backstage view. At the bottom of the center pane, click the **Edit Header & Footer** link.

    - Display the presentation in Notes Page view. On the **Insert** tab, in the **Text** group, click the **Header & Footer** button.

2. Do any of the following:

    - Select the **Date and time** check box. Then click **Update automatically**, and click the format you want to display the date and time in, or click **Fixed**, and then enter the date and time as you want to display them.

- Select the **Page number** check box.

- Select the **Header** check box, and then in the text box, enter the text you want to display at the top of the page.

- Select the **Footer** check box, and then in the text box, enter the text you want to display at the bottom of the page.

3. Click **Apply to All**.

To export handouts to Word

1. Display the **Export** page of the Backstage view.

2. In the center pane, click **Create Handouts**, and then in the right pane, click the **Create Handouts** button to open the Send To Microsoft Word dialog box.

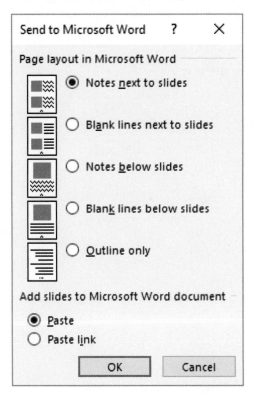

The page layout options are more detailed than those for handouts printed from PowerPoint

3. In the **Page layout in Microsoft Word** area of the dialog box, click the page layout you want.

9

4. In the **Add slides to Microsoft Word document** area, do either of the following:

   - To embed the slides in the document without retaining a link to the presentation, click **Paste**.

   - To embed and link the slides so you can easily update the document with changes to the presentation, click **Paste link**.

5. Click **OK**. Word starts and creates the notes page, handout, or outline you selected. You can enter additional notes and make other changes that you want in the Word document.

Skills review

In this chapter, you learned how to:

- Add notes to slides

- Configure slides for presentation or printing

- Inspect and finalize presentations

- Print presentations and handouts

Practice tasks

The practice files for these tasks are located in the PowerPoint2016SBS\
Ch09 folder. You can save the results of the tasks in the same folder.

Add notes to slides

Open the AddNotes presentation, and then perform the following tasks:

1. Display slide **1** in Normal view, and open the **Notes** pane.

2. In the **Notes** pane, enter the following three lines of text, pressing **Enter** at the
   end of each line:

   Welcome and introductions

   Logistics

   Establish knowledge level

3. Set the height of the **Notes** pane to match the three lines of text.

4. Display slide **2**. In the **Notes** pane, enter **Talk about the main concepts**.

5. Display slide **3**. In the **Notes** pane, enter **Complementary energies**. Then switch
   to Notes Page view, and insert the **YinYang** image from the practice file folder.
   Drag the image down below the *Complementary energies* note, using the smart
   guide to align the image with the slide.

6. Display slide **4** in Notes Page view. Insert the **Hierarchy List** SmartArt graphic,
   and position it in the center of the note pane. You can leave the placeholder
   graphic empty for the purposes of this task.

7. Switch to Normal view. Notice that the graphic on slide **3** and the diagram on
   slide **4** are not visible in the Notes pane in this view.

8. Save and close the presentation.

Configure slides for presentation or printing

Open the ConfigureSlides presentation, and then perform the following tasks:

1. Display the presentation in Slide Sorter view.

2. Change the slide size to **Standard**, and scale the slide content to ensure that it fits on the slides. Notice the effect of this change on the slides.

3. Undo the change to the slide size. Then change the slide size to **Standard**, and maximize the size of the slide content. Notice the effect of this change on the slides, and consider the differences between the two scaling options.

4. Note the slides that contain background images that didn't scale correctly.

5. Display slide **1**, and then display the slide layout in Slide Master view. Select the *Microsoft PowerPoint 2016 Step by Step* image, and then change the image scaling to maintain the original aspect ratio.

6. Close Slide Master view, and notice the change to the slide background image.

7. Save and close the presentation.

Inspect and finalize presentations

Open the InspectPresentations presentation, and then perform the following tasks:

1. Start the **Document Inspector**. Select all the issue categories, and then inspect the presentation.

2. Review the results of the inspection. Consider which content you would not want to distribute with the presentation, and remove it. Then reinspect the presentation to ensure that the issues were resolved.

3. Check the presentation for accessibility issues.

4. Review the results in the Accessibility Checker pane. Locate each of the slide elements, and make any changes that you consider necessary.

5. Mark the presentation as final, and notice the effect on the Info page of the Backstage view, and on the ribbon commands.

6. Display slide **2**. In the title, select the word **Review**, and confirm that you can't delete it while the presentation is read-only.

7. Close the presentation.

Print presentations and handouts

Open the PrintSlides presentation, and then perform the following tasks:

1. Display the **Print** page of the Backstage view.

2. Select a printer that is connected to your computer.

3. Configure the print settings to print slides **1–3** and **5** of the presentation in the **2 Slides** handout format, with frames around the slides.

4. Preview the printout as it would appear when sending color, grayscale, or pure black and white to the printer.

5. If you have a color printer and a black-and-white printer, select the other type of printer and note the differences.

6. Print the selected slides in grayscale on the selected printer.

7. Save and close the presentation.

Prepare
and deliver
presentations

If your presentation includes information that you want to deliver to some audiences but not others, you can create custom slide shows that each contain a subset of the slides in the presentation. The custom slide shows are saved with the presentation, so you need to maintain only one presentation for all audiences rather than individual presentations for each.

Before you deliver a presentation, you can rehearse it and, if you want to, set specific times for the slides to advance without you having to click or press anything. You can set slide timings to match the speed of your narration, or if the slide show will run on its own, to provide the right amount of time for audience members to read the information on each slide.

While you deliver a presentation, you can use the tools that are available in Slide Show view to navigate through the slides, draw attention to specific information with a digital laser pointer, and even draw on or annotate the slides with an on-screen pen or highlighter. If you're presenting on a remote screen, you can use Presenter view to display your slide notes and cue yourself to upcoming slides.

This chapter guides you through procedures related to adapting presentations for different audiences, rehearsing a presentation and setting slide timings, and presenting slide shows.

In this chapter

- Adapt presentations for different audiences
- Rehearse a presentation and set slide timings
- Present slide shows

Practice files

For this chapter, use the practice files from the PowerPoint2016SBS\Ch10 folder. For practice file download instructions, see the introduction.

Adapt presentations for different audiences

If you're going to deliver a presentation to a live audience, you can manually control the movement between slides, or configure slide timings to automatically move between slides. If your presentation will run unaccompanied—for example, as an informational display in a trade show booth—you can set it up to run continuously without external input.

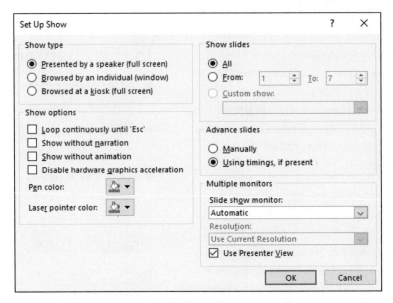

The default slide show settings and other options

If you plan to deliver variations of the same presentation to different audiences, you can save time by preparing one presentation that contains the slides for all the audiences, and then creating a custom slide show for each audience. Each custom slide show displays only the slides you select.

After you create a custom slide show, you can start it by selecting it from the Custom Slide Show menu on the Slide Show tab. If you want to set the custom slide show as the default show that runs when you click the From Beginning button or press F5, you can do so from the Set Up Show dialog box.

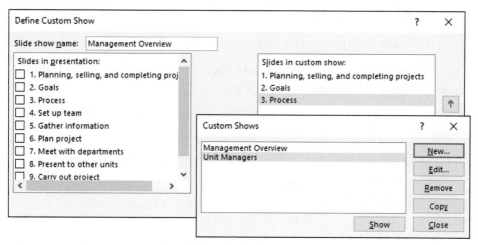

Customize slide shows for different audiences

To set up a slide show to run manually

1. On the **Slide Show** tab, in the **Set Up** group, click the **Set Up Slide Show** button.

2. In the **Set Up Show** dialog box, do the following, and then click **OK**.

   - In the **Show type** area, click **Presented by a speaker (full screen)**.

   - In the **Advance slides** area, click **Manually**.

To set up a slide show so that it runs automatically

1. On the **Slide Show** tab, in the **Set Up** group, click the **Set Up Slide Show** button to open the Set Up Show dialog box.

2. In the **Show type** area, do either of the following:

   - Click **Browsed at a kiosk (full screen)** to loop the show continuously until someone presses **Esc**.

   - Click **Browsed by an individual (window)** if the presentation will be viewed by viewers one at a time. In this case, the presentation will loop continuously by default, but you can disable this setting.

> **TIP** Any narration or animation attached to the presentation will play with the presentation unless you select the Show Without Narration or Show Without Animation check box. For information about narration, see "Rehearse a presentation and set slide timings" later in this chapter. For information about animation, see Chapter 8, "Add sound and movement to slides."

To create a custom slide show from scratch

1. Open the presentation you want to customize for different audiences.

2. On the **Slide Show** tab, in the **Start Slide Show** group, click the **Custom Slide Show** button, and then click **Custom Shows**.

3. In the **Custom Shows** dialog box, click **New** to open the Define Custom Show dialog box.

4. In the **Slide show name** box, enter a name for the custom slide show (for example, a name that identifies the audience).

5. In the **Slides in presentation** list, select the check box for each slide you want to include in the custom slide show.

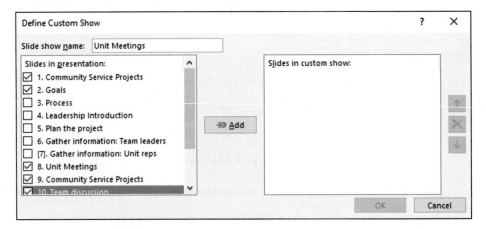

Hidden slides are indicated by square brackets around the slide number

6. Click **Add** to transfer the selected slides to the Slides In Custom Show list.

7. If you want to reorder the slides in the custom slide show, click a slide that you want to move in the Slides In Custom Show list, and then click the **Up** or **Down** button. The slide order in the slide show doesn't affect the slide order in the presentation.

> **TIP** To remove a slide from the custom slide show, click the slide in the Slides In Custom Show list, and then click the Delete button.

8. Click **OK** to return to the Custom Shows dialog box.

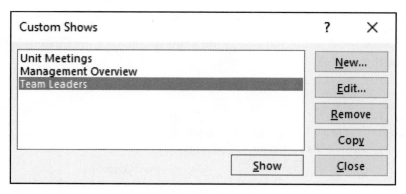

Manage custom slide shows from this dialog box

9. To test the custom slide show, click the slide show name, and then click **Show**.

To create a custom slide show based on an existing slide show

1. On the **Slide Show** tab, in the **Start Slide Show** group, click the **Custom Slide Show** button, and then click **Custom Shows**.

2. In the **Custom Shows** dialog box, click the slide show that you want to start from, and then click **Copy** to create a copy in the list.

3. With the *Copy of* slide show selected, click **Edit** to open the Define Custom Show dialog box.

4. In the **Slide show name** box, rename the custom slide show.

5. Modify the slide show by doing any of the following:

   - Add slides from the **Slides in presentation** list to the **Slides in custom show** list.

   - Delete slides from the **Slides in custom show** list.

   - Reorder slides in the **Slides in custom show** list.

6. Click **OK** to return to the Custom Shows dialog box.

10

To start a custom slide show

1. Open the presentation that includes the custom slide show.

2. On the **Slide Show** tab, in the **Start Slide Show** group, click the **Custom Slide Show** button.

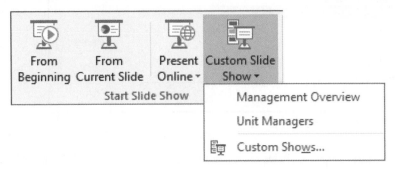

Custom slide shows are saved with the presentation

3. On the **Custom Slide Show** menu, click the custom slide show that you want to start.

To set a custom slide show as the default

1. On the **Slide Show** tab, in the **Set Up** group, click the **Set Up Slide Show** button to open the Set Up Show dialog box.

2. In the **Show slides** area, click **Custom show** to activate the Custom Show list.

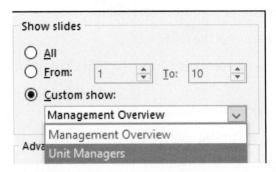

The default slide show runs when you press F5 or click the From Beginning button

3. In the list, click the custom slide show that you want to start by default. Then click **OK** to close the dialog box.

Rehearse a presentation and set slide timings

When you deliver a presentation, you can move from slide to slide manually by clicking the mouse button, pressing keys, or clicking on-screen commands. (You can also use a remote controller, but that is beyond the scope of this book.) If you prefer to not have to manually advance the slides, you can have PowerPoint display each slide for a predefined length of time and then move to the next slide. The length of time the slide remains on screen is the slide timing. You can set slide timings for every slide in a presentation, or for only specific slides.

The "Add and manage slide transitions" topic in Chapter 8, "Add sound and movement to slides," touched briefly on slide timings, because you can set a slide exit time that accomplishes the same thing from the Transitions tab. This topic discusses setting the slide timing from the Slide Show tab as part of the process of rehearsing and timing the delivery of a slide show.

Rehearsing a presentation is an opportunity to practice delivering your narrative or to review the content from the point of view of the audience to ensure that it is legible and clearly conveys your message. When you rehearse a presentation, PowerPoint automatically tracks and sets the slide timings for you, reflecting the amount of time you spend on each slide during the rehearsal. Then, during your actual delivery of the presentation, PowerPoint displays each slide for the length of time you indicated during the rehearsal.

While you rehearse the presentation, PowerPoint displays the slides in Slide Show view (at full screen) with the Recording toolbar in the corner of the screen.

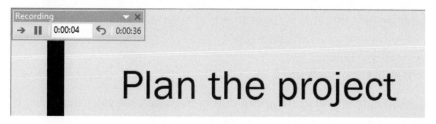

You can drag the toolbar to whatever location is convenient

10

The Recording toolbar has three buttons and two timers.

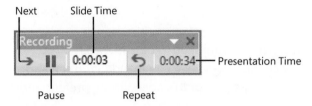

You can pause and restart the timing process

You can use these tools to manage the timing process as follows:

- Next moves to the next slide. You can also use the standard methods of clicking, clicking on-screen buttons, or pressing keyboard keys.

- Pause pauses the slide timing. If you're interrupted during the rehearsal, you can pause the timing process to help keep your timing accurate.

- The Slide Time counter shows the time that the current slide has been displayed.

- The Repeat button pauses the slide timing and resets the Slide Time counter so you can start the timing of the current slide from scratch.

- The Presentation Time counter shows the total slide show time during the rehearsal session.

When you complete the rehearsal, PowerPoint displays the total time and asks whether to save it (and overwrite any previously recorded slide timings).

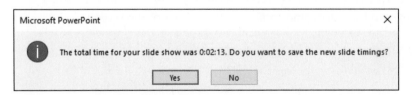

Clicking Yes overwrites any previous slide timings

It isn't vital to get the slide timing exactly right during the rehearsal; you can modify it manually after you complete the process.

When you finish the rehearsal and save the slide timings, they're visible in Slide Sorter view. Unlike the exit timings that you can set with transitions, the slide timings are not visible in the Thumbnails pane of Normal view.

Hidden slide   Slide timings

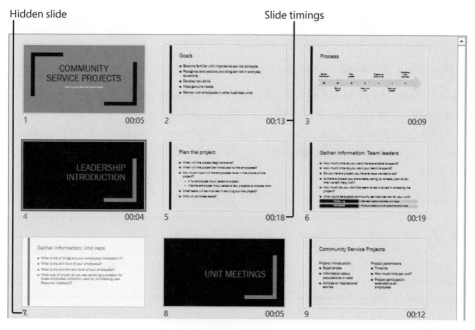

The rehearsal process doesn't display or time hidden slides

> ⚠ **IMPORTANT** By default, each slide timing is divided equally among the animated items on a particular slide. So if a slide has a title and four bullet points that are all animated, and you assign a timing of one minute to the slide, the five elements will appear at 12-second intervals.

10

You can review the slide timings and then, if you want to modify any of them, you can do so manually.

If you want to record your delivery of a presentation, the process is similar to that of rehearsing it. You can record from the beginning of the presentation or from a specific slide, and you can include your audio narration and on-screen annotations, if you want to. You can use your recording to review your work, or you can distribute it to people or post it online for people to watch on their own.

If you're not satisfied with the narration for a slide, you can clear the narration from the slide, and then re-record the narration for only that slide. If you decide that you don't want to use slide timings or narration, you can remove those elements from the slides.

To rehearse a slide show and record slide timings

1. Display the presentation in any development view.

2. On the **Slide Show** tab, in the **Set Up** group, click the **Rehearse Timings** button.

3. Narrate the slide at the speed you intend to when you present the slide show, or wait a sufficient amount of time for your intended audience members to read and comprehend the slide. Then advance to the next slide by clicking the **Next** button on the **Recording** toolbar, or by using any of the methods described in the next topic, "Present slide shows."

4. Repeat step 3 through to the end of the slide show.

> ✓ **TIP** Use the buttons on the Recording toolbar to pause the rehearsal or restart the timing for a slide. If you want to stop partway through the slide show, click the Close button (the X) on the Recording toolbar. You will have the option to save the slide timings.

5. When the slide show ends, PowerPoint displays the total delivery time and asks whether you want to save the recorded slide timings. Click **Yes** to save the timings or **No** to discard them.

To manually adjust the time for a slide

1. Select or display the slide.

2. On the **Transitions** tab, in the **Timing** group, to the right of the slide timing in the **After** box, type or select the time you want.

To record a presentation and review the recording

> ⚠ **IMPORTANT** Ensure that your computer has a working sound card, audio input device (internal or external microphone), and audio output device (headset or speakers) if you intend to record and review narrations.

1. Display the presentation in any development view.

2. On the **Slide Show** tab, in the **Set Up** group, do either of the following to open the Record Slide Show dialog box:

   - To record the presentation starting with slide 1, click the **Record Slide Show** button.

- To record the presentation starting with the current slide, click the **Record Slide Show** arrow, and then click **Start Recording from Current Slide**.

3. In the Record Slide Show dialog box, if you don't want to record timings, clear the **Slide and animation timings** check box. If you don't want to record annotations, clear the **Narrations, ink, and laser pointer** check box.

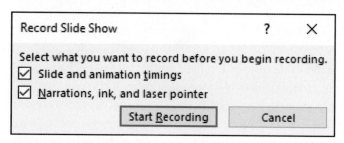

Recording narrations requires an audio input device

4. Click **Start Recording**. PowerPoint switches to Slide Show view, starts the presentation, and displays the Recording toolbar in the upper-left corner of the screen.

5. Use the techniques described in the previous procedure to move through the slide show and to pause, restart, and end the recording.

To test recorded narration

1. Display slide **1** (or the first slide that has recorded narration) and then switch to Reading view, where each slide is accompanied by its recorded narration.

To manage slide timings and narration

1. On the **Slide Show** tab, in the **Set Up** group, click the **Record Slide Show** button, click **Clear**, and then click any of the following:

   - **Clear Timing on Current Slide**

   - **Clear Timings on All Slides**

   - **Clear Narration on Current Slide**

   - **Clear Narrations on All Slides**

 TIP You can also clear the narration from a slide by displaying the slide in Normal view, and then deleting the audio icon that represents the narration.

Prepare presentations for travel

If you'll be delivering a presentation on a different computer than you created it on, you need to ensure that all the fonts, linked objects, and other presentation components will be available when and where you need them.

You can use the Package For CD feature to assemble a package that contains one or more presentations and the linked and embedded content (including fonts, sound effects, and audio and video files), and copy the package to a CD, a USB flash drive, or any connected storage location. You can run the Document Inspector or assign a password to each presentation as part of the packaging process. You can then run the presentation from the package by using PowerPoint or the Microsoft PowerPoint Viewer, which you can download and install for free from the Microsoft Download Center.

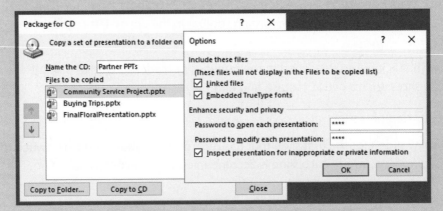

Package a presentation with all its supporting files for delivery from any computer

To package the open presentation, follow these steps:

1. If you want to burn the package to a CD or copy it to a USB flash drive, insert the CD or flash drive. If an AutoPlay or other dialog box related to the media opens, close it.

2. Display the **Export** page of the Backstage view. In the center pane, click **Package Presentation for CD**, and then in the right pane, click the **Package for CD** button.

3. In the **Package for CD** dialog box, do any of the following:

   - Replace the default name (*PresentationCD*) with a name of 16 or fewer characters.

   - To include more presentations in the package, click **Add**, browse to and select the presentations, and then click **Add**.

   - To reorder presentations in the package, click a presentation and then click the **Up** or **Down** button to move it.

4. If you want to change the standard options, click **Options**. In the **Options** dialog box, do any of the following, and then click **OK**:

   - To exclude linked files or embedded fonts from the package, clear that check box.

   - To password-protect the presentation, enter a password in one or both boxes. (Be sure to remember it, because you can't retrieve it if you lose it.)

   - If you want to run the Document Inspector on each presentation before creating the package, select the **Inspect presentation for inappropriate or private information** check box.

5. In the **Package for CD** dialog box, do either of the following:

   - To copy the package to a USB flash drive or any connected storage location, click **Copy to Folder**, browse to the storage drive or location, and then click **OK**.

   - To burn the package to a CD, click **Copy to CD**.

6. Confirm the actions in each message box that appears, and interact with the Document Inspector if you selected the option to run it. PowerPoint creates the folder, an AutoRun file that you can use to play the presentations in order, the presentations, and a subfolder that contains the supporting content.

SEE ALSO For more information about the Document Inspector, see "Inspect and finalize presentations" in Chapter 9, "Review presentations." To download the Microsoft PowerPoint Viewer, go to *www.microsoft.com/en-us/download /details.aspx?id=13*, click the Download button, and then follow the on-screen prompts.

10

Present slide shows

You're finally ready to deliver your slide show to the audience! Here's what you need to know.

Start the slide show

You can start a slide show from the first slide in the presentation, or from the slide that's currently selected in PowerPoint. The default view for a slide show is Slide Show view, which shows the slides at full-screen size.

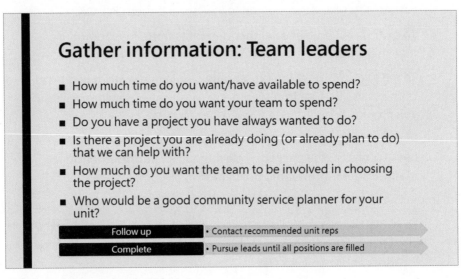

Slide Show view maximizes the slide size

The alternative view for a slide show is Presenter view, which is designed to display Slide Show view to the audience on one monitor, and a presentation control panel to the presenter on another monitor. The presenter's control panel displays a large version of the current slide, a small version of the next slide, and the slide notes.

Presenter view is intended for use with two displays, but you can also display it on one monitor if you want to.

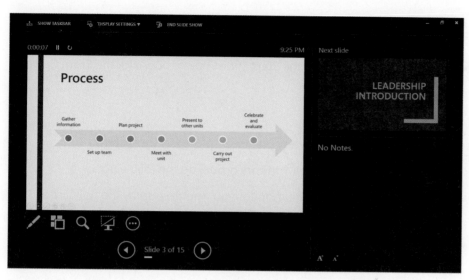

Presenter view provides additional information and options not visible to the audience

PowerPoint has default slide show settings based on the number of monitors connected to your computer:

- If you have only one monitor, slide shows open by default in Slide Show view. From there, you can switch to Presenter view if you want to.

- If you have multiple monitors, slide shows open by default in Presenter view. You can specify which monitor you want to display the full-screen slide show and which you want to display the presenter's control panel. If you prefer to open slide shows in Slide Show view, you can turn off the automatic display of Presenter view.

To start a slide show in the default view

1. To start the slide show from the first slide, do any of the following:

   - On the Quick Access Toolbar, click the **Start From Beginning** button.

   - On the **Slide Show** tab, in the **Start Slide Show** group, click the **From Beginning** button.

   - On the status bar, in the **View Shortcuts** area, click the **Slide Show** button.

   - Press **F5**.

   Or

10

To start the slide show from a specific slide, display the slide you want to start with, and then do either of the following:

- On the **Slide Show** tab, in the **Start Slide Show** group, click the **From Current Slide** button.

- Press **Shift+F5**.

To change the default slide show view on a multiple-monitor system

1. On the **Slide Show** tab, in the **Monitors** group, do the following:

    - In the **Monitor** list, click the monitor you want to display the full-screen slide show on.

    - Select or clear the **Use Presenter View** check box.

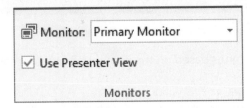

Select the default full-screen slide show monitor

Or

1. On the **Slide Show** tab, in the **Set Up** group, click the **Set Up Slide Show** button to open the Set Up Show dialog box.

2. In the **Multiple monitors** section of the dialog box, do the following:

    - In the **Slide show monitor** list, click the monitor you want to display the full-screen slide show on.

    - In the **Resolution** list, click the screen resolution you want the monitor to display the slide show at, if it's different from the current setting.

    > **TIP** The available screen resolution settings vary based on the screen resolutions that the selected monitor supports.

    - Select or clear the **Use Presenter View** check box.

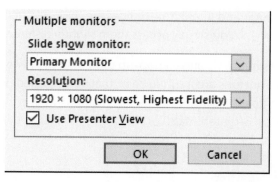

Set the default monitor and screen resolution

3. Click **OK**.

To switch from Slide Show view to Presenter view

1. Do either of the following:

   - At the right end of the pop-up toolbar or presenter's control panel tool-
     bar, click the **Slide Show Options (labeled ...)** button, and then click **Show
     Presenter View**.

   - Right-click the slide, and then click **Show Presenter View**.

Use the slide show tools

After you start the slide show, if you've configured slide timings, the slides advance
according to the timings, until the end of the slide show, when a black screen labeled
End Of Slide Show appears. Then you click or press any key to exit the slide show.

> **TIP** You can configure the PowerPoint options to not display the End Of Slide Show
> screen. For information about managing Slide Show view options, see the final proce-
> dure in this topic. For information about slide timings, see "Add and manage slide transitions"
> in Chapter 8, "Add sound and movement to slides," and "Rehearse a presentation and set slide
> timings" earlier in this chapter.

If you haven't configured slide timings, you can advance the slides manually by clicking the mouse button, pressing keyboard keys, or using the on-screen navigation
tools. In Slide Show view, these are on the pop-up toolbar that appears in the lower-
left corner of the screen when you move the mouse. In Presenter view, the navigation
tools are displayed below the current slide.

10

The tools you use to move through and interact with slides are basically the same in Slide Show view and Presenter view; you simply access them slightly differently.

In Slide Show view, moving the mouse displays a pop-up toolbar in the lower-left corner of the slide. The toolbar buttons are a subtle color that varies based on the background but doesn't draw attention away from the slide content. (It also isn't very easy to see.) Pointing to a button brightens its color.

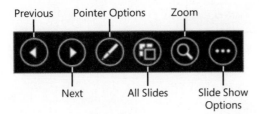

Control the slide show with the mouse, keyboard, or pop-up toolbar controls

Clicking the Slide Show Options button at the right end of the pop-up toolbar displays a menu of additional options.

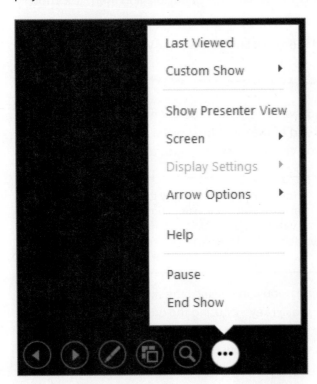

Less-frequently used commands are available from the Slide Show Options menu

TIP The pop-up toolbar is turned on by default but can be turned off in the PowerPoint Options dialog box.

Presenter view provides additional information about the slide show and has a fixed toolbar with larger buttons.

In Presenter view, slide show controls aren't visible to the audience

During a presentation, you can direct the audience's attention to specific information on the slide by pointing to slide elements with the laser pointer, drawing on the slides with an electronic "pen," or highlighting text with a highlighter. You have an unlimited choice of colors for the pen and highlighter, and three for the laser pointer.

⚠ **IMPORTANT** When the pen or highlighter tool is active in Slide Show view, clicking the mouse button does not advance the presentation to the next slide. You can advance with the pen or highlighter active by clicking the Next button, or you can turn off the tool and then click the slide to advance.

10

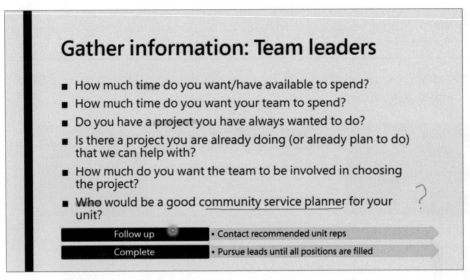

Annotate key points and focus the audience's attention on the current topic

While you're delivering a presentation, you might find it necessary to provide information that is not directly related to the current slide—perhaps in response to a question from an audience member. You can opt to pause the display of a presentation if it uses slide timings, and to display a blank black or white slide, so the audience understands that you're discussing a subject other than that of the slide.

To set the default annotation colors

1. On the **Slide Show** tab, in the **Set Up** group, click the **Set Up Slide Show** button to open the Set Up Show dialog box.

2. In the **Show options** section, do either of the following:

   - In the **Pen color** list, click the color you want to set as the default for the pen. You can choose from the Theme Colors palette or the Standard Colors palette, or you can click More Colors and choose or enter any color.

   - In the **Laser pointer color** list, click the red, green, or blue color swatch.

   > **TIP** The default highlighter color is always yellow, but you can change it within the slide show.

3. Click **OK**.

To display the pop-up toolbar in Slide Show view

1. Move the mouse.

To move through slides in any view

1. To advance to the next slide, do any of the following:

    -   Click the slide.

    -   Click the **Next** button.

    -   Press the **N**, **Spacebar**, **Enter**, **Down Arrow**, **Right Arrow**, or **Page Down** key.

    -   Right-click the slide, and then click **Next**.

2. To return to the previous slide, do any of the following:

    -   Click the **Previous** button.

    -   Right-click the slide, and then click **Previous**.

    -   Press the **P**, **Backspace**, **Up Arrow**, **Left Arrow**, or **Page Up** key.

3. To move to a specific slide, press the slide number key and then press **Enter**. (For example, to move to slide 4, press 4 and then press Enter.)

4. To move to any other slide, do either of the following to display all the slides, and then click the thumbnail of the slide you want to move to:

    -   Click the **All Slides** button.

    -   Press **Ctrl+S**.

5. To return to the previously viewed slide, click the **Slide Show Options** button, and then click **Last Viewed**.

6. To return to slide 1, press and hold the left and right mouse buttons.

 SEE ALSO For a complete list of keyboard shortcuts, see "Keyboard shortcuts" at the end of this book.

10

To select and use annotation tools

1. Do any of the following:

   - On the pop-up toolbar or presenter's control panel toolbar, click the **Pointer Options** button, and then click **Laser Pointer**, **Pen**, or **Highlighter**.

   - Right-click the slide, click **Pointer Options**, and then click **Laser Pointer**, **Pen**, or **Highlighter**.

   - Press **Ctrl+L** to change the pointer to a laser pointer.

   - Press **Ctrl+P** to change the pointer to a pen.

   - Press **Ctrl+I** to change the pointer to a highlighter.

2. Do any of the following:

   - Move the pointer over the slide to point with the laser pointer.

   - Drag to write on the slide with the pen.

   - Drag to highlight slide content.

3. To turn off the active tool, press the **Esc** key.

To change the pen or highlighter color during a slide show

1. With the pen or highlighter active, do either of the following:

   - Click the **Pointer Options** button.

   - Right-click the slide, click **Pointer Options**, and then click **Ink Color**.

You can switch to white, black, or the 10 standard colors

2. Click any of the 12 available colors.

TIP You can't change the laser pointer color during the slide show; you can only change the default color in the Set Up Show dialog box.

To remove annotations from a slide

1. To hide the annotations, do any of the following:

   - Click the **Slide Show Options** button, click **Screen**, and then click **Hide Ink Markup**.

   - Right-click the slide, click **Screen**, and then click **Show/Hide Ink Markup**.

   - Press **Ctrl+M**.

Or

1. To delete the annotations, do any of the following:

   - Click the **Pointer Options** button, and then click **Eraser**. Then click or drag across each individual annotation that you want to delete.

   - Click the **Pointer Options** button, and then click **Erase All Ink on Slide**.

   - Right-click the slide, click **Pointer Options**, and then click **Erase All Ink on Slide**.

   - Press **Ctrl+E** to change the pointer to an eraser. Then click or drag across each individual annotation that you want to delete.

   - Press **E** to erase all pen and highlighter markup on the slide.

To change the magnification of all or part of a slide

1. To zoom in or out of the entire slide, do either of the following:

   - To zoom in, press the **Plus Sign** key or **Ctrl+Plus Sign**.

   - To zoom out, press the **Minus Sign** key or **Ctrl+Minus Sign**.

2. To magnify a specific area of the screen, do either of the following, then move the magnifier to highlight the area you want to magnify, and click:

   - Click the **Zoom In** button.

   - Right-click the slide, and then click **Zoom In**.

3. To stop using the Zoom tool, press the **Esc** key.

10

To pause the play of a timed presentation

1. Do any of the following:

    - Click the **Slide Show Options** button, and then click **Pause**.

    - Right-click the slide, and then click **Pause**.

    - Press the **S** key on your keyboard.

To display a blank black or white screen during a slide show

1. Do any of the following:

    - Click the **Slide Show Options** button, click **Screen**, and then click **Black Screen** or **White Screen**.

    - Right-click the slide, click **Screen**, and then click **Black Screen** or **White Screen**.

    - Press **B** or the **Period** key to display a black screen.

    - Press **W** or the **Comma** key to display a white screen.

To return from a blank screen to the slide show

1. Do any of the following:

    - Click the **Slide Show Options** button, click **Screen**, and then click **Unblack Screen** or **Unwhite Screen**.

    - Right-click the slide, click **Screen**, and then click **Unblack Screen** or **Unwhite Screen**.

    - Press **B** or the **Period** key to hide a black screen.

    - Press **W** or the **Comma** key to hide a white screen.

To resume the play of a timed presentation

1. Do any of the following:

    - Click the **Slide Show Options** button, and then click **Resume**.

    - Right-click the slide, and then click **Resume**.

    - Press the **S** key on your keyboard.

To end the presentation of a slide show

1. Do any of the following:

   - On the **Slide Show Options** menu, click **End Show**.

   - Right-click the slide, and then click **End Show**.

   - Press **Esc** or **Ctrl+Break**.

   If you used the Pen or Highlighter tool to draw on any of the slides in the presentation, PowerPoint prompts you to keep or discard the annotations.

2. Do either of the following:

   - Click **Keep** to keep the annotations in the presentation.

   - Click **Discard** to delete the annotations.

To manage Slide Show view options

1. In the Backstage view, click **Options** to open the PowerPoint Options dialog box.

2. Display the **Advanced** page, and then scroll to the **Slide Show** section.

Slide Show

☑ Show menu on right mouse click ⓘ
☑ Show popup toolbar ⓘ
☑ Prompt to keep ink annotations when exiting
☑ End with black slide

Default slide show options that can be turned off

3. Select or clear any of the following check boxes:

   - **Show menu on right mouse click**

   - **Show popup toolbar**

   - **Prompt to keep ink annotations when exiting**

   - **End with black slide**

10

Skills review

In this chapter, you learned how to:

- Adapt presentations for different audiences

- Rehearse a presentation and set slide timings

- Present slide shows

Practice tasks

The practice files for these tasks are located in the PowerPoint2016SBS\
Ch10 folder. You can save the results of the tasks in the same folder.

Adapt presentations for different audiences

Open the CreateShows presentation, and then perform the following tasks:

1. Create a custom slide show named **Managers** that includes slides **1** through **6**, **9**, **10**, and **14** through **16**.

2. Start the **Managers** custom slide show.

3. Advance through all the slides, including the blank one at the end of the show. As you move from slide to slide, notice the slide numbers in the lower-right corner of the screen.

4. Remove slide **3** from the **Managers** slide show.

5. Set the **Managers** slide show as the default slide show.

6. Save and close the presentation.

Rehearse a presentation and set slide timings

Open the RecordTimings presentation, and then perform the following tasks:

1. Rehearse the presentation, and then save the recorded slide timings.

2. Display the presentation in Slide Sorter view and locate the slide timings.

3. Adjust the slide timing for slide **1** until it is a whole number of seconds.

4. If you have audio input and output devices on your computer, record the presentation, and read the slide content aloud. Then display the presentation in Reading view and listen to your narration.

5. Save and close the presentation.

Present slide shows

Open the DeliverShows presentation, and then perform the following tasks:

1. Open the **Set Up Show** dialog box, and then do the following:

   - Set the default pen color to a color of your choice.

   - Set the default laser pointer color to green.

   - Examine your settings in the **Multiple monitors** section. Find out what screen resolutions are available on your computer, and consider reasons that you might specify a screen resolution here.

   - If your computer is connected to multiple monitors, select the **Presenter view** check box to continue this set of practice tasks in Presenter view. Otherwise, you'll be in Slide Show view.

2. Close the dialog box, and then start the slide show.

3. Advance to slide **2**.

4. Move directly from slide **2** to slide **6**.

5. Return directly to slide **2**.

6. Move to slide **3**, and use the **Laser Pointer** to point to each bullet as you read it.

7. Zoom in on the bulleted list, and then return to the standard magnification.

8. Highlight the words *unique* and *successful*.

9. Draw a line in the default color below the word *shared*.

10. Erase all the ink annotations on the slide.

11. Move to slide **4**.

12. Change the pen color to **Dark Red**.

13. Draw a line below the word *overview.*

14. End the slide show, and discard your ink annotations.

15. Save and close the presentation.

Part 5

Use advanced PowerPoint functions

Work in PowerPoint more efficiently

After you become accustomed to using PowerPoint 2016, you might notice certain default behaviors that don't fit the way you work. For example, you might always select a non-default paste option. The default PowerPoint functionality is based on the way that most people work with presentations, or in some cases, because one option had to be selected as the default. You can modify the default behavior of many functions so that you can work more efficiently. You can also change aspects of the program to make it more suitable for the kinds of presentations you create.

When working in PowerPoint, you interact with commands (in the form of buttons, lists, and galleries) on the various tabs of the ribbon. Most people use a few commands from each tab often, and others not at all. You can centralize and streamline your interactions with the ribbon by adding the commands (from ribbon tabs other than Home) that you use most often to the Quick Access Toolbar, and positioning the Quick Access Toolbar below the ribbon so it's closer to the presentation content. You can also hide or display specific ribbon tabs and modify the content that appears on the ribbon.

This chapter guides you through procedures related to changing the default PowerPoint options, customizing the Quick Access Toolbar and the ribbon, and managing add-ins and security options.

In this chapter

- Change default PowerPoint options
- Customize the Quick Access Toolbar
- Customize the ribbon
- Manage add-ins and security options

Practice files

No practice files are necessary to complete the practice tasks in this chapter.

Change default PowerPoint options

Many of the options available in the PowerPoint Options dialog box are discussed in context in other chapters in this book. This topic includes information about all the available options, including a few that power users of PowerPoint might particularly find useful to modify.

All the options I discuss in this topic are available in the PowerPoint Options dialog box, which you open from the Backstage view. Each Office app has its own Options dialog box. Because so many options are available for each app and for Office, they are divided among pages (and in some cases, additional dialog boxes that you open from the pages). The pages are represented by page tabs in the left pane of the PowerPoint Options dialog box.

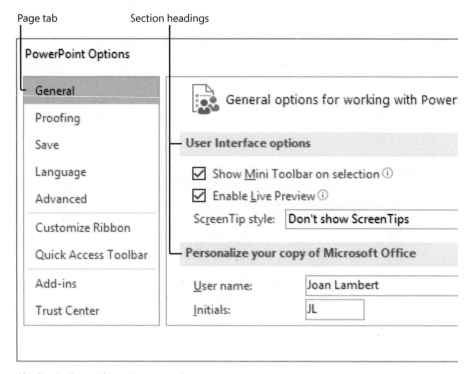

Shading indicates the active page tab

The left pane of the PowerPoint Options dialog box is divided into three sections:

- The first section contains the General, Proofing, Save, Language, and Advanced page tabs. These are the pages of options that standard PowerPoint users will most commonly make changes to when customizing the app functionality.

- The second section contains the Customize Ribbon and Quick Access Toolbar page tabs. These are the pages on which you customize the presentation of commands in the user interface.

- The third section contains the Add-ins and Trust Center page tabs. These pages are access points for higher-level customizations that can affect the security of your computer, are not often necessary to modify.

> **SEE ALSO** This topic discusses the options on the General, Proofing, Save, Language, and Advanced pages. For information about customizing the ribbon, Quick Access Toolbar, add-ins, and security options, see the related topics later in this chapter.

A brief description of the page content appears at the top of each page. Each page is further divided into sections of related options. The General page contains information that is shared among the Office apps. Other pages contain options that are specific to the app or to the file you're working in.

The images in this topic depict the default selections for each option. Many options have only on/off settings as indicated by a selected or cleared check box. Options that have settings other than on or off are described in the content that follows the image.

11

Manage general Office and PowerPoint options

Options that affect the user interface and startup behavior of PowerPoint are available from the General page of the PowerPoint Options dialog box.

General options for working with PowerPoint.

User Interface options

☑ Show Mini Toolbar on selection ⓘ
☑ Enable Live Preview ⓘ
ScreenTip style: [Show feature descriptions in ScreenTips ⌄]

Personalize your copy of Microsoft Office

User name: [Samantha Smith]
Initials: [SS]
☐ Always use these values regardless of sign in to Office.
Office Background: [No Background ⌄]
Office Theme: [Colorful ⌄]

Start up options

Choose the extensions you want PowerPoint to open by default: [Default Programs...]
☑ Tell me if Microsoft PowerPoint isn't the default program for viewing and editing presentations.
☑ Show the Start screen when this application starts

General options for working with PowerPoint

The options in the User Interface Options and Personalize sections of the General page are shared among all the Office apps installed on the computer you're working on, and include the following:

- You can turn off the Mini Toolbar, which hosts common formatting commands and appears by default when you select content.

- You can turn off the Live Preview feature if you find it distracting to have content formatting change when the pointer passes over a formatting command.

- You can minimize or turn off the display of ScreenTips when you point to buttons.

- You can specify the user name and initials you want to accompany your comments and tracked changes, and override the display of information from the account associated with your installation of Office.

- You can choose the background graphics and color scheme (Office theme) that you want to use for all the Office apps. You can also set these on the Account page of the Backstage view.

SEE ALSO For information about Office backgrounds and themes, see "Manage Office and app settings" in Chapter 1, "PowerPoint 2016 basics."

In addition to these shared options, you can turn off the Start screen that appears when you start PowerPoint without opening a specific file. When the Start screen is turned off, starting the app without opening a specific file automatically creates a new, blank file.

To open the PowerPoint Options dialog box

1. Click the **File** tab to display the Backstage view.

2. In the left pane, click **Options**.

To display a specific page of the PowerPoint Options dialog box

1. Open the PowerPoint Options dialog box.

2. In the left pane, click the tab of the page that you want to display.

To close the PowerPoint Options dialog box

1. Do either of the following:

   - To commit to any changes, click **OK**.

   - To cancel any changes, click **Cancel** or click the **Close** button (**X**) in the upper-right corner of the dialog box.

To enable or disable the Mini Toolbar

1. Open the **PowerPoint Options** dialog box, and display the **General** page.

2. In the **User Interface options** section, select or clear the **Show Mini Toolbar on selection** check box.

To enable or disable the Live Preview feature

1. Display the **General** page of the **PowerPoint Options** dialog box.

2. In the **User Interface options** section, select or clear the **Enable Live Preview** check box.

To control the display of ScreenTips

1. Display the **General** page of the **PowerPoint Options** dialog box.

2. In the **User Interface options** section, display the **ScreenTip style** list, and then click any of the following:

   - Show feature descriptions in ScreenTips

   - Don't show feature descriptions in ScreenTips

   - Don't show ScreenTips

To change the user identification that appears in comments and tracked changes

 IMPORTANT The User Name and Initials settings are shared by all the Office apps, so changing them in any one app immediately changes them in all the apps.

1. Display the **General** page of the **PowerPoint Options** dialog box.

2. In the **Personalize your copy of Microsoft Office** section, do the following:

   - In the **User name** and **Initials** boxes, enter the information you want to use.

   - Select the **Always use these values regardless of sign in to Office** check box.

To enable or disable the PowerPoint Start screen

1. Display the **General** page of the **PowerPoint Options** dialog box.

2. In the **Start up options** section, select or clear the **Show the Start screen when this application starts** check box.

Manage proofing options

Options that affect the spelling and grammar-checking and automatic text replacement functions of PowerPoint are available from the Proofing page of the PowerPoint Options dialog box.

ABC✓ Change how PowerPoint corrects and formats your text.

AutoCorrect options

Change how PowerPoint corrects and formats text as you type: [AutoCorrect Options...]

When correcting spelling in Microsoft Office programs

☑ Ignore words in UPPERCASE
☑ Ignore words that contain numbers
☑ Ignore Internet and file addresses
☑ Flag repeated words
☐ Enforce accented uppercase in French
☐ Suggest from main dictionary only

[Custom Dictionaries...]

French modes: [Traditional and new spellings ▾]
Spanish modes: [Tuteo verb forms only ▾]

When correcting spelling in PowerPoint

☑ Check spelling as you type
☐ Hide spelling and grammar errors
☐ Check grammar with spelling

[Recheck Document]

Editorial options for working with slide content

The options on this page are more relevant when you're working with large amounts of closely spaced text in Microsoft Word documents than with short sections of text on PowerPoint slides. One set of options that you might find useful on this page are the spelling and grammar correction options in the When Correcting Spelling In PowerPoint section of the page. These options control whether PowerPoint displays squiggly red and blue lines under words that don't meet its spelling and grammar guidelines while you're developing a presentation. If you find those lines to be distracting, you can turn them off here.

When reviewing spelling in a presentation, you have options to ignore one or all instances of suspected spelling errors. If you choose to ignore all instances of a flagged spelling error in a presentation, either from the shortcut menu or from the

11

Spelling pane, PowerPoint remembers your selection and removes the squiggly underlines from all instances of that word. If you want PowerPoint to forget those settings and conduct a fresh spelling check, you can do that from this page.

The AutoCorrect settings affect the way PowerPoint processes specific text and character combinations that you enter, so it's good to be familiar with them.

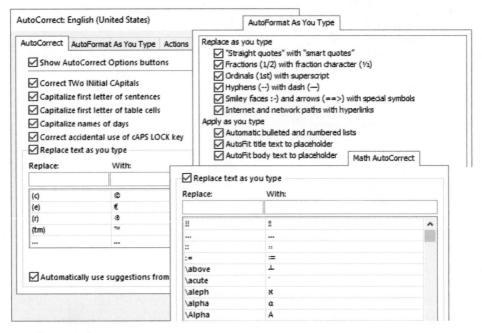

AutoCorrect options

Reasons to modify the AutoCorrect settings include:

- If you find that PowerPoint is consistently changing text that you enter, in a way that you don't want it to.

- If you consistently make a spelling mistake that you would like PowerPoint to correct for you.

- If you want to create a shortcut for entering longer text segments. (For example, if you want PowerPoint to enter *Wide World Importers* whenever you type *WW*.)

To turn off the automatic spelling checking function

1. Display the **Proofing** page of the **PowerPoint Options** dialog box.

2. In the **When correcting spelling in PowerPoint** section, clear the **Check spelling as you type** check box.

To hide squiggly underlines that indicate spelling or grammar errors

1. Display the **Proofing** page of the **PowerPoint Options** dialog box.

2. In the **When correcting spelling in PowerPoint** section, select the **Hide spelling and grammar errors** check box.

To clear the results of a previous spelling check

1. Display the **Proofing** page of the **PowerPoint Options** dialog box.

2. In the **When correcting spelling in PowerPoint** section, click the **Recheck Document** button.

To stop PowerPoint from automatically correcting a specific type of text entry

1. Display the **Proofing** page of the **PowerPoint Options** dialog box.

2. In the **AutoCorrect options** section, click the **AutoCorrect Options** button.

3. In the **AutoCorrect** dialog box, on the **AutoCorrect** or **AutoFormat As You Type** tab, locate the correction that you want to turn off, and clear the check box. Then click **OK**.

11

To automatically change a specific text entry to another

1. Display the **Proofing** page of the **PowerPoint Options** dialog box.

2. In the **AutoCorrect options** section, click the **AutoCorrect Options** button.

3. In the **AutoCorrect** dialog box, on the **AutoCorrect** tab, do the following, and then click **OK**:

   - In the **Replace** box, enter the misspelling or abbreviated text. The list scrolls to display the closest entries.

   - In the **With** box, enter the corrected spelling or full-length text you want PowerPoint to replace the original entry with.

Manage file locations

The Save page of the PowerPoint Options dialog box contains two sections of options that control the behavior of the app, and one section that is specific to the presentation you're working in.

Options that affect where and when PowerPoint saves and looks for presentations and templates are available in the Save Presentations and Offline Editing Options sections. These options can be rather important—not necessarily to change them, but to know where PowerPoint stores files so that you can browse to them if necessary.

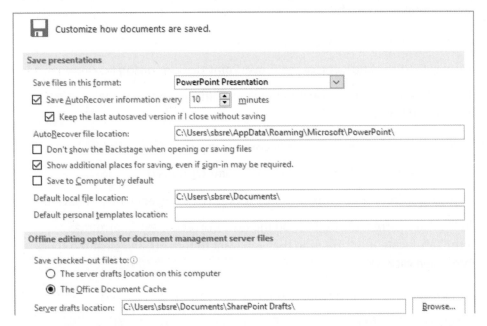

Customize your save options

Two options that you might find useful are these:

- If you're making a lot of changes that you don't want to lose, or feel that your system might run into trouble (for example, if you're in a location that is experiencing frequent power outages and you don't have battery backup) you can automatically save drafts more frequently than the default of every 10 minutes.

- You can specify the folder that PowerPoint displays in the Save As dialog box when you select This PC in the Places list. The default is your Documents folder, but if you routinely save in another location, you can save yourself a few clicks by choosing that instead. (Or you can pin the location to the top of the location list.)

The location specified in the Offline Editing section is where PowerPoint stores local copies of online files it's working with. It's best to not change anything in this section.

Options for saving fonts with the current presentation are available in the Preserve Fidelity section. When you distribute a PowerPoint presentation electronically (as a .pptx file), the fonts in the presentation render correctly on-screen only if they are installed on the computer that's displaying the presentation. If you use fonts in your presentation other than those that come with Office, or if you have reason to believe that the fonts you use won't be available on a computer or device that displays the presentation, you can embed the fonts in the presentation.

Preserve fidelity when sharing this presentation:	Presentation1 ∨
☐ Embed fonts in the file ⓘ	
◉ Embed only the characters used in the presentation (best for reducing file size)	
○ Embed all characters (best for editing by other people)	

Embed nonstandard fonts in presentations so they display correctly on other computers

Embedding fonts in a presentation increases the size of the file. You can minimize the increase by embedding only the characters that are used in the presentation. Letters, numbers, and symbols that aren't in the presentation when you embed the fonts will not be available. Embedding all the characters of a font requires more storage space, especially if you use multiple fonts in the presentation, but makes the characters available on other systems so the presentation content can be gracefully edited.

To change the automatic draft saving frequency

1. Display the **Save** page of the **PowerPoint Options** dialog box.

2. In the **Save presentations** section, set the saving frequency in the **Save AutoRecover information every** box.

11

To change the default local folder

1. Start File Explorer and browse to the folder you want to set as the default.

2. Do either of the following to copy the folder path to the Clipboard:

   - Click the folder icon at the left end of the **Address** box to display the folder path. Then press **Ctrl+C**.

   - Right-click the **Address** box, and then click **Copy address as text**.

3. Display the **Save** page of the **PowerPoint Options** dialog box.

4. In the **Save presentations** section, select the content of the **Default local file location** box.

5. Do either of the following to paste the folder path into the box:

   - Press **Ctrl+V**.

   - Right-click the selection, and then click **Paste**.

To embed fonts in a presentation

1. Display the **Save** page of the **PowerPoint Options** dialog box.

2. In the **Preserve fidelity when sharing this presentation** section, select the **Embed fonts in the file** check box.

3. If you want to embed the entire character set of all fonts used in the presentation, click **Embed all characters**.

Manage language options

Most people use only one editing and display language when working in presentations, but people who work in a multilingual environment might be able to use additional languages. The Language page of the PowerPoint Options dialog box contains options for adding, removing, and prioritizing language options in all the Office apps that are installed on the computer.

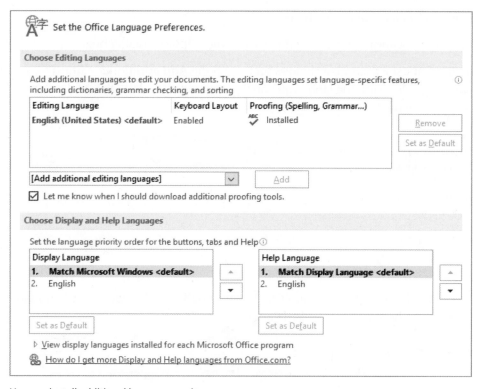

You can install additional language packs

You can configure two types of language options on the Language page:

- Editing languages, which control the keyboard and proofing settings

- Display languages, which control the language of user interface labels (such as ribbon tab names and button names) and built-in user assistance features (such as ScreenTips)

The keyboard languages are installed through Windows, but you can start the process from this page. If you've already installed a language on your computer through Windows, that language is automatically available to you in Office as a keyboard language. The Office proofing tools and display languages are specific to Office and aren't provided by Windows.

To add an editing language to Office

1. Display the **Language** page of the **PowerPoint Options** dialog box.

2. In the **Choose Editing Languages** section, in the **Add additional editing languages** list, click the language you want to add. Then click the **Add** button adjacent to the list.

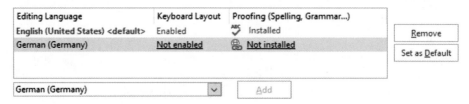

You must specifically install the proofing tools through Office

To enable the keyboard layout for a language

1. In the **Editing Language** pane, click the **Not enabled** link to open the Language window of the Windows Control Panel.

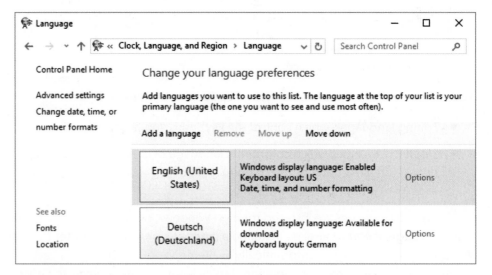

Languages that you install through Windows are available to you as keyboard languages

2. On the **Language** page, click **Add a language**.

3. On the **Add a language** page, locate the language that you want to enable the keyboard for. Click the language, and then click **Add**.

To install the proofing tools for a language or to install a display language

1. In the **Editing Language** pane, click the **Not installed** link to display the Language Accessory Pack For Office 2016 page of the Office website.

2. On the **Language Accessory Pack** page, locate the language that you want to install the proofing tools for.

German	de-de	Deutsch	Full	The pack includes:	Download
				▪ Display in selected language	
				▪ Help in selected language	
				▪ Proofing tools for selected language	

The language accessory pack includes the proofing tools and display language, if available

3. Click the **Download** link for the language.

4. In the prompt that appears, click **Run** to begin the installation of the selected language accessory pack. An Office message box informs you that you must close all Office apps and Internet Explorer to install the language pack.

To set a default editing language

1. In the **Editing Language** pane, click the language that you want to set as the default.

2. To the right of the pane, click the **Set as Default** button.

To remove an editing language

1. In the **Editing Language** pane, click the language that you want to remove.

2. To the right of the pane, click the **Remove** button.

To prioritize a display language or Help language

1. In the **Display Language** or **Help Language** pane, click the language you want to prioritize.

2. Click the **Move Up** button adjacent to the pane.

11

Manage advanced options

The most interesting and useful options are, of course, gathered on the Advanced page of the PowerPoint Options dialog box. There are many options here; some affect the app behavior, and others are specific to the presentation you're working in.

The Advanced page is divided into nine sections.

Manage the ways you can edit content

The options in the Editing Options and Cut, Copy, And Paste sections are self-explanatory, other than the Use Smart Cut And Paste option. This option is very useful when working with text in a Word document because it controls whether the app tries to merge content into adjacent lists when you cut it from one location and paste it in another.

Manage the impact of images on file size

Most of the options in the Image Size And Quality and Chart sections are specific to the current presentation. These options can frequently be useful:

- **Discard editing data** When you insert images in a presentation and then edit them by using the tools on the Format tool tab for pictures, PowerPoint saves the editing data so you can undo your changes. You can decrease the file size of a presentation by discarding the editing data.

- **Do not compress images in file** When you're finalizing a presentation for distribution, you have the option to compress the media within the file. This results in a smaller file size, but also a lower quality. You also have the option to exclude images from the media compression.

> **SEE ALSO** For information about compressing media, see "Compress media to decrease file size" in Chapter 8, "Add sound and movement to slides."

The options in the Chart section control whether custom data labels and formatting stay with data points in charts. It seems likely that this would always be the better option, but if you find that it presents a problem, you can turn it off here.

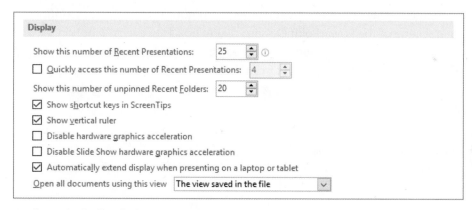

Configure the display of information in the Backstage view and in the app window

Options in the Display section are among those that you might want to configure for the way you work. You can change the number of presentations that appear in the Recent file list in the right pane of the Open page of the Backstage view. You can also display your most recently edited presentations directly in the left pane of the Backstage view, below the Options button, for easy access. This can be very convenient, but the option is not turned on by default.

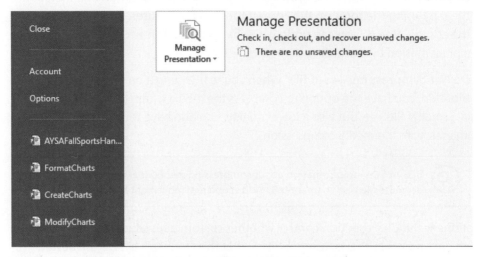

Quickly access recent presentations from the left pane of the Backstage view

You configure the display of ScreenTips and whether they include feature descriptions on the General page of the PowerPoint Options dialog box. However, the option to display keyboard shortcuts within ScreenTips is here in the Display section of the Advanced page. If you're a person who likes to work from the keyboard and you don't have the full list of keyboard shortcuts memorized, you can learn them by including them in ScreenTips.

 SEE ALSO For an extensive list of keyboard shortcuts that you can use in PowerPoint 2016 and globally throughout Office 2016, see "Keyboard shortcuts" at the end of this book.

Another option in the Display section that can be useful is specifying the view that PowerPoint opens all presentations in. The default is to open a presentation in the view it was saved in; if the person who edited a presentation before you closed it in Outline view, the presentation will open in Outline view.

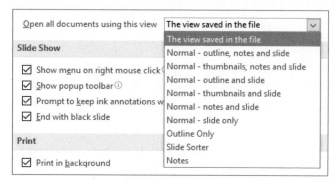

Choose a default opening view for consistency

You can configure this option so that you have a consistent experience when opening files. One situation in which this can be useful is if you're processing a series of presentations that you need to apply transitions to or reset layouts in, and you want to do this in Slide Sorter view. You can set this option to open all presentations in Slide Sorter view, and then you don't have to switch to that view in each presentation.

Configure options for presenting slide shows on this computer

11

In the Slide Show section, you can turn off any of the standard Slide Show view options—for example, if you don't want to display a black slide at the end of a presentation.

Print

☑ Print in background
☐ Print TrueType fonts as graphics
☐ Print inserted objects at printer resolution
☐ High quality
☐ Align transparent graphics at printer resolution

When printing this document: 📄 Presentation1 ⌄

⦿ Use the most recently used print settings ⓘ
○ Use the following print settings: ⓘ
 Print what: Full Page Slides ⌄
 Color/grayscale: Color ⌄
  ☐ Print hidden slides
  ☐ Scale to fit paper
  ☐ Frame slides

General

☐ Provide feedback with sound
☐ Show add-in user interface errors

Save specific print options with the current presentation

There are two sections of printing options; the first are general printing options and the second are specific to the presentation you're working in. You can configure the same options for printing the current presentation on the Print page of the Backstage view. The advantage to configuring the document-specific options here is that they travel with the presentation.

Customize the Quick Access Toolbar

By default, buttons representing the Save, Undo, and Redo commands appear on the Quick Access Toolbar. If you regularly use a few commands that are scattered on various tabs of the ribbon and you don't want to switch between tabs to access the commands, you might want to add them to the Quick Access Toolbar so that they're always available to you.

You can add commands to the Quick Access Toolbar directly from the ribbon, or from the Quick Access Toolbar page of the PowerPoint Options dialog box.

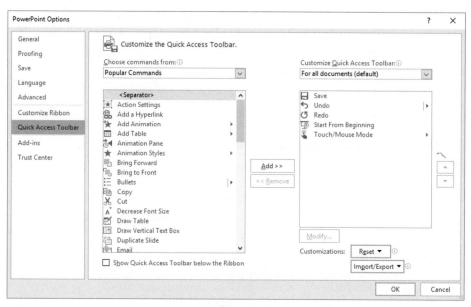

The Quick Access Toolbar is a convenient command organization option

> ✓ **TIP** You can display a list of commands that do not appear on the ribbon by clicking Commands Not In The Ribbon in the Choose Commands From list on the Quick Access Toolbar or Customize Ribbon page of the app-specific Options dialog box.

11

You can customize the Quick Access Toolbar in the following ways:

- You can define a custom Quick Access Toolbar for all presentations (referred to in the PowerPoint Options dialog box as documents), or you can define a custom Quick Access Toolbar for a specific document.

- You can add any command from any group of any tab, including tool tabs, to the toolbar.

- You can display a separator between different types of buttons.

- You can move commands around on the toolbar until they are in the order you want.

- You can reset everything back to the default Quick Access Toolbar configuration.

After you add commands to the Quick Access Toolbar, you can reorganize them and divide them into groups to simplify the process of locating the command you want.

As you add commands to the Quick Access Toolbar, it expands to accommodate them. If you add a lot of commands, it might become difficult to view the text in the title bar, or all the commands on the Quick Access Toolbar might not be visible, defeating the purpose of adding them. To resolve this problem and also position the Quick Access Toolbar closer to the file content, you can move the Quick Access Toolbar below the ribbon.

To add a command to the Quick Access Toolbar from the ribbon

1. Do either of the following:

   - Right-click a command on the ribbon, and then click **Add to Quick Access Toolbar**. You can add any type of command this way; you can even add a drop-down list of options or gallery of thumbnails.

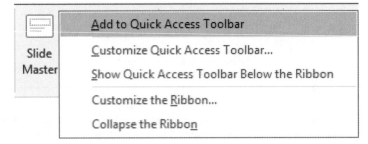

Add any button to the Quick Access Toolbar directly from the ribbon

   - At the right end of the Quick Access Toolbar, click the **Customize Quick Access Toolbar** button. On the menu of commonly used commands, click a command you want to add.

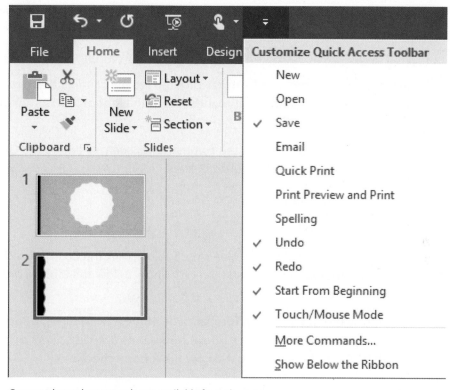

Commonly used commands are available from the menu

To display the Quick Access Toolbar page of the PowerPoint Options dialog box

1. Do any of the following:

   - At the right end of the Quick Access Toolbar, click the **Customize Quick Access Toolbar** button, and then click **More Commands**.

   - Click the **File** tab and then, in the left pane of the Backstage view, click **Options**. In the left pane of the **PowerPoint Options** dialog box, click **Quick Access Toolbar**.

   - Right-click any ribbon tab or empty area of the ribbon, and then click **Customize Quick Access Toolbar**.

11

To add a command to the Quick Access Toolbar from the PowerPoint Options dialog box

1. Display the **Quick Access Toolbar** page of the **PowerPoint Options** dialog box.

2. In the **Choose commands from** list, click the tab the command appears on, or click **Popular Commands**, **Commands Not in the Ribbon**, **All Commands**, or **Macros**.

3. In the left list, locate and click the command you want to add to the Quick Access Toolbar. Then click the **Add** button.

To move the Quick Access Toolbar

1. Do either of the following:

   - At the right end of the Quick Access Toolbar, click the **Customize Quick Access Toolbar** button, and then click **Show Below the Ribbon** or **Show Above the Ribbon**.

   - Display the **Quick Access Toolbar** page of the **PowerPoint Options** dialog box. In the area below the **Choose commands from** list, select or clear the **Show Quick Access Toolbar below the Ribbon** check box.

To define a custom Quick Access Toolbar for a specific presentation

1. Display the **Quick Access Toolbar** page of the **PowerPoint Options** dialog box.

2. In the **Customize Quick Access Toolbar** list (above the right pane) click **For** *file name*.

3. Add the commands to the toolbar that you want to make available to anyone who edits the file, and then click **OK**. The app displays the file-specific Quick Access Toolbar to the right of the user's own Quick Access Toolbar.

 TIP If a command is on a user's Quick Access Toolbar and also on a file-specific Quick Access Toolbar, it will be shown in both toolbars.

To display a separator on the Quick Access Toolbar

1. Display the **Quick Access Toolbar** page of the **PowerPoint Options** dialog box.

2. In the right pane, click the command after which you want to insert the separator.

3. Do either of the following:

   - In the left pane, double-click **<Separator>**.

   - Click **<Separator>** in the left pane, and then click the **Add** button.

To move buttons on the Quick Access Toolbar

1. Display the **Quick Access Toolbar** page of the **PowerPoint Options** dialog box.

2. In the right pane, click the button you want to move. Then click the **Move Up** or **Move Down** arrow until it reaches the position you want.

To reset the Quick Access Toolbar to its default configuration

1. Display the **Quick Access Toolbar** page of the **PowerPoint Options** dialog box.

2. In the lower-right corner, click **Reset**, and then click either of the following:

   - Reset only Quick Access Toolbar

   - Reset all customizations

3. In the **Microsoft Office** message box verifying the change, click **Yes**.

> ⚠ **IMPORTANT** Resetting the Quick Access Toolbar does not change its location. You must manually move the Quick Access Toolbar by using either of the procedures described earlier.

11

Customize the ribbon

The ribbon was designed to make all the commonly used commands visible so that people can more easily discover the full potential of each Office app. But many people perform the same set of tasks all the time, and for them, buttons that they never use might be considered just another form of clutter.

If you don't want to entirely hide the ribbon, you can modify its content. From the Customize Ribbon page of the PowerPoint Options dialog box, you can control the tabs that appear on the ribbon, and the groups that appear on the tabs.

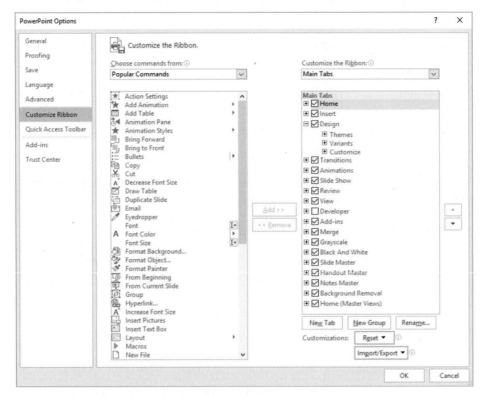

You can hide and display individual ribbon tabs

On this page, you can customize the ribbon in the following ways:

- You can hide an entire tab.

- You can remove a group of commands from a tab. (The group is not removed from the app, only from the tab.)

- You can move or copy a group of commands to another tab.

- You can create a custom group on any tab and then add commands to it. (You cannot add commands to a predefined group.)

- You can create a custom tab. For example, you might want to do this if you use only a few commands from each tab and you find it inefficient to flip between them.

Don't be afraid to experiment with the ribbon to come up with the configuration that best suits the way you work. If at any point you find that your new ribbon is harder to work with rather than easier, you can easily reset everything back to the default configuration.

> ⚠️ **IMPORTANT** Although customizing the default ribbon content might seem like a great way of making the app yours, I don't recommend doing so. A great deal of research has been done about the way that people use the commands in each app, and the ribbon has been organized to reflect the results of that research. If you modify the default ribbon settings, you might end up inadvertently hiding or moving commands that you need. Instead, consider the Quick Access Toolbar to be the command area that you customize and make your own. If you add all the commands you use frequently to the Quick Access Toolbar, you can hide the ribbon and have extra vertical space for document display. (This is very convenient when working on a smaller device.) Or, if you really want to customize the ribbon, do so by gathering your most frequently used commands on a custom tab, and leave the others alone.

To display the Customize Ribbon page of the PowerPoint Options dialog box

1. Do either of the following:

   - Display the **PowerPoint Options** dialog box. In the left pane, click **Customize Ribbon**.

   - Right-click any ribbon tab or empty area of the ribbon, and then click **Customize the Ribbon**.

To permit or prevent the display of a tab

1. Display the **Customize Ribbon** page of the **PowerPoint Options** dialog box.

2. In the **Customize the Ribbon** list, click the tab set you want to manage:

   - All Tabs

   - Tool Tabs

   - Main Tabs

3. In the right pane, select or clear the check box of any tab other than the File tab. (You can't hide the File tab.)

To remove a group of commands from a tab

1. Display the **Customize Ribbon** page of the **PowerPoint Options** dialog box.

2. In the **Customize the Ribbon** list, click the tab set you want to manage.

11

3. In the **Customize the Ribbon** pane, click the **Expand** button (+) to the left of the tab you want to modify.

4. Click the group you want to remove, and then in the center pane, click the **Remove** button.

To create a custom tab

1. Display the **Customize Ribbon** page of the **PowerPoint Options** dialog box.

2. On the **Customize Ribbon** page, click the **New Tab** button to insert a new custom tab below the active tab in the Customize The Ribbon pane. The new tab includes an empty custom group.

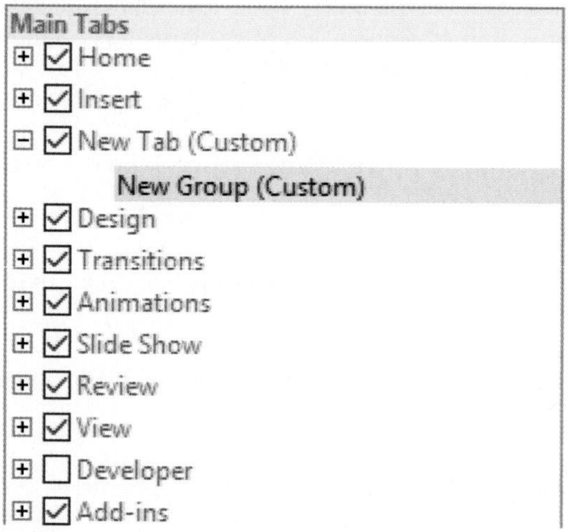

```
Main Tabs
⊞ ☑ Home
⊞ ☑ Insert
⊟ ☑ New Tab (Custom)
          New Group (Custom)
⊞ ☑ Design
⊞ ☑ Transitions
⊞ ☑ Animations
⊞ ☑ Slide Show
⊞ ☑ Review
⊞ ☑ View
⊞ ☐ Developer
⊞ ☑ Add-ins
```

Creating a new tab and group

To rename a custom tab

1. Display the **Customize Ribbon** page of the **PowerPoint Options** dialog box.

2. In the **Customize the Ribbon** pane, click the custom tab. Then click the **Rename** button.

3. In the **Rename** dialog box, replace the existing tab name with the tab name you want, and then click **OK**.

To rename a custom group

1. Click the custom group, and then click the **Rename** button to open the **Rename** dialog box in which you can specify an icon and display name for the group.

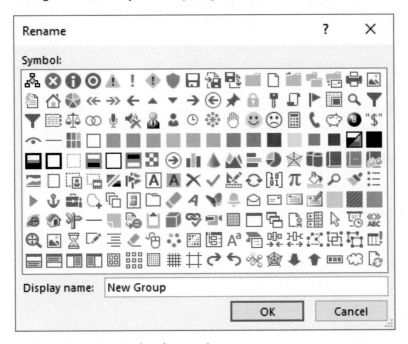

Assign an icon to appear when the group is narrow

2. In the **Rename** dialog box, do the following, and then click **OK**:

   - In the **Display name** box, replace the current name with the group name that you want to display.

   - In the **Symbol** pane, click an icon that you want to display when the ribbon is too narrow to display the group's commands.

To create a custom group

1. Display the **Customize Ribbon** page of the **PowerPoint Options** dialog box.

2. On the **Customize Ribbon** page, in the right pane, click the tab you want to add the group to. Then click the **New Group** button to add an empty custom group.

11

To add commands to a custom group

1. Display the **Customize Ribbon** page of the **PowerPoint Options** dialog box.

2. In the **Customize the Ribbon** list, expand the tab set you want to manage, and then click the group you want to add the commands to.

3. In the **Choose commands from** list, click the tab the command appears on, or click **Popular Commands**, **Commands Not in the Ribbon**, **All Commands**, or **Macros**.

4. In the left list, locate and click the command you want to add to the group. Then click the **Add** button.

To reset the ribbon to its default configuration

1. Display the **Customize Ribbon** page of the **PowerPoint Options** dialog box.

2. In the lower-right corner, click **Reset**, and then click either of the following:

   - Reset only selected Ribbon Tab

   - Reset all customizations

Manage add-ins and security options

The final section of pages in the PowerPoint Options dialog box contains the settings that you should definitely think carefully about before changing, because they can affect the security of your system.

Manage add-ins

Add-ins are utilities that add specialized functionality to a program but aren't full-fledged programs themselves. PowerPoint includes two primary types of add-ins: COM add-ins (which use the Component Object Model) and PowerPoint add-ins.

There are several sources of add-ins:

- You can purchase add-ins from third-party vendors; for example, you can purchase an add-in that allows you to assign keyboard shortcuts to PowerPoint commands that don't already have them.

- You can download free add-ins from the Microsoft website or other websites.

- When installing a third-party program, you might install an add-in to allow it to interact with Microsoft Office 2016 programs.

> ✓ **TIP** Be careful when downloading add-ins from websites other than those you know and trust. Add-ins are executable files that can easily be used to spread viruses and otherwise wreak havoc on your computer. For this reason, default settings in the Trust Center intervene when you attempt to download or run add-ins.

Information about the add-ins that are installed on your computer, and access to manage them, is available from the Add-ins page of the PowerPoint Options dialog box.

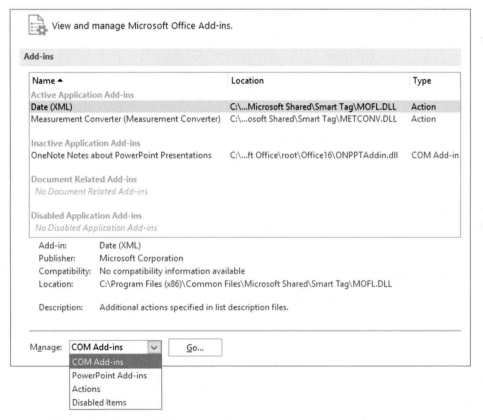

The Add-ins page displays installed add-ins of all types

11

Each type of add-in has its own management interface. You can add and remove add-ins, turn off installed add-ins, and enable add-ins that have been disabled.

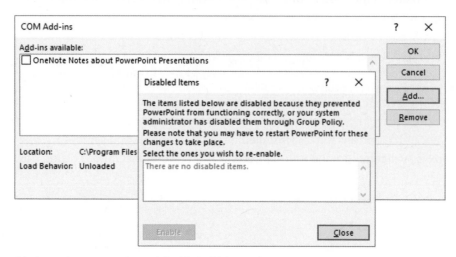

Display and manage active and disabled add-ins

Many add-ins install themselves, but to use some add-ins, you must first install them on your computer and then load them into your computer's memory.

To display management options for a type of add-in

1. Display the **Add-Ins** page of the **PowerPoint Options** dialog box.

2. In the **Manage** list at the bottom of the page, click the type of add-in you want to manage. Then click the adjacent **Go** button.

To install an add-in

1. Display the dialog box for the type of add-in you want to manage.

2. In the dialog box, click **Add** or **Add New**.

3. In the **Add Add-In** dialog box, navigate to the folder where the add-in you want to install is stored, and double-click its name.

4. In the list of available add-ins in the **Add-In** dialog box, select the check box of the new add-in, and then click **OK** or **Load** to make the add-in available for use in PowerPoint.

Configure Trust Center options

The Trust Center is a separate multipage dialog box in which you can configure security and privacy settings. You open the Trust Center from the Trust Center page of the PowerPoint Options dialog box.

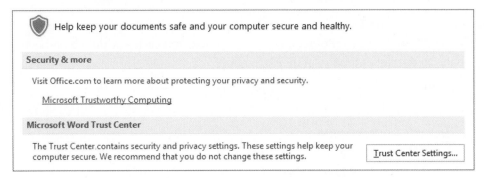

Continue at your own risk

The Trust Center settings aren't exposed directly on the page; you must click a button next to a warning informing you that you shouldn't change any of the settings. It's certainly true that if you don't take care when modifying the Trust Center settings, you could expose PowerPoint, your computer, and your network to malicious software. It's more common to modify these settings in Word than in PowerPoint, but review the available settings so you can evaluate whether any of them would be appropriate to change in your specific situation.

The Trust Center has the following 11 pages of options that you can configure:

- Trusted Publishers

- Trusted Locations

- Trusted Documents

- Trusted Add-in Catalogs

- Add-ins

- ActiveX Settings

- Macro Settings

11

- Protected View

- Message Bar

- File Block Settings

- Privacy Options (Trust Center)

When you first open the Trust Center from the Backstage view, the Macro Settings page is active. As in the PowerPoint Options dialog box, you click a page tab name in the left pane to display that page in the right pane.

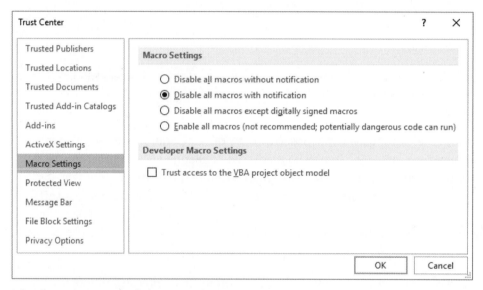

It is safest to run macros only from trusted sources

Most pages display options that are very specific to the page name. When you're working in PowerPoint, some circumstances will send you directly to this dialog box—for example, if you open a presentation that contains macros, and then click the info bar to enable them, PowerPoint takes you to this page.

Many of the Trust Center options are beyond the scope of any needs that you'd usually have when creating presentations. Some of those that might be of interest are those that make it easier to work in presentations that you trust, but that PowerPoint might not know are safe.

When you open a presentation from an online location (such as a cloud storage location or email message) or from a location that has been deemed unsafe, PowerPoint opens the file in Protected view, with most editing functions disabled. The purpose of this is to prevent any malicious code that is embedded in the file from gaining access to your computer. If you're uncertain about the origin of a file that you're opening, you can choose to open the file in Protected view.

In Protected view, the title bar displays *Read-Only* in brackets to the right of the file name, and a yellow banner at the top of the content pane provides information about why the file has been opened in Protected view. If you know that the presentation is from a safe location or sender, and you want to edit the file content, you can choose to enable editing.

If you find that you frequently need to edit presentations that open in Protected view, you can modify options on three pages of the Trust Center to affect this:

- If you want to open any presentation that is stored in a specific location without going into Protected view, you can add that folder (and its subfolders, if you want) to your Trusted Locations list.

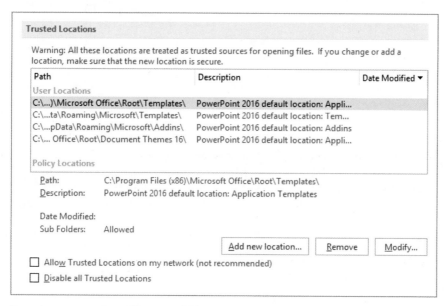

Trust the contents of specific storage folders

If you want to trust folders on other computers on your network, you must first specifically choose that option. Otherwise, when you try to add a network folder as a trusted location, the Trust Center displays a message that it is not permitted by your current security settings. Before selecting the option to allow network locations, consider what people or computers have access to the network locations you intend to allow, and whether the locations are secure or could host malicious content.

- If you want to be able to edit all files of a specific type (based on the file extension) you can modify the File Block settings.

Block specific types of files or permit editing in Protected view

- You can exclude an entire class of files (files originating from the Internet, stored in unsafe locations, or received as email attachments) from Protected view.

Turn off Protected view for a class of files

Before doing any of these things, you should carefully consider whether the "rule" you're making will always yield the results you want.

If you frequently work with a specific PowerPoint presentation that contains active content, and you feel that the security prompts are unnecessarily slowing you down, you can choose to trust the presentation. When you do so, it is added to the Trusted Documents list. You can manage the Trusted Documents list from the Trusted Documents page of the Trust Center. You can stipulate whether to trust presentations that aren't stored locally, turn off the Trusted Documents function completely (to stop trusting all presentations), or clear the Trusted Documents list to start over.

Trusted Documents

Warning: Trusted Documents open without any security prompts for macros, ActiveX controls and other types of active content in the document. For a Trusted Document, you will not be prompted the next time you open the document, even if new active content was added to the document or changes were made to existing active content. Therefore, you should only trust documents if you trust the source.

☑ Allow documents on a network to be trusted

☐ Disable Trusted Documents

Clear all Trusted Documents so that they are no longer trusted   [Clear]

If you experience trouble with a trusted presentation, you can reset the list here

Some, but not all, of the Trust Center pages include buttons that you can click to reset that set of options to the defaults, so take care when making changes; if you're uncertain whether you should invoke a change, click Cancel to close the Trust Center without committing to the changes.

As with options in the PowerPoint Options dialog box, you should take the time to familiarize yourself with the Trust Center settings so you know what changes it is possible to make, in the event that it is appropriate to do so in your computing environment.

11

To open the Trust Center

1. In the left pane of the Backstage view, click the **Trust Center** page tab.

2. On the **Trust Center** page, click the **Trust Center Settings** button.

Skills review

In this chapter, you learned how to:

- Change default PowerPoint options
- Customize the Quick Access Toolbar
- Customize the ribbon
- Manage add-in and security options

Practice tasks

No practice files are necessary to complete the practice tasks in this chapter.

Change default PowerPoint options

Start PowerPoint, display any presentation, and then perform the following tasks:

1. Open the **PowerPoint Options** dialog box.

2. Explore each page of the dialog box.

3. On the **General**, **Proofing**, **Save**, **Language**, and **Advanced** pages, do the following:

   - Notice the sections and the options in each section.

   - Note the options that apply only to the current file.

   - Modify the options on the page as necessary to fit the way you work.

4. Close the **PowerPoint Options** dialog box.

Customize the Quick Access Toolbar

Start PowerPoint, display any presentation, and then perform the following tasks:

1. Move the Quick Access Toolbar below the ribbon. Consider the merits of this location versus the original location.

2. From the **Customize Quick Access Toolbar** menu, add the **Sort Ascending** command to the Quick Access Toolbar.

3. From the **Insert** tab of the ribbon, add the following commands to the Quick Access Toolbar:

   - From the **Slides** group, add the **New Slide** command (the arrow half, not the default button half).

   - From the **Text** group, add the **WordArt** command.

   Notice that each of the commands is represented on the Quick Access Toolbar exactly as it is on the ribbon. Clicking the New Slide arrow displays a list, and clicking WordArt displays a gallery.

4. From the **Show** group on the **View** tab, add the **Ruler** command and the **Gridlines** command to the Quick Access Toolbar. Notice that the commands are represented on the Quick Access Toolbar as check boxes.

5. Point to the commands you added to the Quick Access Toolbar and then to the same commands on the View tab. Notice that ScreenTips for commands on the Quick Access Toolbar are identical to those for commands on the ribbon.

6. Display the **Quick Access Toolbar** page of the **PowerPoint Options** dialog box, and then do the following:

    - In the left pane, display the commands that appear on the **Slide Show** tab.

    - Add the **Hide Slide** button from the Slide Show tab to the Quick Access Toolbar.

    - In the right pane, move the **New Slide** button to the bottom of the list so that it will be the rightmost button on the Quick Access Toolbar (immediately to the left of the Customize Quick Access Toolbar button).

    - Insert a separator between the original commands and the commands you added in this task set.

    - Insert two separators between the **WordArt** and **Ruler** commands.

7. Close the **PowerPoint Options** dialog box and observe your customized Quick Access Toolbar. Note the way that a single separator sets off commands, and the way that a double separator sets off commands.

8. Redisplay the **Quick Access Toolbar** page of the **PowerPoint Options** dialog box.

9. Reset the Quick Access Toolbar to its default configuration, and then close the dialog box. Notice that resetting the Quick Access Toolbar does not change its location.

10. Close the presentation without saving it.

Customize the ribbon

Start PowerPoint, display any presentation, and then perform the following tasks:

1. Display the **Customize Ribbon** page of the **PowerPoint Options** dialog box.

2. Remove the **Review** tab from the ribbon, and add the **Developer** tab (if it isn't already shown).

3. Create a custom tab and name it MyShapes.

4. Move the **MyShapes** tab to the top of the right pane so that it will be the left-most optional ribbon tab (immediately to the right of the File tab).

5. Change the name of the custom group on the **MyShapes** tab to Curved Shapes, and select a curved or circular icon to represent the group.

6. Create another custom group on the **MyShapes** tab. Name the group Angular Shapes, and select a square or triangular icon to represent the group.

7. In the **Choose commands from** list, click **Commands Not in the Ribbon**. From the list, add the **Arc** and **Oval** commands to the **Curved Shapes** group. Then add the **Isosceles Triangle** and **Rectangle** commands to the **Angular Shapes** group.

8. Close the **PowerPoint Options** dialog box and display your custom tab. Click the **Arc** command, and then drag on the page to draw an arc.

9. Change the width of the app window to collapse at least one custom group, and verify that the group button displays the icon you selected.

10. Restore the app window to its original width and redisplay the **Customize Ribbon** page of the **PowerPoint Options** dialog box.

11. Reset the ribbon to its default configuration, and then close the dialog box.

12. Close the presentation without saving it.

Manage add-ins and security options

Start PowerPoint, display any presentation, and then perform the following tasks:

1. Open the **PowerPoint Options** dialog box.

2. Display the **Add-ins** page, and then do the following:

   - Review the add-ins that are installed on your computer.

   - Notice the types of add-ins that are active, and display the dialog box for that type of add-in.

   - Notice add-ins that are turned on or off, and modify the setting if you want to.

   - Close the dialog box.

3. Display the **Trust Center** page, and then do the following:

   - Open the Trust Center.

   - Review the settings therein, but don't make any changes.

   - Close the Trust Center.

4. Close the **PowerPoint Options** dialog box.

Create custom presentation elements

In addition to using the built-in design elements of PowerPoint 2016, you can create your own designs, themes, theme color and font sets, layouts, and templates. This makes it easy to create consistent presentations that reflect the branding elements—such as colors, fonts, and visual imagery—associated with your organization.

Creating a fully custom PowerPoint presentation template involves two processes. The layout of content on slides is controlled by slide layouts, and the colors, fonts, and visual effect styles of the presentation are controlled by the theme. The slide layouts and theme are both part of the slide master. To create a custom template, you create a theme, modify the slide master and its slide layouts, and then save the modified package as a template. You can reuse the custom theme in Microsoft Word documents and Microsoft Excel workbooks, and incorporate it into custom templates for those apps.

This chapter guides you through procedures related to creating custom themes, customizing slide masters and layouts, and saving custom presentation templates.

In this chapter

- Create custom themes
- Customize slide masters and layouts
- Save custom presentation templates

Practice files

For this chapter, use the practice files from the PowerPoint2016SBS\Ch12 folder. For practice file download instructions, see the introduction.

Create custom themes

As you learned in Chapter 3, "Create and manage slides," a simple, yet elegant, way to dress up a presentation is to apply a theme that makes the colors, fonts, formatting, graphic effects, and other elements consistent across the entire presentation. Understanding theme colors and theme fonts can help you create professional-looking presentations that use an appealing balance of color and text. Every theme includes a color set, a font set, and an effect set.

The color set includes 12 complementary colors that are designed to be used for the following elements of a slide:

- **Text/background** These four colors are for dark text on a light background or light text on a dark background.

- **Accent 1 through Accent 6** These six colors are for objects other than text.

- **Hyperlink** This color is to draw attention to hyperlinks.

- **Followed Hyperlink** This color is to indicate visited hyperlinks.

The Theme Colors menu displays 8 of the 12 theme colors, and the Theme Colors gallery displays a palette of 6 light to dark variations of 10 of the theme colors. (The two hyperlink colors do not appear in this palette.) If you like all the elements of a theme except its color scheme, you can choose a different predefined set of theme colors without otherwise affecting the overall look of the theme.

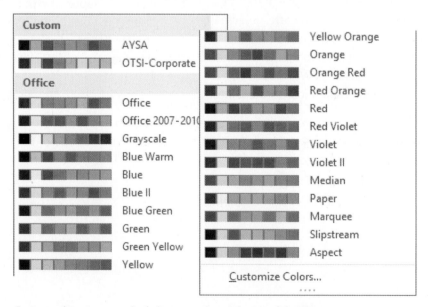

Custom color sets appear in their own section at the top of the Themes menu

If none of the sets of theme colors is exactly what you're looking for, you can create your own.

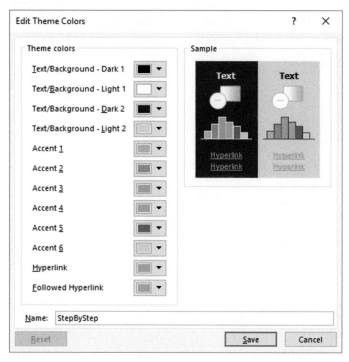

The order in which you select theme colors specifies the elements that they affect

 SEE ALSO For information about using non-theme colors, see the sidebar "Non-theme colors" in Chapter 3, "Create and manage slides."

The color set of the theme is available from all the color galleries in the presentation. Changing the color set automatically updates all presentation elements that are formatted with theme colors. Any elements that have colors from outside of the Theme Colors palette do not change.

 TIP When you change the color set, the colors in the Theme Colors palette are replaced with the colors that are in the same column of the new color set.

In addition to changing the theme colors, you can change the theme fonts. The Fonts gallery—which you can display from either the Variants group on the Design tab in Normal view or the Background group on the Slide Master tab in Slide Master view—shows a list of all the predefined combinations. In each combination, the first font (called the *heading font*) is used for slide titles, and the second font (called the *body font*) is used for other slide text.

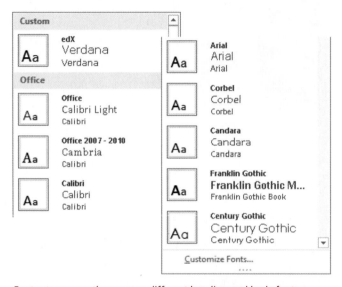

Font sets can use the same or different heading and body fonts

If the specific pairing of fonts that you want to use isn't available in the Office fonts list, or if your organization uses a font that doesn't come with Office, you can create a custom font set.

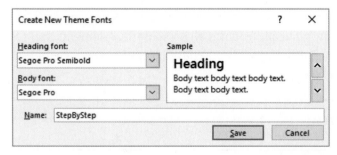

You can use any font that is installed on your computer and available within Office apps

> **✓ TIP** When you create a new theme color set or font set, you do so by modifying an existing set. If an existing color set contains colors that you want to use in your custom color set, you can save time by choosing that color set as a starting point.

Each theme also has a set of theme effects. You can't create your own effect set, but you can choose a different set from the Effects gallery.

After you choose or create the color set, font set, and effect set, you save them as a custom theme. If you intend to use the custom theme in most or all of the presentations you create, you can set it as the default theme.

You can create custom color sets, font sets, and themes from the Design tab in any of the presentation development views, or from any of the Master views. Regardless of where you create these elements, they're available from within all the Office apps.

To create a custom theme color set

1. Do the following to open the Create New Theme Colors dialog box:

   a. Display the presentation in any development view.

   b. On the **Design** tab, in the **Variants** group, click the **More** button to expand the Variants gallery and menu.

   c. On the **Variants** menu, click **Colors**, and then click **Customize Colors**.

   Or

   a. Display the presentation in any Master view.

   b. On the **Slide Master** tab, the **Handout Master** tab, or the **Notes Master** tab, in the **Background** group, click the **Colors** button, and then click **Customize Colors**.

2. For each color in the **Theme colors** section, click the current color swatch, and then do either of the following:

   - In the **Theme Colors** or **Standard Colors** palette, click the color swatch you want to assign to that element.

12

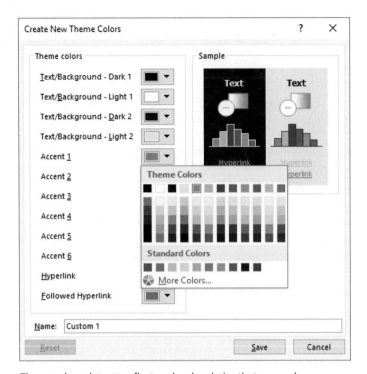

The sample updates to reflect each color choice that you make

- Click **More Colors** to open the Colors dialog box.

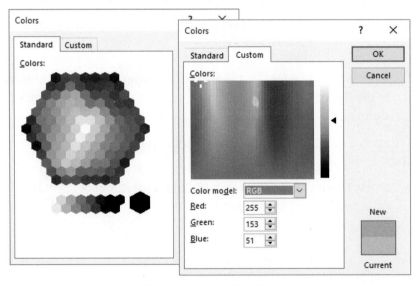

Choose a standard color or define one by using RGB values

Click a color swatch on the **Standard** tab, or define the RGB or HSL values of the color you want to use on the Custom tab. Then click **OK**.

> **SEE ALSO** For more information about working with themes and colors, see "Apply themes" in Chapter 3, "Create and manage slides."

3. In the **Name** box at the bottom of the **Create New Theme Colors** dialog box, enter a name for the new theme color set.

4. Click **Save** to create the color set and apply it to the current presentation.

To edit a custom color set

1. On the **Colors** menu, in the **Custom** section, right-click the color set, and then click **Edit**.

To delete a custom color set

1. On the **Colors** menu, in the **Custom** section, right-click the color set, click **Delete**, and then click **Yes** to confirm the deletion.

To create a custom theme font set

1. Do the following to open the Create New Theme Fonts dialog box:

   a. Display the presentation in any development view.

   b. On the **Design** tab, in the **Variants** group, click the **More** button to expand the Variants gallery and menu.

   c. On the **Variants** menu, click **Fonts**, and then click **Customize Fonts**.

   Or

   a. Display the presentation in any Master view.

   b. On the **Slide Master** tab, the **Handout Master** tab, or the **Notes Master** tab, in the **Background** group, click the **Fonts** button, and then click **Customize Fonts**.

12

2. In the **Heading font** list, click the font you want to use for slide titles and subtitles, and for document headings when the font set is applied in a Word document.

3. In the **Body font** list, click the font you want to use for slide text content (such as lists) and for normal paragraphs, lists, tables, and other document content when the font set is applied in Word.

4. In the **Name** box, enter a name for the new theme font set.

5. Click **Save** to create the font set and apply it to the current presentation.

To edit a custom font set

1. On the **Font** menu, in the **Custom** section, right-click the font set, and then click **Edit**.

To delete a custom font set

1. On the **Font** menu, in the **Custom** section, right-click the font set, click **Delete**, and then click **Yes** to confirm the deletion.

To select a theme effect set

1. Do the following to display the Effects gallery:

   a. Display the presentation in any development view.

   b. On the **Design** tab, in the **Variants** group, click the **More** button to expand the Variants gallery and menu.

   c. On the **Variants** menu, click **Effects**.

   Or

   a. Display the presentation in any Master view.

   b. On the **Slide Master** tab, the **Handout Master** tab, or the **Notes Master** tab, in the **Background** group, click the **Effects** button.

2. In the **Effects** gallery, click the effect set that you want to use with the theme.

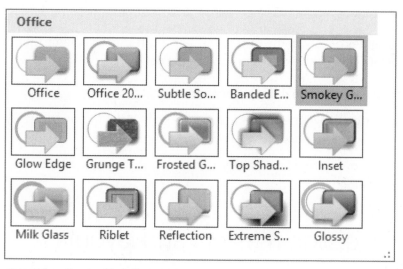

Choose from the 15 Office effect sets

To save the current theme elements as a custom theme

1. Do the following to open the Save Current Theme dialog box:

   a. Display the presentation in any development view.

   b. On the **Design** tab, in the **Themes** group, click the **More** button to display the Themes gallery and menu.

   c. On the **Themes** menu, click **Save Current Theme**.

   Or

   a. Display the presentation in any Master view.

   b. On the **Slide Master** tab, the **Handout Master** tab, or the **Notes Master** tab, in the **Edit Theme** group, click the **Themes** button, and then click **Save Current Theme**.

   > **TIP** The dialog box displays the contents of the Document Themes folder, which is located at C:\Users\<*user name*>\AppData\Roaming\Microsoft\Templates \Document Themes. Custom theme colors and theme fonts are saved in subfolders of this folder so that they are available in their galleries for use in other presentations, documents, and workbooks.

2. In the **File name** box, enter a name for the custom theme, and then click **Save**.

12

To delete a custom theme

1. In the **Themes** gallery, in the **Custom** section, right-click the theme thumbnail, click **Delete**, and then click **Yes** to confirm the deletion.

To set a custom theme as the default theme

1. On the **Design** tab, in the **Themes** group, click the **More** button to display the Themes gallery and menu.

2. In the **Custom** section of the gallery, right-click the theme, and then click **Set as Default Theme**.

Customize slide masters and layouts

When you create a presentation, the slides take on the characteristics of the template on which the presentation is based. PowerPoint templates use *masters* to determine their basic design. By default, each PowerPoint presentation has three masters:

-   **Slide master** This set of masters controls the look of all the slides in a presentation, including the theme, text placement, background graphics, and other slide elements. The set contains a master design for most of the layouts you are likely to need when using that particular template.

-   **Handout master** This master controls the look of any handouts you prepare for distribution to your audience.

-   **Notes master** This master controls the look of slide notes in Notes Page view and if you choose to print them.

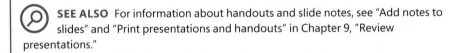

SEE ALSO For information about handouts and slide notes, see "Add notes to slides" and "Print presentations and handouts" in Chapter 9, "Review presentations."

This topic provides information specifically about slide masters, but you can use the procedures described in this topic to work with handout masters and notes masters.

Each slide master has one master layout that is the basis for one or more slide layouts. (For example, most slide masters include slide layouts for presentation title slides, section headers, and content slides that usually include a title and one or more content placeholders.) A PowerPoint presentation can have multiple slide masters if they're necessary to define multiple base slides.

The master layout defines the theme and default slide background, and can define locations and formatting of placeholders for the title, text, date, slide number, and footer that can be part of each slide layout. The slide layouts define the location and formatting of the slide content, and the types of content placeholders on the slide.

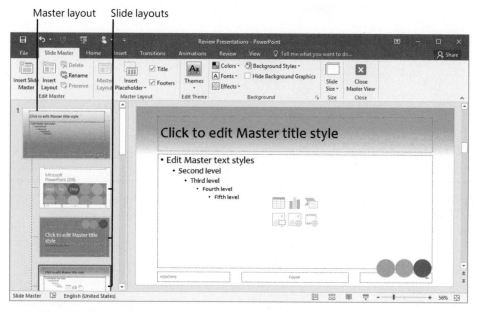

Each slide master includes one master slide and multiple slide layouts

The master layout and slide layouts are visible in Slide Master view, where you can edit them. Thumbnails of the slide layouts are visible in Normal view and Slide Sorter view, where you can apply them. In the presentation development views, the slide layouts are available on the Home tab from the New Slide menu (to create a slide that has a specific layout) and from the Layout menu (to change the layout of an existing slide).

12

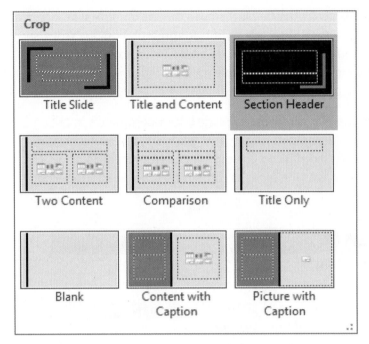

Each slide layout has a unique title

> 🔍 **SEE ALSO** For information about creating slides from slide layouts, applying slide layouts, and resetting slides to slide layouts, see "Add and remove slides" in Chapter 3, "Create and manage slides."

When you modify the slide master, you can make changes to the master layout or to the individual slide layouts. The best place to make a change depends on the type of change and whether you want it to affect all slides or only some slides. Here are some guidelines:

- On the master layout, you can specify which base slide elements the master layout controls, modify the placeholders for those elements, format the placeholder content, format the background of all slides, and add fixed text and images that appear on all slides. Any change that you make to the master layout affects those elements on the associated slide layouts, unless you customize the elements for the specific slide layout.

- On the individual slide layouts, you can add, modify, and hide placeholders; format placeholder content; format the individual slide background; and add fixed text or images that will appear only on slides based on that layout.

When editing a slide master in Slide Master view, you work with the commands on the Slide Master tab to create, delete, and rename slide layouts; insert placeholders; hide or display base elements; and manage theme elements and slide backgrounds. You can also set the slide size from this tab, as you can from the Design tab in the development views.

The items available in the Master Layout group depend on whether a master layout or slide layout is selected

A subset of the commands that you use in the development views are available on the other ribbon tabs in Slide Master view. You can use these commands to insert and format placeholder text, images, transitions, and animations. You can also use the commands on the Review tab to review any boilerplate text that you're including on the slide masters rather than on the slides. The Design and Slide Show tabs are hidden in Slide Master view.

You can easily develop high-quality presentations without ever venturing into Slide Master view, but for maximum efficiency, any change that you want to make consistently throughout a presentation should be made on the slide master.

Here are some of the tasks that you might want to accomplish that are most efficient to perform on the slide master rather than on individual slides:

- Move or resize a content placeholder
- Change the default size, font, or position of text in a placeholder
- Add an element, such as a logo, to every slide or to every slide of a specific slide layout
- Create a custom slide layout that arranges or formats content differently than the existing slide layouts

Changes to the slide master do not affect the master layout or slide layouts in the original design template that is available from the New page of the Backstage view or the Themes gallery on the Design tab.

12

To switch to Slide Master view

1. On the **View** tab, in the **Master Views** group, click **Slide Master**.

To specify the slide elements that are controlled by the slide master

1. In Slide Master view, select the master slide (not a slide layout).

2. On the **Slide Master** tab, in the **Master Layout** group, click the **Master Layout** button.

The slide master can control these elements for the associated layouts

3. In the **Master Layout** dialog box, select the check boxes of the elements you want the slide master to control. Then click **OK**.

To apply a different theme to a slide master

1. On the **Slide Master** tab, in the **Edit Theme** group, click **Themes**, and then click the theme you want to apply.

To change theme elements of a slide master

1. On the **Slide Master** tab, in the **Background** group, do any of the following:

   - In the **Colors** list, click the color set you want to use.

   - In the **Fonts** list, click the font set you want to use.

   - In the **Effects** gallery, click the effect style you want to use.

To change the background of one or more slide layouts

1. Do either of the following:

    -   To change the background of one slide layout, display that slide layout.

    -   To change the background of all slide layouts, select the master slide.

     TIP You can make changes to one slide layout and then apply the change to all of them afterward, from the Format Background pane.

2. On the **Slide Master** tab, in the **Background** group, click the **Background Styles** button, and then do either of the following:

    -   Click one of the 12 preconfigured background styles.

        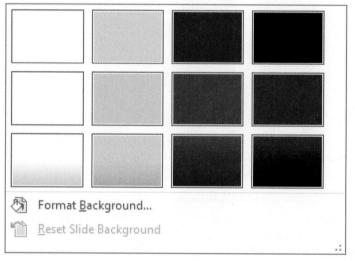

        The preconfigured background styles are based on the four Text/Background theme colors

    -   Click **Format Background** to open the Format Background pane, in which you can select the fill style and specify the fill color, picture, texture, or pattern.

12

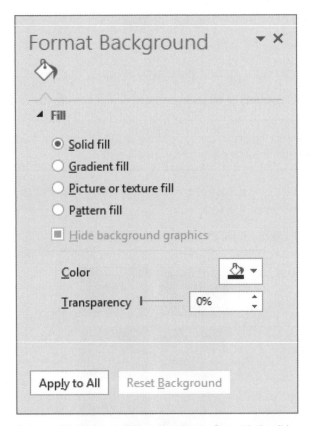

Select a slide background that doesn't interfere with the slide content

 SEE ALSO For information about working in the Format Background pane, see "Change slide backgrounds" in Chapter 3, "Create and manage slides."

3. If you modify the background of one slide and then want to apply your changes to the others, open the **Format Background** pane, and then click **Apply to All**.

To remove the slide master background from a slide layout

1. Display the slide layout.

2. In the **Background** group, select the **Hide Background Graphics** check box.

To add a placeholder to a slide layout

1. Display the slide layout you want to modify.

2. On the **Slide Master** tab, in the **Master Layout** group, do either of the following:

- If you want to insert a content placeholder that defines multilevel list formatting and includes buttons for inserting text, tables, charts, SmartArt graphics, pictures, and media clips, click the **Insert Placeholder** button, or click the **Insert Placeholder** arrow, and then click **Content**.

- If you want to insert a placeholder that supports a specific type of content, click the **Insert Placeholder** arrow, and then click the content type.

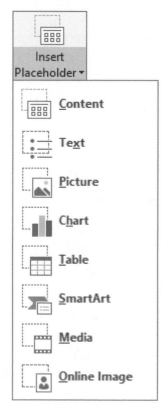

Use content-specific placeholders to guide the creation of slide content

3. Point to the slide where you want the upper-left corner of the placeholder. The cursor shape is a plus sign.

4. Do either of the following:

- Click the slide to insert a one-inch square placeholder.

- Drag down and to the right to draw a placeholder.

When you release the mouse button, the placeholder is selected for editing and the Format tool tab is active.

To format a placeholder

1. Select the placeholder, and then do any of the following:

   - ·To move the placeholder, drag it or press the arrow keys.
   - To resize the placeholder, drag the placeholder sizing handles, or set the **Height** and **Width** in the **Size** group.
   - To rotate the placeholder, drag the placeholder rotation handle, or click the **Rotate** command in the **Arrange** group on the Format tool tab, and then click a specific rotation.
   - To format the placeholder outline, fill, or visual effects, use the commands in the **Shape Styles** group.

To format the text in a placeholder

1. Do either of the following:

   - To modify all the text in the placeholder, point to the placeholder border and then click to select it.
   - To modify specific text within a placeholder, select that text.

2. Apply character and paragraph formatting from the Mini Toolbar, by using commands on the **Home** tab, or by using keyboard shortcuts.

To create a slide layout

1. Do either of the following:

   - To create a copy of an existing layout, in the **Thumbnails** pane, right-click a slide layout that you want to copy, and then click **Duplicate Layout**.

     The duplicate layout has the same name as the original layout, but is preceded by 1_ (or a higher number if the copied layout name started with a number).

   - To create a generic layout, select the slide layout after which you want to insert the new slide layout. Then on the **Slide Master** tab, in the **Edit Master** group, click the **Insert Layout** button to insert a generic slide.

The new layout has the name *Custom Layout Layout* (or if that name already exists, the new layout name is preceded by a number and underscore).

To display the name and usage of a slide layout

1. In the **Thumbnails** pane, point to a slide layout to display a ScreenTip that contains the slide layout name and the slide numbers that use the slide layout.

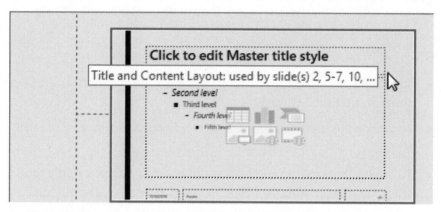

Quickly display the layout name and slides that use it

To rename a slide layout

1. Select the slide layout.

2. On the **Slide Master** tab, in the **Edit Master** group, click the **Rename** button to open the Rename Layout dialog box.

3. In the **Layout name** box, enter a new name for the layout, and then click **Rename**.

To manage the display of the title and footer on a slide layout

1. On the **Slide Master** tab, in the **Master Layout** group, select or clear the **Title** and **Footers** check boxes to specify whether to include these elements on the slide layout.

To manage slide master footer content

1. On the **Insert** tab, in the **Text** group, click the **Header & Footer** button.

12

2. On the **Slide** tab of the **Header and Footer** dialog box, do any of the following:

- Select the **Date and time** check box. Then click **Update automatically**, and click the format you want to display the date and time in, or click **Fixed**, and then enter the date and time as you want to display them.

- Select the **Slide number** check box.

- Select the **Footer** check box, and then in the text box, enter the text you want to display at the bottom of the page.

3. Do any of the following to change the default scope of the footer:

- To include the footer elements on the **Title Slide** layout, clear the **Don't show on title slide** check box.

- To display the specific footer selections only on the current slide, click **Apply**.

- To display the specific footer selections on all slides, click **Apply to All**.

 IMPORTANT Regardless of your selection, the footer content is shown only on slide layouts that have the Footers check box in the Master Layout group selected.

To delete one or more slide layouts from a slide master

1. In the **Thumbnails** pane, select the slide layout or layouts you want to remove. Then do any of the following:

- On the **Slide Master** tab, in the **Edit Master** group, click the **Delete** button.

- Right-click the selection, and then click **Delete Layout**.

- Press the **Delete** key.

 TIP Only slide layouts that are not currently in use can be deleted. Pointing to a slide layout displays, in a ScreenTip, a list of slides to which the layout is applied.

To close Slide Master view and return to the presentation

1. Do either of the following:

- On the **Slide Master** tab, in the **Close** group, click the **Close Master View** button.

- On the **View Shortcuts** toolbar at the right end of the status bar, click any view button.

Save custom presentation templates

You can save any presentation as a custom template, which will be available to you on the New page of the Backstage view. Depending on the version of PowerPoint 2016 you're running, you must click the Custom or Personal heading to display the custom templates. The additional heading is available only after you have saved a presentation template to the default personal templates location.

Access your custom templates by clicking the Custom or Personal link

By default, PowerPoint saves custom templates to the Custom Office Templates subfolder of the Documents folder associated with your user account. If you want to change the default location (for example, if you want to save them in the Public folder

12

structure or a shared folder so they're available to multiple users or from multiple computers), you can do so. (You can always save the custom templates elsewhere, but for them to appear in the Custom view of the New page, you must change the default personal templates location.)

To save a presentation as a template

1. Remove any content that you don't want to save with the template.

2. On the **Save As** page of the Backstage view, click **Browse** to open the Save As dialog box. (You don't have to select a location.)

3. In the **Save as type** list, click **PowerPoint Template (*.potx)** to change the location to the default personal template location.

4. In the **File name** box, enter a name for the custom template. Then click **Save**.

To create a presentation based on a custom template

1. Display the **New** page of the Backstage view.

2. Click the **Custom** or **Personal** link near the top of the page, and then do either of the following:

   - Click the thumbnail of the template you want to use, and then click **Create** in the dialog box that opens.

   - Double-click the thumbnail of the template you want to use.

To set the default personal templates location

1. In the Backstage view, click **Options** to open the PowerPoint Options dialog box.

2. In the left pane of the **PowerPoint Options** dialog box, click the **Save** page tab.

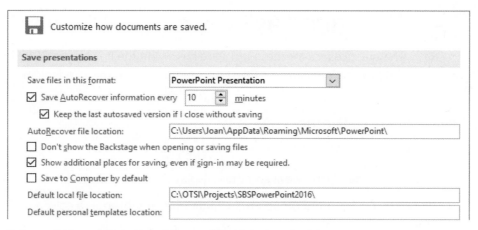

Enter any folder path in the Default Personal Templates Location box

3. In the **Save presentations** section of the page, in the **Default Personal Templates Location** box, enter the folder you want to use. Then click **OK**.

Skills review

In this chapter, you learned how to:

- Create custom themes
- Customize slide masters and layouts
- Save custom presentation templates

12

Practice tasks

The practice files for these tasks are located in the PowerPoint2016SBS\
Ch12 folder. You can save the results of the tasks in the same folder.

Create custom themes

Open the CreateThemes presentation, and then perform the following tasks:

1. Switch to Slide Master view, and then display the master layout.

2. From the **Background** group on the **Slide Master** tab, apply a color set of your choice.

3. Create a custom color set based on the color set you chose. Change at least one of the colors, and notice that the preview image reflects the change. Save the custom color set as **MyColors**.

4. Apply the **Candara** font set.

5. Create a custom font set that uses **Franklin Gothic Medium** as the heading font and Candara as the body font. Save the custom color set as **MyFonts**.

6. Apply the **Glossy** effect style.

7. Save the new color, font, and effect combination as a custom theme named MySlideTheme.

8. Save and close the presentation.

Customize slide masters and layouts

Open the CustomizeMasters presentation, and then perform the following tasks:

1. Display slide **2**, and then switch to Slide Master view.

2. Change the default slide size to **Widescreen**.

3. Configure the slide background to display the **Background** picture from the practice file folder. Set the transparency of the picture to **70%**.

4. Apply the background picture to all slide layouts in the slide master.

5. Remove the date from the master layout.

6. Increase the font size of the placeholder title text to the next largest font size.

7. Remove the background from the title slide. Then remove the Footer and page number from the title slide, leaving only the date in the footer area.

8. Insert a new slide layout that has two small picture placeholders on the left side of the slide, and a text placeholder on the right side of the slide.

9. Rename the new slide layout **Two Pictures and Text**.

Save custom presentation templates

Open the SaveTemplates presentation, and then perform the following tasks:

 TIP This task assumes that you haven't previously designated a default personal templates folder. If you have already done so, you can do steps 1-3 and 7-9.

1. Remove existing text and other content from the slides.

2. Save the presentation as a template named **MySlideTemplate** in the default folder (**Custom Office Templates**).

3. Close the file.

4. Create a new presentation based on the template.

5. Close the new presentation without saving it.

6. Delete the template from your Custom Office Templates folder if you want to.

Save and share presentations

Many presentations are developed collaboratively by a team of people. You might be the lead developer of some presentations that are reviewed by others, or you might be a reviewer of some presentations that have been developed by colleagues. With PowerPoint 2016, you can easily email a presentation to someone for review, or you can present it online for a group collaboration session. If you want to send it to someone who doesn't have PowerPoint 2016 installed on his or her computer, you can save the presentation in a different file format. If you want to be sure that only authorized people can review a presentation, you can assign a password.

When reviewing a PowerPoint presentation on a computer, you can insert comments and queries, and respond to comments made by others. If the presentation is saved in a shared location, several people can make changes that PowerPoint seamlessly incorporates into the same file.

This chapter guides you through procedures related to saving presentations in other formats, sharing presentations from PowerPoint, restricting access to presentations by using passwords, adding and reviewing comments, and coauthoring presentations with other people.

In this chapter

- Save presentations in other formats
- Share presentations from PowerPoint
- Restrict access by using passwords
- Add and review comments
- Coauthor presentations

Practice files

For this chapter, use the practice files from the PowerPoint2016SBS\Ch13 folder. For practice file download instructions, see the introduction.

Save presentations in other formats

In Chapter 2, "Create and manage presentations," you learned about saving PowerPoint presentations as files on your local computer or in an online storage location. When you've completed a presentation and want to share it with other people, there are some situations in which it is advantageous or necessary to save the presentation in a different format. Some of the options to consider include these:

- **PowerPoint Show** A presentation that runs only as a slide show. The slide show can be viewed in PowerPoint or in the free PowerPoint Reader app.

- **Video** A video presentation can be saved in MPEG-4 or WMV format. It supports animations, transitions, and media playback, and can include your recorded narration and slide timings.

- **Picture presentation** This format saves each slide as one picture. The slide components aren't active and can't be edited.

- **PDF or XPS** A file that people can view but not interact with. The file can include the entire presentation or only select slides.

All these formats are available from the Export page of the Backstage view and some from the File Type list in the Save As dialog box. The Export page offers more information about the file types and is a bit more user friendly.

> **SEE ALSO** For information about packaging presentations for CD, see the sidebar "Prepare presentations for travel" in Chapter 10, "Prepare and deliver presentations." For information about creating handouts, see "Print presentations and handouts" in Chapter 9, "Review presentations."

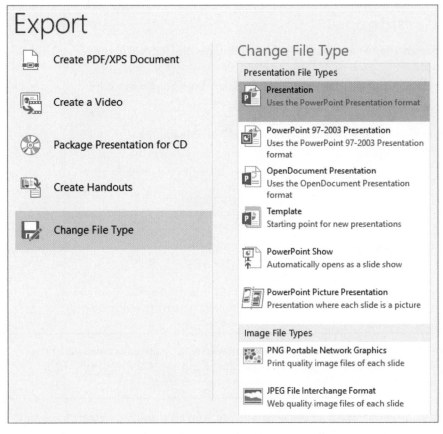

Consider which format will best suit your audience and delivery method

Creating a video of a PowerPoint slide show is a quite simple task. A benefit of a video is that viewers can see it exactly as you deliver it, with your narration and any animations and transitions you've incorporated. If you don't want or need to provide narration and slide timings, PowerPoint displays each slide for a length of time that you specify (five seconds is the default).

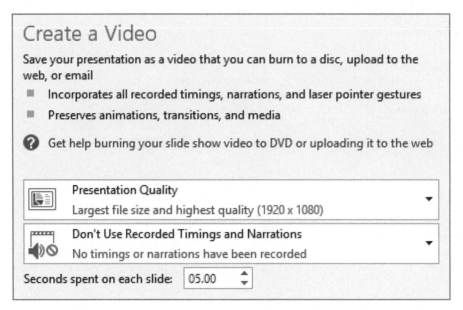

Creating a video preserves your work so viewers can appreciate all aspects of the slide show

> ✓ **TIP** Video files can be quite large if they contain media, so consider compressing the media before creating the video. For more information, see "Compress media to decrease file size" in Chapter 8, "Add sound and movement to slides."

When you save a presentation as a PDF or XPS file, you lose any animated elements of the presentation. You can include the entire presentation, or you can select slides. You make this selection from the Options dialog box, in which you can also specify whether to frame slides, include hidden slides, and include comments and markup.

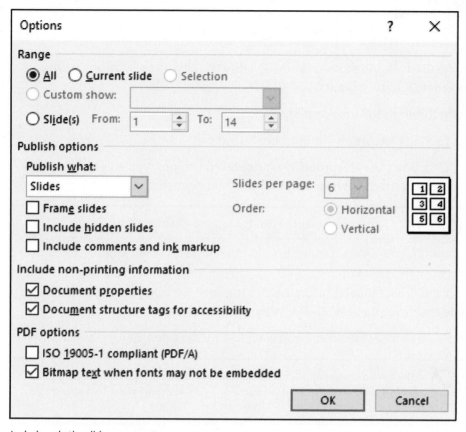

Include only the slides you want

To save a presentation as a PowerPoint Show

1. In the Backstage view, display the **Export** page, and then click **Change File Type**.

2. On the **Change File Type** page, click **PowerPoint Show**, and then click the **Save As** button to open the Save As dialog box with *PowerPoint Show* selected in the Save As Type box.

3. Navigate to the folder where you want to save the PowerPoint Show, and then click **Save**.

13

To save a presentation as a video

1. On the **Export** page of the Backstage view, click **Create a Video**.

2. In the **Create a Video** pane, in the **Quality** list, click **Presentation Quality**, **Internet Quality**, or **Low Quality**.

3. In the **Timings & Narrations** list, do either of the following:

   - Click **Use Recorded Timings and Narrations**.

   - Click **Don't Use Recorded Timings and Narrations**, and adjust the setting in the **Seconds spent on each slide** box as needed.

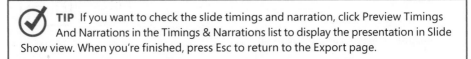

   TIP If you want to check the slide timings and narration, click Preview Timings And Narrations in the Timings & Narrations list to display the presentation in Slide Show view. When you're finished, press Esc to return to the Export page.

4. Click the **Create Video** button to open the **Save As** dialog box. In the **Save as type** list, click either **MPEG-4** or **Windows Media Video**.

5. Navigate to the folder where you want to save the video, and then click **Save**.

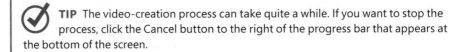

   TIP The video-creation process can take quite a while. If you want to stop the process, click the Cancel button to the right of the progress bar that appears at the bottom of the screen.

To save a presentation as a Picture Presentation

1. On the **Change File Type** page, click **PowerPoint Picture Presentation**, and then click the **Save As** button to open the Save As dialog box with *PowerPoint Picture Presentation* selected in the Save As Type box.

2. Navigate to the folder where you want to save the PowerPoint Picture Presentation, and then click **Save**.

3. Click **OK** to acknowledge the message that the Picture Presentation has been saved in the selected folder.

To save a presentation as a PDF or XPS file

1. On the **Export** page of the Backstage view, click **Create PDF/XPS Document**.

2. On the **Create a PDF/XPS Document** page, click the **Create PDF/XPS** button to open the Save As dialog box.

3. In the **Save as type** list, click **PDF Document** or **XPS Document**.

4. Navigate to the folder where you want to save the file, and then click **Publish**.

To save specific slides in PDF or XPS format

1. In Normal view or Slide Sorter view, select the slides you want to save in the file.

2. On the **Create a PDF/XPS Document** page, click the **Create PDF/XPS** button to open the **Save As** dialog box.

3. Click the **Options** button.

4. In the **Options** dialog box, in the **Range** area, click **Selection**. Then click **OK**.

5. In the **Save as type** list, click **PDF Document** or **XPS Document**.

6. Navigate to the folder where you want to save the file containing the selected slides, and then click **Publish**.

13

Share presentations from PowerPoint

When Microsoft Outlook is set as your default email app, you can send a presentation from PowerPoint while you're working in the file. You have the option of sending a copy of the file as a message attachment or, if the file is stored in a shared location, you can send a link to the file.

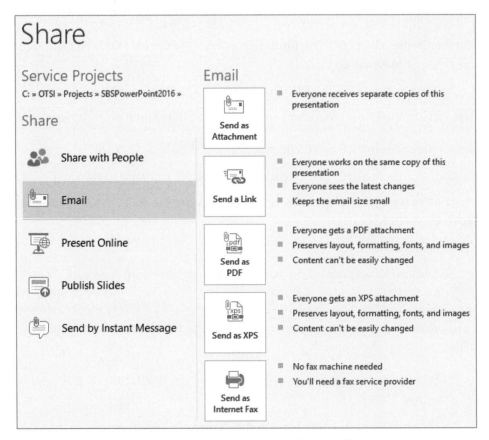

You can share an Office document as an attachment to an Outlook email message

> ⚠ **IMPORTANT** To use the Email sharing option, you must have Outlook installed and configured on your computer. If you're running another email app, the Email option will be available on the Share page of the Backstage view but might not generate an email message.

When you use the Share function, an interesting option that you have is to send a presentation as a PDF or XPS file. When you choose one of these options, PowerPoint creates the selected version of the presentation and attaches it to an email message for you to send. The PDF or XPS file is not saved to your computer.

> **TIP** If you have an account with a fax service provider that permits the transmission of fax messages by email, you can click the Send As Internet Fax button and provide the fax number to address the message in the format required by the fax service. For example, if your fax service provider is Contoso and the fax number is (425) 555-0199, the email might be addressed to 14255550199@contoso.com. The fax service relays the message electronically to the recipient's fax number.

If you want to share the presentation with team members but you don't want to provide them with the file, you have the option of presenting it as an online slide show. The specific options that are available to you depend on the communication services you have access to. If your organization uses Skype for Business, you can present in a Skype meeting. If you don't have Skype for Business, but you have a Microsoft account, you can use the free Microsoft Office Presentation Service to present the slideshow in a browser window.

To send a presentation by email from within PowerPoint

1. In the presentation, click the **File** tab to display the Backstage view.

2. On the **Share** page of the Backstage view, click **Email** to display the email options.

3. In the **Email** pane, do one of the following:

   - Click **Send as Attachment** to attach a copy of the presentation to an email message.

   - Click **Send a Link** to insert a link to the shared file into an email message.

     > **TIP** The Send A Link button is available only if the presentation is saved in a shared location.

   - Click **Send as PDF** or **Send as XPS** to save a version of the presentation in that format and attach it to an email message.

13

4. If Outlook isn't already running, PowerPoint starts it before generating the email message. Enter your password if you are prompted to do so.

 SEE ALSO For information about the many fabulous features of Outlook 2016, refer to *Microsoft Outlook 2016 Step by Step* by Joan Lambert (Microsoft Press, 2015).

To present a slide show online

1. On the **Share** page of the Backstage view, click **Present Online** to display the online presentation options. Depending on your available resources, there might be a list of options at the top of the right pane that you can expand.

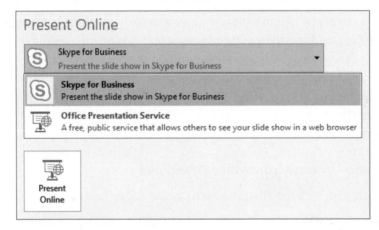

The Office Presentation Service is available to anyone

2. If you have multiple online presentation options, select the one you want from the list.

3. If you're going to use the Office Presentation Service and want to allow people to download a copy of your presentation, select the **Enable remote viewers to download the presentation** check box.

4. Click the **Present Online** button.

5. If you're using the Office Presentation Service, PowerPoint begins the online presentation, displays the Present Online commands on the ribbon, and opens the Present Online window. Send the URL in the window to the people you want to invite to the presentation, and then click **Present Online** to begin.

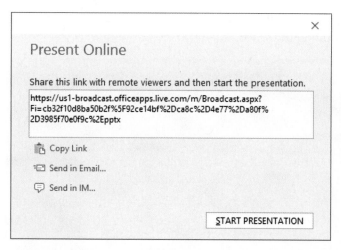

Use the commands in the window to send the link, or copy it and send it through your preferred messaging service

6. If you're using Skype for Business, the Present This Slide Show In A Skype Meeting window opens. Select an existing conversation, and then click **OK**, or start a new meeting.

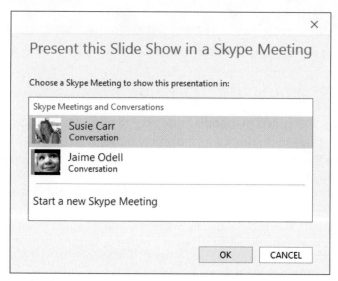

Choose an existing conversation or start a new meeting

13

Skype uploads the slide show and provides on-screen controls for moving through and annotating the slides.

Clicking the pen in the upper-right corner of the slide displays a full selection of annotation tools

Restrict access by using passwords

Sometimes, you might want only certain people to be able to open and change a presentation. The simplest way to do this for an individual presentation is to assign a password to protect the file so that a person who wants to modify the presentation must enter a password when opening it to permit changes.

You can assign a password to a presentation while working in the presentation or when saving the presentation. PowerPoint offers two levels of password protection:

- **Encrypted** The presentation is saved in such a way that people who do not know the password cannot open it at all.

- **Unencrypted** The presentation is saved in such a way that only people who know the password can open it, make changes, and save the file. People who don't know the password can open a read-only version. If they make changes and want to save them, they have to save the presentation with a different name or in a different location, preserving the original.

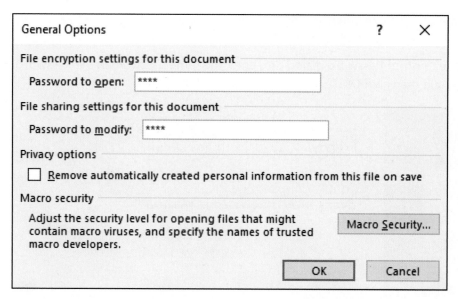

Assigning a password to open a presentation encrypts the file; assigning a password to modify the presentation does not

 IMPORTANT After assigning a password, make a note of it in a safe place. If you forget it, you won't be able to open the password-protected presentation.

To prevent unauthorized access to a presentation

1. Display the **Info** page of the Backstage view.

2. Click the **Protect Presentation** button, and then click **Encrypt with Password**.

Use a password that you will remember

13

3. In the **Encrypt Document** dialog box, enter the password you want to assign in the **Password** box, and then click **OK**.

4. In the **Confirm Password** dialog box, enter the same password in the **Password** box, and then click **OK**.

The Info page displays the protected status of the presentation

5. Close the presentation and save your changes.

Or

1. Display the **Save As** page of the Backstage view.

2. In the **Places** list, select the storage location where you want to save the presentation. Then click **Browse** to open the Save As dialog box.

3. If you want to protect a copy of the presentation instead of the original, enter a name for the copy in the **File name** box.

4. Near the lower-right corner of the **Save As** dialog box, click the **Tools** button. Then in the **Tools** list, click **General Options**.

5. In the **General Options** dialog box, in the **Password to open** box, enter the password you want to assign to the presentation. Then click **OK** to open the Confirm Password dialog box.

6. Enter the same password in the **Reenter password to open** box, and then click **OK** to set the password.

PowerPoint obscures the password as you enter it

7. In the **Save As** dialog box, click **Save**. If PowerPoint prompts you to overwrite the original presentation, click **Yes**.

To prevent unauthorized changes to a presentation

1. Display the **Save As** page of the Backstage view.

2. In the **Places** list, select the storage location where you want to save the presentation. Then click **Browse** to open the Save As dialog box.

3. If you want to protect a copy of the presentation instead of the original, enter a name for the copy in the **File name** box.

4. Near the lower-right corner of the **Save As** dialog box, click the **Tools** button. Then in the **Tools** list, click **General Options**.

5. In the **General Options** dialog box, in the **Password to modify** box, enter the password you want to assign to the presentation. Then click **OK** to open the **Confirm Password** dialog box.

6. Enter the same password in the **Reenter password to modify** box, and then click **OK** to set the password.

7. In the **Save As** dialog box, click **Save**. If PowerPoint prompts you to overwrite the original presentation, click **Yes**.

13

To test the security of a password-protected presentation

1. Open the presentation and verify that PowerPoint opens the **Password** dialog box.

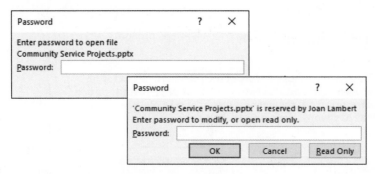

The Password dialog box content depends on the type of encryption

2. Enter an incorrect password, click **OK**, and verify that PowerPoint denies you access to the presentation.

To open a password-protected presentation for reading

1. Open the presentation, and then do either of the following:

   - In the **Password** dialog box, click the **Read Only** button to open a read-only version of the presentation.

      TIP When using the default settings, PowerPoint opens the presentation in Read Mode.

   - In the **Password** dialog box, enter the password that you assigned to the presentation, and then click **OK** to open a read-write version of the presentation.

To remove password protection from a presentation

1. Open the presentation and enter the correct password.

2. On the **Info** page of the Backstage view, in the **Protect Presentation** list, click **Encrypt with Password**.

3. In the **Encrypt Presentation** dialog box, delete the password from the **Password** box, and then click **OK**.

Or

1. On the **Save As** page of the Backstage view, in the **Current Folder** area, click the current folder.

2. At the bottom of the **Save As** dialog box, in the **Tools** list, click **General Options**.

3. In the **General Options** dialog box, select the contents of the **Password to open** or **Password to modify** box, press **Delete**, and then click **OK**.

4. In the **Save As** dialog box, click **Save**.

Add and review comments

The development of a presentation—especially one that will be delivered to clients, shareholders, or other important people—is often a collaborative effort, with several people contributing ideas and feedback. Even if you are developing a presentation for your own purposes, you might want to ask other people to review and comment on it before declaring it final.

If you are asked to review a presentation, you can give feedback about a slide without disrupting its text and layout by entering comments. You can do this by using the tools in the Comments group on the Review tab or by using the Comments pane. In either area, you can do the following:

- Add new comments.
- Skip to the next comment.
- View the previous comment.
- Reply to comments.
- Delete comments.

> ✓ **TIP** In addition to deleting comments, you can also delete any ink, or markups, you've applied to the slide. For information about marking up slides while working with a presentation, see "Present slide shows" in Chapter 10, "Prepare and deliver presentations."

If you add a comment without first selecting an object on the slide, the comment icon appears in the upper-left corner of the slide. If you select an object on the slide and then add the comment, the comment icon appears in the upper-right corner of the object.

13

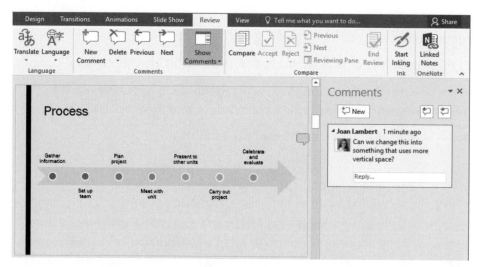

The comment icon location provides an indication of what the comment references

The comment text attached to a slide appears in the Comments pane to the right of that slide. When the Comments pane is closed, you can click any comment icon to display the pane and the comment associated with that icon.

You can move directly to comments in the presentation to review and respond to them. If you find the comment icons distracting, you can hide them. You can delete comments individually when they're no longer required, or delete all the comments on a slide or in a presentation at one time.

To add comments to a presentation

1. Display the slide in Normal view. If you want to attach the comment to a specific object, select that object.

2. Do either of the following:

   - On the **Review** tab, in the **Comments** group, click the **New Comment** button.

   - In the **Comments** pane, click the **New** button.

   A comment icon appears on the slide. The Comments pane opens if it wasn't already open, and an active comment box appears in the pane.

3. Enter your comment in the active comment box, and then click away from the comment box to finish.

> **TIP** To close the Comments pane, click the Close button in the upper-right corner of the pane. Alternatively, click the Show Comments button in the Comments group on the Review tab.

To open the Comments pane

1. Do either of the following:

   - On the **Review** tab, in the **Comments** group, click the **Show Comments** button.

   - On a slide, click a comment icon.

To close the Comments pane

1. Do either of the following:

   - On the **Review** tab, in the **Comments** group, click the **Show Comments** button.

   - Click the **Close** button (the **X**) in the upper-right corner of the pane.

To edit a comment

1. In the **Comments** pane, click the original comment text to activate it.

2. Make the changes you want, and then click away from the comment box to finish.

To review comments

1. In the **Comments** group on the **Review** tab, or in the **Comments** pane, do either of the following:

   - Click the **Next** button to move to the next comment.

   - Click the **Previous** button to move to the previous comment.

To reply to a comment

1. In the **Comments** pane, click the **Reply** box below the comment you want to respond to.

2. Enter your response, and then click away from the comment box to finish.

13

To hide and redisplay comments

1. On the **Review** tab, in the **Comments** group, click the **Show Comments** arrow, and then click **Show Markup** to hide or display all comments and other markup. (A check mark indicates that the command is active.)

To delete a comment

1. Do either of the following:

   - In the **Comments** pane, point to the comment box, and then click the **Delete** button that appears.

   - Click the comment in the slide or in the **Comments** pane, and then on the **Review** tab, in the **Comments** group, click the **Delete** button.

To delete all comments from a slide or presentation

1. In the **Comments** group, click the **Delete** arrow, and then do either of the following:

   - Click **Delete All Comments and Ink on This Slide**.

   - Click **Delete All Comments and Ink in This Presentation**, and then in the message box requesting confirmation, click **Yes**.

Coauthor presentations

Whether you work for a large organization or a small business, you might need to collaborate with other people on the development of a presentation. No matter what the circumstances, it can be difficult to keep track of different versions of a presentation produced by different people. If you store a presentation in a shared location such as a Microsoft SharePoint document library or OneDrive folder, multiple people can edit the presentation simultaneously.

After you save a presentation to a shared location, you can open and edit the presentation that is stored on the site just as you would if it were stored on your computer. Other people can also open and edit the presentation either by browsing to it or from an invitation that you send. This facilitates efficient collaboration between people regardless of location, schedule, or time zone.

When other people open a shared file for editing, PowerPoint alerts you by updating the Share button label on the ribbon and in the Share pane.

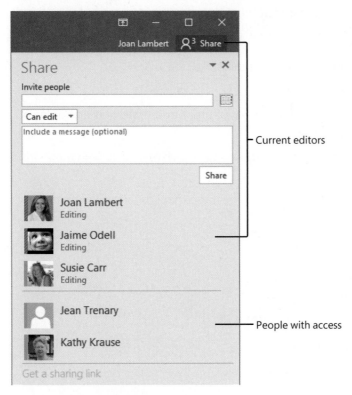

Multiple people can work in a presentation at the same time

To make a presentation available for coauthoring

1. Save the presentation to a SharePoint document library or OneDrive folder.

To begin coauthoring a presentation

1. Open the presentation directly from the SharePoint document library or OneDrive folder. If the presentation is stored in a document library, do NOT check it out.

2. Edit the presentation as you would normally.

13

To display the Share pane

1. Do either of the following:

   - Click the **Share** button located at the right end of the ribbon.

   - On the **Share** page of the Backstage view, click the **Share with People** button.

To invite other people to edit a shared presentation

1. Open the **Share** pane.

2. In the **Invite people** box, enter the names or email addresses of the people you want to send a presentation link to.

3. In the message box, enter any specific message you want to include in the sharing invitation.

4. Click the **Share** button to send an email message that contains a link to the presentation.

To display changes made by coauthors

1. Do either of the following:

   - Save the presentation.

   - On the status bar, click the **Updates Available** button.

The Updates Available button appears on the status bar when other editors save changes

To configure PowerPoint to quickly make your changes available to coauthors

1. Open the **Share** pane.

2. In the **Automatically share changes** list, click **Always**.

Skills review

In this chapter, you learned how to:

- Save presentations in other formats

- Share presentations from PowerPoint

- Restrict access by using passwords

- Add and review comments

- Coauthor presentations

Practice tasks

The practice files for these tasks are located in the PowerPoint2016SBS\Ch13 folder. You can save the results of the tasks in the same folder.

Save presentations in other formats

Open the SaveSlides presentation, and then perform the following tasks:

1. Save the presentation as a PowerPoint Show. Then close the presentation.

2. Open the PowerPoint Show you just created, and watch the presentation as it advances automatically from slide to slide while playing the embedded music. Then close the PowerPoint Show.

3. Reopen the **SaveSlides** presentation, and save it as a Picture Presentation with the name **MyPicturePresentation**. Then close the file.

4. Open the Picture Presentation. On slide **1**, click the title, and notice that handles surround the entire slide. Then close the Picture Presentation.

5. Reopen the **SaveSlides** presentation, and save it as a video. A progress bar on the status bar displays the progress. When the process finishes, close the file.

6. Play the video. Then close the video playback window.

7. Open the **SaveSlides** presentation and save only slides 1, 3, and 5 as a PDF file.

8. Open the PDF file and confirm its content.

9. Close the presentation and any other files that remain open.

Share presentations from PowerPoint

> ⚠ **IMPORTANT** These steps assume that Microsoft Outlook is your default email program.

Open the ShareSlides presentation, and then perform the following tasks:

1. Send the presentation as an attachment to an email message to yourself, directly from PowerPoint.

2. Start an online presentation, using either the Microsoft Office Presentation Service or another service that is available to you on the Present Online page. Invite at least one person to your presentation. Experiment with the slide markup tools that are available to you. Then end the online presentation.

3. Close the presentation.

Restrict access by using passwords

Open the RestrictAccess presentation, and then perform the following tasks:

1. Assign the password **P@ssword** to open the presentation. Then save and close the presentation.

> ✓ **TIP** In this example, we use a common word that is easy to enter as the password. For maximum protection, use a password of at least eight characters that includes a combination of capital and small letters, digits, and punctuation symbols.

2. Reopen the presentation to test the password protection, and enter the password to open the presentation.

3. Remove the password and save the presentation.

4. Assign the password **P@ssword** to modify the presentation. Then save and close the presentation.

5. Reopen the presentation to test the password protection. In the **Password** box, click **Read Only**.

6. On slide **1**, double-click the presentation title, and then press the **Delete** key. Notice that you cannot modify the presentation content.

7. Close and reopen the presentation.

8. In the **Password** box, enter the password, and then verify that you can modify the presentation content.

9. Save and close the presentation.

Add and review comments

Open the AddComments presentation, and then perform the following tasks:

1. Display slide **1**, and then do the following:

   - Without selecting anything on the slide, insert a comment that says **Great job on this!**

   - In the slide title, select the word *completing*, and then insert the comment **Replace with "carrying out"?**

   - Notice the locations of the comment icons on the slide.

2. Display slide **4**. Select the bulleted list, and then insert the comment **A graphic would be helpful here.**

3. Click away from the comment, and then edit it to insert the word **colorful** to the left of the word *graphic*.

4. Use the commands on the ribbon or in the **Comments** pane to move forward and backward among the comments.

5. Hide the comments, and then redisplay them.

6. Delete the first comment, and then delete all remaining comments in the presentation.

7. Close the presentation without saving it.

Coauthor presentations

There are no practice tasks for this topic.

Keyboard shortcuts

Throughout this book, we provide information about how to perform tasks quickly and efficiently by using keyboard shortcuts. This section presents information about keyboard shortcuts that are built in to PowerPoint 2016 and Microsoft Office 2016, and about custom keyboard shortcuts.

 TIP In the following lists, keys you press at the same time are separated by a plus sign (+), and keys you press sequentially are separated by a comma (,).

PowerPoint 2016 keyboard shortcuts

This section provides a comprehensive list of keyboard shortcuts built into PowerPoint 2016. The list has been excerpted from PowerPoint Help and formatted in tables for convenient lookup.

Move between panes

Action	Keyboard shortcut
Move clockwise among panes in Normal view	F6
Move counterclockwise among panes in Normal view	Shift+F6
Switch between Normal view and Outline view	Ctrl+Shift+Tab

Work in an outline

Action	Keyboard shortcut
Promote a paragraph	Alt+Shift+Left Arrow
Demote a paragraph	Alt+Shift+Right Arrow
Move selected paragraphs up	Alt+Shift+Up Arrow

Action	Keyboard shortcut
Move selected paragraphs down	Alt+Shift+Down Arrow
Show heading level 1	Alt+Shift+1
Expand text below a heading	Alt+Shift+Plus Sign
Collapse text below a heading	Alt+Shift+Minus Sign

Show or hide a grid or guides

Action	Keyboard shortcut
Show or hide the grid	Shift+F9
Show or hide guides	Alt+F9

Work with shapes and objects

Action	Keyboard shortcut
Select a single shape	Tab or Shift+Tab
Group selected shapes	Ctrl+G
Ungroup a group of shapes	Ctrl+Shift+G
Copy object attributes	Ctrl+Shift+C
Paste object attributes	Ctrl+Shift+V

Select text and objects

Action	Keyboard shortcut
Select one character to the right	Shift+Right Arrow
Select one character to the left	Shift+Left Arrow
Select to the end of a word	Ctrl+Shift+Right Arrow

Action	Keyboard shortcut
Select to the beginning of a word	Ctrl+Shift+Left Arrow
Select one line up	Shift+Up Arrow
Select one line down	Shift+Down Arrow
Select an object (when the object content is active)	Esc
Select another object (when one object is selected)	Tab or Shift+Tab until the object you want is selected
Select text within an object (with an object selected)	Enter
Select all thumbnails in the Thumbnails pane, all slides in Slide Sorter view, all content on a slide, or all text in a text box	Ctrl+A

Delete and copy text and objects

Action	Keyboard shortcut
Delete one character to the left	Backspace
Delete one word to the left	Ctrl+Backspace
Delete one character to the right	Delete
Delete one word to the right (the cursor must be between words to do this)	Ctrl+Delete
Cut selected object or text	Ctrl+X
Copy selected object or text	Ctrl+C
Paste cut or copied object or text	Ctrl+V
Undo the last action	Ctrl+Z
Redo the last action	Ctrl+Y
Copy formatting only	Ctrl+Shift+C
Paste formatting only	Ctrl+Shift+V
Open the Paste Special dialog box	Ctrl+Alt+V

Move around in text

Action	Keyboard shortcut
Move one character to the left	Left Arrow
Move one character to the right	Right Arrow
Move one line up	Up Arrow
Move one line down	Down Arrow
Move one word to the left	Ctrl+Left Arrow
Move one word to the right	Ctrl+Right Arrow
Move to the end of a line	End
Move to the beginning of a line	Home
Move up one paragraph	Ctrl+Up Arrow
Move down one paragraph	Ctrl+Down Arrow
Move to the end of a text box	Ctrl+End
Move to the beginning of a text box	Ctrl+Home
Move to the next title or body text placeholder, or, from the last placeholder on a slide, create a new slide	Ctrl+Enter
Move to repeat the last Find action	Shift+F4

Move around in and work in tables

Action	Keyboard shortcut
Move to the next cell	Tab
Move to the preceding cell	Shift+Tab
Move to the next row	Down Arrow
Move to the preceding row	Up Arrow
Insert a tab in a cell	Ctrl+Tab
Start a new paragraph	Enter
Add a new row at the bottom of the table	Tab at the end of the last row

Edit a linked or embedded object

Follow these steps:

1. Press **Tab** or **Shift+Tab** to select the object you want.

2. Press **Shift+F10** to display the shortcut menu.

3. Press the **Down Arrow** key until the Object command is selected, press the **Right Arrow** key to select Edit, and then press **Enter**.

> ✓ **TIP** The name of the command in the shortcut menu depends on the type of embedded or linked object. For example, an embedded Microsoft Excel worksheet has the command Worksheet Object, whereas an embedded Microsoft Visio Drawing has the command Visio Object.

Format and align characters and paragraphs

Change or resize the font

Action	Keyboard shortcut
Open the Font dialog box to change the font	Ctrl+Shift+F
Increase the font size	Ctrl+Shift+>
Decrease the font size	Ctrl+Shift+<

Apply character formats

Action	Keyboard shortcut
Open the Font dialog box to change the formatting of characters	Ctrl+T
Change the case of letters between sentence case, lowercase, and uppercase	Shift+F3
Apply bold formatting	Ctrl+B
Apply an underline	Ctrl+U
Apply italic formatting	Ctrl+I

Action	Keyboard shortcut
Apply subscript formatting (automatic spacing)	Ctrl+=
Apply superscript formatting (automatic spacing)	Ctrl+Shift+Plus Sign
Remove manual character formatting, such as subscript and superscript	Ctrl+Spacebar
Insert a hyperlink	Ctrl+K

Copy text formats

Action	Keyboard shortcut
Copy formats	Ctrl+Shift+C
Paste formats	Ctrl+Shift+V

Align paragraphs

Action	Keyboard shortcut
Center a paragraph	Ctrl+E
Justify a paragraph	Ctrl+J
Left-align a paragraph	Ctrl+L
Right-align a paragraph	Ctrl+R

Manage a presentation

Use the following keyboard shortcuts while running a presentation in Slide Show view.

Run a slide show

Action	Keyboard shortcut
Start a presentation from the beginning	F5
Perform the next animation or advance to the next slide	N, Enter, Page Down, Right Arrow, Down Arrow, or Spacebar

Action	Keyboard shortcut
Perform the previous animation or return to the previous slide	P, Page Up, Left Arrow, Up Arrow, or Backspace
Go to a specific slide number	Slide number+Enter
Display a blank black slide, or return to the presentation from a blank black slide	B or Period
Display a blank white slide, or return to the presentation from a blank white slide	W or Comma
Stop or restart an automatic presentation	S
End a presentation	Esc or Hyphen
Erase on-screen annotations	E
Go to the next slide, if the next slide is hidden	H
Re-record slide narration and timing	R
Return to the first slide	Press and hold right and left mouse buttons
Show or hide the arrow pointer	A or =
Change the pointer to a pen	Ctrl+P
Change the pointer to an arrow	Ctrl+A
Change the pointer to an eraser	Ctrl+E
Show or hide ink markup	Ctrl+M
Hide the pointer and navigation button immediately	Ctrl+H
Hide the pointer and navigation button in 15 seconds	Ctrl+U
View the All Slides dialog box	Ctrl+S
View the computer task bar	Ctrl+T
Display the shortcut menu	Shift+F10
Go to the first or next hyperlink on a slide	Tab
Go to the last or previous hyperlink on a slide	Shift+Tab
Perform the "mouse click" behavior of the selected hyperlink	Enter
Start a slide show presentation to a remote audience	Ctrl+F5

Use media shortcuts during a slide show

Action	Keyboard shortcut
Stop media playback	Alt+Q
Switch between play and pause	Alt+P
Go to the next bookmark	Alt+End
Go to the previous bookmark	Alt+Home
Increase the sound volume	Alt+Up
Decrease the sound volume	Alt+Down
Seek forward	Alt+Shift+Page Down
Seek backward	Alt+Shift+Page Up
Mute the sound	Alt+U

 TIP Press F1 during a presentation to display a list of controls.

Office 2016 keyboard shortcuts

This section provides a comprehensive list of keyboard shortcuts available in all Office 2016 programs, including PowerPoint.

Display and use windows

Action	Keyboard shortcut
Switch to the next window	Alt+Tab
Switch to the previous window	Alt+Shift+Tab
Close the active window	Ctrl+W or Ctrl+F4
Restore the size of the active window after you maximize it	Alt+F5

Action	Keyboard shortcut
Move to a pane from another pane in the program window (clockwise direction)	F6 or Shift+F6
If pressing F6 does not open the pane that you want, press Alt to put the focus on the ribbon, and then press Ctrl+Tab to move to the pane	
Switch to the next open window	Ctrl+F6
Switch to the previous window	Ctrl+Shift+F6
Maximize or restore a selected window	Ctrl+F10
Copy a picture of the screen to the Clipboard	Print Screen
Copy a picture of the selected window to the Clipboard	Alt+Print Screen

Use dialog boxes

Action	Keyboard shortcut
Move to the next option or option group	Tab
Move to the previous option or option group	Shift+Tab
Switch to the next tab in a dialog box	Ctrl+Tab
Switch to the previous tab in a dialog box	Ctrl+Shift+Tab
Move between options in an open drop-down list, or between options in a group of options	Arrow keys
Perform the action assigned to the selected button; select or clear the selected check box	Spacebar
Select an option; select or clear a check box	Alt+ the underlined letter
Display a selected drop-down list	Alt+Down Arrow
Select an option from a drop-down list	First letter of the list option
Close a selected drop-down list; cancel a command and close a dialog box	Esc
Run the selected command	Enter

Use edit boxes within dialog boxes

An edit box is a blank box in which you enter or paste an entry.

Action	Keyboard shortcut
Move to the beginning of the entry	Home
Move to the end of the entry	End
Move one character to the left or right	Left Arrow or Right Arrow
Move one word to the left	Ctrl+Left Arrow
Move one word to the right	Ctrl+Right Arrow
Select or unselect one character to the left	Shift+Left Arrow
Select or unselect one character to the right	Shift+Right Arrow
Select or unselect one word to the left	Ctrl+Shift+Left Arrow
Select or unselect one word to the right	Ctrl+Shift+Right Arrow
Select from the insertion point to the beginning of the entry	Shift+Home
Select from the cursor to the end of the entry	Shift+End

Use the Open and Save As dialog boxes

Action	Keyboard shortcut
Open the Open dialog box	Ctrl+F12 or Ctrl+O
Open the Save As dialog box	F12
Open the selected folder or file	Enter
Open the folder one level above the selected folder	Backspace
Delete the selected folder or file	Delete
Display a shortcut menu for a selected item such as a folder or file	Shift+F10
Move forward through options	Tab
Move back through options	Shift+Tab
Display the Look In list	F4 or Alt+I
Refresh the file list	F5

Use the Backstage view

Action	Keyboard shortcut
Display the Open page of the Backstage view	Ctrl+O
Display the Save As page of the Backstage view (when saving a file for the first time)	Ctrl+S
Continue saving an Office file (after giving the file a name and location)	Ctrl+S
Display the Save As page of the Backstage view (after initially saving a file)	Alt+F, A
Back out of the Backstage view	Esc

Navigate the ribbon

Follow these steps:

1. Press **Alt** to display the KeyTips over each feature in the current view.

2. Press the letter shown in the KeyTip over the feature that you want to use.

 TIP To cancel the action and hide the KeyTips, press Alt.

Change the keyboard focus without using the mouse

Action	Keyboard shortcut
Select the active tab of the ribbon and activate the access keys	Alt or F10; press either of these keys again to move back to the document and cancel the access keys
Move to another tab of the ribbon	F10 to select the active tab, and then Left Arrow or Right Arrow
Expand or collapse the ribbon	Ctrl+F1

Action	Keyboard shortcut
Display the shortcut menu for the selected item	Shift+F10
Move the focus to select each of the following areas of the window: ■ Active tab of the ribbon ■ Any open panes ■ Status bar at the bottom of the window ■ Your document	F6
Move the focus to each command on the ribbon, forward or backward, respectively	Tab or Shift+Tab
Move among the items on the ribbon	Arrow keys
Activate the selected command or control on the ribbon	Spacebar or Enter
Display the selected menu or gallery on the ribbon	Spacebar or Enter
Activate a command or control on the ribbon so that you can modify a value	Enter
Finish modifying a value in a control on the ribbon, and move focus back to the document	Enter
Get help on the selected command or control on the ribbon	F1

Undo and redo actions

Action	Keyboard shortcut
Cancel an action	Esc
Undo an action	Ctrl+Z
Redo or repeat an action	Ctrl+Y

Access and use panes and galleries

Action	Keyboard shortcut
Move to a pane from another pane in the program window	F6
When a menu is active, move to a pane	Ctrl+Tab
When a pane is active, select the next or previous option in the pane	Tab or Shift+Tab
Display the full set of commands on the pane menu	Ctrl+Spacebar
Perform the action assigned to the selected button	Spacebar or Enter
Open a drop-down menu for the selected gallery item	Shift+F10
Select the first or last item in a gallery	Home or End
Scroll up or down in the selected gallery list	Page Up or Page Down
Close a pane	Ctrl+Spacebar, C
Open the Clipboard	Alt+H, F, O

Access and use available actions

Action	Keyboard shortcut
Display the shortcut menu for the selected item	Shift+F10
Display the menu or message for an available action or for the AutoCorrect Options button or the Paste Options button	Alt+Shift+F10
Move between options in a menu of available actions	Arrow keys
Perform the action for the selected item on a menu of available actions	Enter
Close the available actions menu or message	Esc

Find and replace content

Action	Keyboard shortcut
Open the Find dialog box	Ctrl+F
Open the Replace dialog box	Ctrl+H
Repeat the last Find action	Shift+F4

Use the Help window

Action	Keyboard shortcut
Open the Help window	F1
Close the Help window	Alt+F4
Switch between the Help window and the active program	Alt+Tab
Return to the Help table of contents	Alt+Home
Select the next item in the Help window	Tab
Select the previous item in the Help window	Shift+Tab
Perform the action for the selected item	Enter
Move back to the previous Help topic (Back button)	Alt+Left Arrow or Backspace
Move forward to the next Help topic (Forward button)	Alt+Right Arrow
Scroll small amounts up or down, respectively, within the currently displayed Help topic	Up Arrow, Down Arrow
Scroll larger amounts up or down, respectively, within the currently displayed Help topic	Page Up, Page Down

Action	Keyboard shortcut
Display a menu of commands for the Help window. This requires that the Help window have the active focus (click in the Help window)	Shift+F10
Stop the last action (Stop button)	Esc
Print the current Help topic If the cursor is not in the current Help topic, press F6 and then press Ctrl+P	Ctrl+P
In a Table of Contents in tree view, select the next or previous item, respectively	Up Arrow, Down Arrow
In a Table of Contents in tree view, expand or collapse the selected item, respectively	Left Arrow, Right Arrow

Glossary

accessible content Content that is packaged and delivered in a way that supports access by all means of input methods and output devices.

action button A ready-made button that you can insert into a presentation and use to define hyperlinks.

add-in A utility that adds specialized functionality to an app but that does not operate as an independent app.

adjustment handle A diamond-shaped handle used to adjust the appearance but not the size of most shapes. For example, you can adjust a rounded rectangle to be more or less rounded.

animation An effect that you can apply to text or an object to produce an illusion of movement.

aspect ratio The ratio of the width of an image to its height.

attribute An individual item of character formatting, such as size or color, that determines how text looks.

AutoCorrect A feature that automatically detects and corrects misspelled words and incorrect capitalization. You can add your own AutoCorrect entries.

background The colors, shading, texture, and graphics, that appear behind the text and objects on a slide.

body font The second font listed in a set of theme fonts, which is by default applied to all text except headings.

bulleted list item An item in a list in which each list entry is preceded by a symbol.

caption Descriptive text associated with a figure, photo, illustration, or screenshot.

case The capitalization (uppercase or lowercase) of a word or phrase. In title case, the first letter of each important word is capitalized. In sentence case, only the first letter of the first word is capitalized.

category axis The horizontal reference line on a grid, chart, or graph that has horizontal and vertical dimensions. Also called the *x-axis*.

cell A box formed by the intersection of a row and column in a worksheet or a table, in which you enter information.

cell address The location of a cell, expressed as its column letter and row number, as in *A1*.

character formatting Formatting you can apply to selected characters.

chart A diagram that plots a series of values in a table or worksheet.

chart area A region in a chart that is used to position chart elements, render axes, and plot data.

clip art A piece of free, ready-made art that is distributed without copyright. Usually a cartoon, sketch, illustration, or photograph.

Clipboard A storage area shared by all Microsoft Office apps, where cut or copied items are temporarily stored so they can be pasted elsewhere.

color gradient A gradual progression from one color to another color or from one shade to another shade of the same color.

column Either the vertical arrangement of text into one or more side-by-side sections, or the vertical arrangement of cells in a table or worksheet.

comment An annotation that is associated with text or an object to provide context-specific information or reviewer feedback.

connection point A point on a shape to which another shape can be connected.

connector A line that connects two shapes and that moves if the shapes are moved.

content placeholder See *placeholder*.

contextual tab See *tool tab*.

cursor A representation on the screen of the input device pointer location.

custom slide show A set of slides extracted from a presentation to create a slide show for an audience that doesn't need to view the entire presentation.

cycle diagram A diagram that shows a continuous process.

data marker A customizable symbol or shape that identifies a data point on a chart. Data markers can be bars, columns, pie or doughnut slices, dots, and various other shapes and can be various sizes and colors.

data point An individual value plotted in a chart.

data series Related data points that are plotted in a chart. One or more data series can be plotted in a chart. A pie chart has just one data series.

design template A file that contains masters that control the formatting of a presentation, including placeholder sizes and positions; background design, graphics, and color schemes; fonts; and the type and size of bullets.

destination file The file into which a linked or embedded object is inserted. When you change information in a destination file, the information is not updated in the source file. See also *source file*.

diagram A graphic in which shapes, text, and pictures are used to illustrate a process, cycle, or relationship.

dialog box launcher On the ribbon, a button at the bottom of some groups that opens a dialog box with features related to the group.

Document Inspector A tool that automates the process of detecting and removing all extraneous and confidential information from a presentation.

dragging A way of moving objects by selecting them and then, while the selection device is active (for example, while you are holding down the mouse button), moving the selection to the new location.

embedded object An object that is wholly inserted into a file. Embedding the object, rather than simply inserting or pasting its contents, ensures that the object retains its original format. If you open the embedded object, you can edit it with the toolbars and menus from the app used to create it.

encrypting To programmatically disguise content to hide its substance.

file format The structure or organization of data in a file. The file format is usually indicated by the file name extension.

file name extension A set of characters added to the end of a file name that identifies the file type or format.

font A graphic design applied to a collection of numbers, symbols, and characters. A font describes a certain typeface, which can have qualities such as size, spacing, and pitch.

font effect An attribute, such as superscript, small capital letters, or shadow, that can be applied to a font.

font size The height (in points) of a collection of characters, where one point is equal to approximately 1/72 of an inch.

font style The emphasis placed on a font by using formatting such as bold, italic, underline, or color.

footer One or more items of information, typically at the bottom of a slide and typically containing elements such as the page number and the date.

gallery Rich, customizable list boxes that can be used to organize items by category, display them in flexible column-based and row-based layouts, and represent them with images and text. Depending on the type of gallery, live preview is also supported.

graphic Any image, such as a picture, photograph, drawing, illustration, or shape, that can be placed as an object on a slide.

grayscale The range of shades of black in an image.

group On a ribbon tab, an area containing buttons related to a specific presentation element or function.

grouping Assembling several objects, such as shapes, into a single unit so that they act as one object. Grouped objects can easily be moved, sized, and formatted.

handle A small circle, square, or set of dots that appears at the corner or on the side of a selected object and facilitates moving, sizing, reshaping, or other functions pertaining to the object.

handout master A template that defines the layout for the printed handout pages distributed to a presentation's audience.

Handout Master view The view from which you can change the overall look of audience handouts.

heading font The first font listed in a set of theme fonts, which is by default applied to all slide titles.

hierarchy diagram A diagram that illustrates the structure of an organization or entity.

hyperlink A connection from a hyperlink anchor such as text or a graphic that you can follow to display a link target such as a file, a location in a file, or a website. Text hyperlinks are usually formatted as colored or underlined text, but sometimes the only indication is that when you point to them, the pointer changes to a hand.

icon A small picture or symbol representing a command, file type, function, app, or tool.

keyboard shortcut Any combination of keystrokes that can be used to perform a task that would otherwise require a mouse or other pointing device.

kiosk mode A display mode in which a single window takes over the whole screen and the desktop is inaccessible.

legend A key that identifies the data series plotted in the chart.

line break A manual break that forces the text that follows it to the next line. Also called a *text wrapping break*.

link See *hyperlink; linked object*.

linked object An object that is inserted into a slide but that still exists in its source file. When information is linked, the slide is updated automatically if the information in the original document changes.

Live Preview A feature that temporarily displays the effect of applying a specific format to the selected slide element.

master A slide or page on which you define formatting for all slides or pages in a presentation. Each presentation has a set of masters for slides, in addition to masters for speaker notes and audience handouts.

Microsoft Office Clipboard See *Clipboard*.

Microsoft PowerPoint Viewer A viewer with which you can display presentations on a computer that does not have PowerPoint installed.

Mini Toolbar A toolbar that is typically displayed after you select text on a slide so that you can quickly format the text.

Normal view A view that displays three panes: Thumbnails, Slide, and Notes.

notes master A template that defines the formatting and content used by slide notes pages.

Notes Master view The view from which you can change the overall look of speaker notes pages.

Notes Page view The view in which you can add speaker notes that contain objects such as tables, charts, and graphics.

Notes pane The pane in Normal view in which you enter notes that you want to accompany a slide. You can print these notes as speaker notes pages.

object An item, such as a graphic, video clip, sound file, or worksheet, that can be inserted into a slide and then selected and modified.

Outline pane The pane that appears in Outline view on the left side of the app window and that displays all the text of the presentation in outline form.

Outline view A view that displays three panes: Outline, Slide, and Notes.

Package for CD A feature to help you gather all the components of a presentation and store them to a CD or another type of removable media so that they can be transported to a different computer.

palette A collection of color swatches that you can click to apply a color to selected text or an object. PowerPoint has three palettes: Theme Colors, Standard, and Recently Used.

paragraph formatting Formatting that controls the appearance of a paragraph. Examples include indentation, alignment, line spacing, and pagination.

password The string of characters that must be entered to open a password-protected presentation for editing.

path A sequence of folders that leads to a specific file or folder. A backslash is used to separate each folder in a Windows path, and a forward slash is used to separate each directory in an Internet path.

photo album A specific kind of presentation into which you can insert and arrange collections of digital images.

picture A photograph, clip art image, illustration, or another type of image created with an app other than PowerPoint.

picture diagram A diagram that uses pictures to convey information, rather than or in addition to text.

pixel The smallest element used to form the composition of an image on a computer monitor. Computer monitors display images by drawing thousands of pixels arranged in columns and rows.

placeholder An area on a slide designed to contain a specific type of content that you supply.

plot area In a two-dimensional chart, the area bounded by the axes, including all data series. In a three-dimensional chart, the area bounded by the axes, including the data series, category names, tick-mark labels, and axis titles.

point The unit of measure for expressing the size of characters in a font, where 72 points equals 1 inch.

PowerPoint Online An app that you can use to review and edit a presentation in your web browser when you're working with a presentation that is stored on a SharePoint site or in a OneDrive folder. The web app runs directly in your web browser instead of on your computer. Web apps are installed in the online environment in which you're working and are not part of the desktop app that you install directly on your computer.

Presenter view A tool with which you can control a presentation on one monitor while the audience views the presentation's slides in Slide Show view on a delivery monitor or projector screen.

process diagram A diagram that visually represents the ordered set of steps required to complete a task.

property Settings of a file that you can change, such as the file's name and read-only status, in addition to attributes that you can't directly change, such as the file's size and creation date.

Quick Access Toolbar A small, customizable toolbar that displays frequently used commands.

read-only A setting that allows a file to be read or copied, but not changed or saved. If you change a read-only file, you can save your changes only if you give the file a new name.

Reading view The view in which each slide fills the screen. You can click buttons on the navigation bar to move through or jump to specific slides.

relationship diagram A diagram that shows convergent, divergent, overlapping, merging, or containment elements.

ribbon A user interface design that organizes commands into logical groups that appear on separate tabs.

Rich Text Format (RTF) A format for text and graphics interchange that can be used with different output devices, operating environments, and operating systems.

rotate handle A small green handle that you can use to adjust the angle of rotation of a shape.

screen clipping An image of all or part of the content displayed on a computer screen. Screen clippings can be captured by using a graphics capture tool such as the Screen Clipping tool included with Office 2016 apps.

ScreenTip A note that appears on the screen to provide information about the app interface or certain types of document content, such as proofing marks and hyperlinks within a document.

selecting To specify, or highlight, an object or block of text so that you can manipulate or edit it in some way.

series axis The third axis in a three-dimensional coordinate system, used in computer graphics to represent depth. Also called the z-axis.

shape An object created by using drawing tools or commands.

size handle A small circle, square, or set of dots that appears at the corner or on the side of a selected object. You drag these handles to change the size of the object horizontally, vertically, or proportionally.

slide library A type of SharePoint document library that is optimized for storing and reusing PowerPoint slides.

slide master The set of slides that stores information about a presentation's design template, including font styles, placeholder sizes and positions, background design, and color schemes.

Slide Master view The view from which you make changes to the slide masters.

Slide pane The area in Normal view that shows the currently selected slide as it will appear in the presentation.

Slide Show view The view in which you deliver an electronic presentation to an audience.

Slide Sorter view The view in which the slides of the presentation are displayed as thumbnails so that you can easily reorganize them.

slide timing The time a slide will be displayed on the screen before PowerPoint moves to the next slide.

smart guide A vertical or horizontal dotted line that appears on a slide to help align slide elements.

SmartArt graphic A predefined set of shapes and text used as a basis for creating a diagram.

source file A file that contains information that is linked, embedded, or merged into a destination file. Updates to source file content are reflected in the destination file when the data connection is refreshed. See also *destination file*.

source app The app used to create a linked or embedded object. To edit the object, you must have the source app installed on your computer.

stack A set of graphics that overlap each other.

status bar An app window element, located at the bottom of the app window, that displays indicators and controls.

subpoint A subordinate item below a bullet point in a list.

tab A tabbed page on the ribbon that contains buttons organized in groups.

table One or more rows of cells commonly used to display numbers and other items for quick reference and analysis. Items in a table are organized in rows and columns.

template A file that can contain predefined formatting, layout, text, or graphics, and that serves as the basis for new presentations with a similar design or purpose.

text box A movable, resizable container used to insert text on a slide with a different position or orientation than the text in placeholders.

theme A set of unified design elements that combine color, fonts, and effects to provide a professional look for a presentation.

theme fonts A set of two fonts: one applied to slide titles (heading font) and one applied to all other text on a slide (body font).

Thesaurus A feature that looks up alternative words, or *synonyms*, for a word.

thumbnail A small representation of an item, such as a slide or theme. Thumbnails are typically used to provide visual identifiers for related items.

Thumbnails pane The pane in Normal view that displays thumbnails of the slides in a presentation and allows you to display a specific slide by clicking its thumbnail.

tick-mark A small line of measurement, similar to a division line on a ruler, that intersects an axis in a chart.

title bar The horizontal bar at the top of a window that contains the name of the window. Most title bars also contain boxes or buttons for closing and resizing the window.

tool tab A tab containing commands that are relevant only when you have selected a particular object type.

transition An effect that specifies how the display changes as you move from one slide to another.

value axis The vertical reference line on a grid, chart, or graph that has horizontal and vertical dimension. Also called the y-axis.

View Shortcuts toolbar A toolbar at the right end of the status bar that contains tools for switching between views of slide content and changing the view of the open presentation.

watermark A faint text or graphic image that appears on the page behind the main content of a slide.

web app See *PowerPoint Online*.

web browser Software that interprets HTML files, formats them into webpages, and displays them. A web browser, such as Internet Explorer, can follow hyperlinks, respond to requests to download files, and play sound or video files that are embedded in webpages.

webpage A World Wide Web document. A webpage typically consists of an HTML file, with associated files for graphics and sets of instructions called *scripts*. It is identified by a Uniform Resource Locator (URL).

WordArt A group of text effects that incorporate qualities such as shadows, reflections, edge glow, beveled edges, 3-D rotation, and transforms.

x-axis The horizontal reference line on a grid, chart, or graph that has horizontal and vertical dimensions. Also called the category axis.

y-axis The vertical reference line on a grid, chart, or graph that has horizontal and vertical dimensions. Also called the value axis.

z-axis The third axis in a three-dimensional coordinate system, used in computer graphics to represent depth. Also called the series axis.

Index

About the author

Joan Lambert has worked closely with Microsoft technologies since 1986, and in the training and certification industry since 1997. As President and CEO of Online Training Solutions, Inc. (OTSI), Joan guides the translation of technical information and requirements into useful, relevant, and measurable resources for people who are seeking certification of their computer skills or who simply want to get things done efficiently.

Joan is the author or coauthor of more than three dozen books about Windows and Office (for Windows, Mac, and iPad), video-based training courses for SharePoint and OneNote, and three generations of Microsoft Office Specialist certification study guides.

Joan is a Microsoft Certified Professional, Microsoft Certified Trainer, Microsoft Office Specialist Master (for all Office versions since Office 2007), Microsoft Certified Technology Specialist (for Windows and Windows Server), Microsoft Certified Technology Associate (for Windows), and Microsoft Dynamics Specialist.

Joan currently lives in a small town in Texas with her simply divine daughter, Trinity; an ever-growing menagerie of dogs, cats, fish, and frogs; and the DeLonghi Gran Dama super-automatic espresso machine that runs the house.

Acknowledgments

I appreciate the time and efforts of Carol Dillingham, Rosemary Caperton, and the team at Microsoft Press—past and present—who made this and so many other books possible.

I would like to thank the editorial and production team members at Online Training Solutions, Inc. (OTSI) and other contributors for their efforts. Angela Martin, Ginny Munroe, Jaime Odell, Jean Trenary, Jeanne Craver, Kate Shoup, Kathy Krause, Meredith Thomas, Steve Lambert, Susie Carr, and Val Serdy all contributed to the creation of this book.

OTSI specializes in the design and creation of Microsoft Office, SharePoint, and Windows training solutions and the production of online and printed training resources. For more information about OTSI, visit *www.otsi.com* or follow us on Facebook at *www.facebook.com/Online.Training.Solutions.Inc.*

I hope you enjoy this book and find it useful. The content of this book was guided in part by feedback from readers of previously published *Step by Step* books. If you find errors or omissions in this book, want to say something nice about it, or would like to provide input for future versions, you can use the feedback process outlined in the introduction.

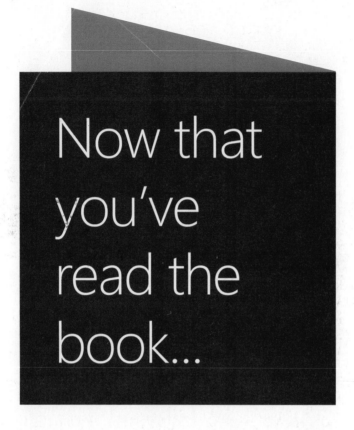

Now that you've read the book...

Tell us what you think!

Was it useful?
Did it teach you what you wanted to learn?
Was there room for improvement?

Let us know at http://aka.ms/tellpress

Your feedback goes directly to the staff at Microsoft Press,
and we read every one of your responses. Thanks in advance!

 Microsoft